Thailand's Political Peasants

New Perspectives in Southeast Asian Studies

Series Editors

Alfred W. McCoy

R. Anderson Sutton

Thongchai Winichakul

Kenneth M. George

Associate Editors

Warwick H. Anderson

Katherine Bowie

Ian Coxhead

Michael Cullinane

Anna M. Gade

Anne Ruth Hansen

Paul D. Hutchcroft

Courtney Johnson

Kris Olds

Thailand's Political Peasants

Power in the Modern Rural Economy

ANDREW WALKER

THE UNIVERSITY OF WISCONSIN PRESS

Publication of this volume has been made possible, in part,
through support from the Center for Southeast Asian Studies
at the University of Wisconsin–Madison.

The University of Wisconsin Press
1930 Monroe Street, 3rd Floor
Madison, Wisconsin 53711-2059
uwpress.wisc.edu

3 Henrietta Street
London WC2E 8LU, England
eurospanbookstore.com

Printed in the United States of America

Library of Congress Cataloging-in-Publication Data
Walker, Andrew, 1961–
Thailand's political peasants : power in the modern rural economy / Andrew Walker.
p.   cm. — (New perspectives in Southeast Asian studies)
Includes bibliographical references and index.
ISBN 978-0-299-28824-2 (pbk. : alk. paper) — ISBN 978-0-299-28823-5 (e-book)
1. Peasants—Political activity—Thailand. 2. Thailand—Politics and government—
1988– 3. Thailand—Rural conditions. 4. Thailand—Economic conditions—1986–
I. Title. II. Series: New perspectives in Southeast Asian studies.
DS586.W26   2012
320.9593088´63—dc23
2011042652

for

DIANE, MALI, *and* JOSH

Contents

Illustrations

Charts

Tables

Acknowledgments

Several people have played a very important part in producing this book. I owe an enormous debt of thanks to my research assistant during much of the time that I worked in Ban Tiam, Rungnapa Kasemrat. Rung has spent much more time in Ban Tiam than I, and her patience, persistence, and detailed reporting gave me a great deal of the local data that I draw on in the chapters that follow. Another research assistant, Supranee Davis, helped me enormously in the bewildering early stages of research. Su did a lot of the foundational surveying on demographics, agriculture, and supernatural power. My friend and colleague, Nicholas Farrelly, also worked with me during some of my early research visits to Ban Tiam. During these visits, and in many conversations since, Nich has helped to shape much of my thinking about how Thai society works.

Of course I must also thank the many people in the village I have called Ban Tiam. I would like to name them; however, some of my public comments on political matters have met with disapproval from the Thai authorities, and I don't want to create any difficulties for my hosts and friends. Some of the sensitive issues discussed in the book also warrant anonymity. The woman I refer to as Aunt Kluay was my generous host for most of the time I worked in Ban Tiam. Together with her husband, mother, and daughter, Kluay always made me very welcome in her home. Many others in the village patiently answered questions, responded to surveys, shared meals and celebrations, gossiped, laughed, provided endless explanations, and did a great deal to make research in the village informative and enjoyable. Special thanks are due to Lek, who facilitated many aspects of my research; Daeng for sharing her extraordinary knowledge on agricultural matters; Tham for her many explanations and wonderful gossip; Wi for his offbeat insights (though not for his many linguistic puns, which I rarely understood); Or, Tan, and Jan for their advice on supernatural matters; and Su, Ta, and Luan for giving me information about projects. Outside Ban Tiam, staff in the municipality, district office, agricultural cooperative, and several shops and restaurants also contributed a great deal to my understanding of local affairs.

I wrote this book while I was employed in two different academic locations in the College of Asia and the Pacific at the Australian National University. I started this research while I was working in the Resource Management in Asia Pacific Program (RMAP). Early on, I fully intended to focus my research on resource management issues, but I soon got distracted by other matters. While working in RMAP several doctoral students helped to shape my thinking about the relationship between state power and peasant communities: Holly High, who worked on development in Laos; Sarinda Singh, who wrote about forests and power in Laos; Jakkrit Sangkamanee, who wrote about water-resource development in Thailand; and Jinghong Zhang, who worked on the *puer* tea "craze" in southern China. In 2009, I transferred to the Department of Political and Social Change under the leadership of Paul Hutchcroft and, a little later, Ed Aspinall. I thank them both, and all of my other new colleagues, for making me very welcome in this new location. Soon after, I was joined by Tyrell Haberkorn, who is always full of useful ideas, suggested readings, and good cheer. I have also benefited from many discussions on peasant politics and economy with Nattakant Akarapongpisak, a doctoral student working on land occupations in northern Thailand. During the final year of writing I was lucky to be able to employ Pongphisoot Busbarat to assist me with some of the research. Pongphisoot is a master compiler of coherent data out of disparate and, at times, inconsistent sources. He chased down an enormous amount of information that has greatly enriched the discussion.

Several others have provided valuable support: Craig Reynolds has been a vital source of inspiration, encouragement, and advice on scholarship in general and Thai matters in particular; Tim Forsyth gave me momentum at a time when it was lagging; Peter Warr, Ikuko Okamoto, and Benchaphun Ekasingh helped me on economic matters; Ryan Lane and David Gilbert provided insightful comments; and Assa Doran suggested some very helpful readings. Chris Baker, Katherine Bowie, and Jonathan Rigg read the full manuscript, and their detailed comments were invaluable in clarifying the arguments and focusing the discussion. Some of the ideas in this book have been road tested on *New Mandala*, the blog I run with Nicholas Farrelly. I have received many useful comments from readers, and some of the critical commentary has helped me to adjust and refine my argument. I would like to thank two readers in particular: Chris Baker and Jean-Philippe Leblond. Both have consistently made incisive comments and suggested important data sources and references that I would have missed otherwise. *New Mandala* also brought me into electronic contact with Rick Doner, whose book *The Politics of Uneven Development* has been very influential in shaping my ideas.

Some parts of this book draw on my previous writing about Ban Tiam: chapter 3 is a reworked version of "Matrilineal Spirits, Descent, and Territorial Power in Northern Thailand," *Australian Journal of Anthropology* 17, no. 2 (2006); chapter 4 is a revised version of "Now the Companies Have Come: Local Values and Contract Farming in Northern Thailand," in *Agrarian Angst and Rural Resistance in Contemporary Southeast Asia*, ed. Sarah Turner and Dominique Caouette (London: Routledge, 2009); some sections in chapter 6 use material from "The Festival, the Abbot, and the Son of the Buddha," in *Tai Lands and Thailand: Community and State in Mainland Southeast Asia*, ed. Andrew Walker (Singapore: National University of Singapore Press, 2010); and chapter 7 is a revised version of "The Rural Constitution and the Everyday Politics of Elections in Northern Thailand," *Journal of Contemporary Asia* 38, no. 1 (2008). I thank the publishers of these works for permission to use them in this book.

Some of the research for this book was supported by the Australian Research Council's *Discovery Projects* funding scheme (project no. DP0881496).

I owe enormous thanks to my family, Diane, Mali, and Josh. They have always been generous in their support and encouragement of my work, even when it occupied too much of my time and energy and regularly took me away from home. This book is dedicated to them.

Thailand's Political Peasants

Introduction

Peasants, Power, and
Political Society

In recent years, Thai public life has been preoccupied with issues of power. In September 2006, the controversial government of billionaire businessman Thaksin Shinawatra was overthrown in a military coup. The tanks that rolled onto the streets of Bangkok had yellow ribbons tied around their gun barrels. Yellow is the color of Thailand's long-reigning king, Bhumibol Adulyadej. By binding the immense potency of the king to their political cause, the coup makers were hoping to demonstrate that it was reasonable to depose a government that derived its legitimacy only from electoral mandate. Royal power, with its illustrious mix of Buddhist virtue and righteous rule, was used to trump parliamentary authority. According to the coup makers, the power of Thaksin, and his formidable party machine, lay in an unsavory tangle of money, violence, patronage, and, quite possibly, unorthodox dealings with dubious supernatural forces. The impure electoral influence of his government arose out of populist appeals to the parochial self-interest of poorly educated voters in the rural north and northeast. With the aging king's health gradually failing, there was real concern among some sections of Thailand's elite that the preeminent power of the royal center was being challenged.

They were right to be worried. Thaksin's dramatic electoral rise showed that power could be produced in new networks of influence. Rural Thailand has experienced decades of economic diversification and administrative integration, and, despite many predictions of its demise, the peasantry has emerged as a powerful political force. Changes within the countryside have nurtured new cultures of inclusion and a reluctance to accept the old political axiom that governments are made in the provinces but unmade in Bangkok.[1]

The rural reaction to the coup itself was muted, although there were some protest rallies and a few cases of arson in the provinces. Members of the royalist government appointed by the military after the coup worked hard to erase Thaksin's populist legacy. They emphasized the need for rural people to be trained in genuine democratic values, and they made the king's "sufficiency economy" philosophy that rural people should live simply and with modest expectations for commercial inclusion a centerpiece of their policy platform. However, there were ominous signs of discontent when most provinces north of Bangkok voted to reject the constitution proposed by the coup makers in a referendum held in August 2007. A few months later the work of the coup was undone when, on the strength of votes from the rural north and northeast, a new government aligned with the exiled Thaksin was formed after the postcoup election of 23 December 2007.

The Bangkok elites could not accept that result. Not long after the election, the anti-Thaksin forces, clad in royal yellow shirts, took to the streets of Bangkok. They occupied Government House and steadily ratcheted up their provocation in the hope of triggering another coup. The new pro-Thaksin government lasted less than a year, falling in the wake of the yellow shirts' occupation of Bangkok's international airport and a series of unfavorable court decisions. A new anti-Thaksin government was cobbled together in December 2008, with strong military backing. The reaction to this second "coup" was much less restrained. Over the new-year (*songkran*) holiday period in April 2009, pent-up anger exploded as the red-shirted supporters of Thaksin rampaged through Bangkok, only to be dispersed by a formidable display of military force. Bangkok's fiery *songkran* riots ushered in another year of political polarization.

The red shirts returned to Bangkok in March 2010 determined to force the government to a new election. The *Bangkok Post* described the arrival of the protesters from the north and northeast as a "rural horde" descending on the capital.[2] It was one of the biggest protest crowds that Bangkok had ever seen. Many thought that the rally would dissipate after a few days—a week or so at the longest—but the protesters demonstrated remarkable resilience and logistical capability. The rural occupation paralyzed parts of central Bangkok for more than two months. Eventually the government could wait no longer, and in mid-May the army moved in. Red-shirt guards responded with slingshots, homemade fireworks, Molotov cocktails, and a seemingly endless supply of burning tires. Some antigovernment hard-liners were armed with rifles and grenade launchers. But the protesters were no match for the military force mobilized against them, and by the time the urban battlefield fell quiet on the evening of 19 May 2010 scores of protesters were dead, and hundreds injured. In the final hours of the confrontation, enraged red shirts torched the vast Central World shopping center, one of Bangkok's glittering symbols of modern retail prosperity.

The next episode in this national power struggle came in July 2011 when Thailand finally went to its second postcoup election. The red shirts and Thaksin's political allies rallied behind the charismatic—but politically in-experienced—figure of his younger sister, Yingluck Shinawatra. In another demonstration of modern Thailand's new political alignments, Yingluck led her party to a decisive victory, winning the vast majority of seats in the rural north and northeast, the heartlands of red-shirt agitation. It was only the second time in Thailand's modern political history that a party had won an absolute majority in parliament (the first time was the Thaksin land-slide in 2005). Yingluck's triumph sent a clear message that the political forces that had brought her brother to power a decade earlier had not dissi-pated. Thaksin had been thrown out of government in September 2006, and his red-shirt followers had been forced out of Bangkok in May 2010, but the fundamental changes in rural society that have been unfolding since the 1970s meant that the balance of power had well and truly shifted toward the provinces.

This book is an exploration of the underlying economic, political, and cul-tural processes that contributed to Thailand's contemporary contests over power. It does not examine Thaksin's political rise or the red-shirt movement directly. Instead, it investigates the rural transformations that have produced a major new player in the Thai political landscape: the middle-income peas-ant. I examine this middle-income peasantry from the perspective of Ban Tiam, a rural village in northern Thailand, located about one hour's drive from the region's major city, Chiang Mai (map 1). Of course it would be ludicrous to argue that life in a single village could fully explain the seismic movements that have shaken an entire country. But it is well to remember the old truism that anthropologists don't study villages, they study *in* villages. At a time when the political motivations of the peasantry are poorly under-stood, detailed ethnographic engagement has the advantage of providing insights that fall below the radar of more totalizing forms of analysis. In sim-ple terms my argument is this: in order to understand the politics of Thai-land's middle-income peasantry—including its strong electoral support for

Thaksin's populist policies, the political passions that brought the red shirts to Bangkok, and the electoral triumph of Yingluck Shinawatra—it is necessary to address how power is perceived in a context of rising living standards and a transformed relationship with the state. Rural politics in contemporary Thailand is not the old rebellious or resistant politics of the rural poor; rather, it is a new middle-income politics of peasants whose livelihoods are now relatively secure. Rural Thailand's new "political society" is energized by a fundamental desire to be productively connected to sources of power.[3] The power of the pro-Thaksin movement lies in a middle-income peasantry whose thoroughly modern political goal is to bind itself to the state, not to oppose it.

Middle-Income Peasants

James C. Scott opens his highly influential *The Moral Economy of the Peasant* by quoting a classic account of marginal subsistence production: "There are districts in which the position of the rural population is that of a man standing permanently up to the neck in water, so that even a ripple is sufficient to drown him."[4] This specific context of livelihood vulnerability—dominated by the specter of hunger and dearth—underpins what Scott calls a "subsistence ethic," which is preoccupied with preventing the livelihood fluctuations that could plunge households and villages into destitution. Economic action operates according to risk-minimization, safety-first principles. Peasant sociality is based on reciprocity, redistribution, and a degree of imposed egalitarianism. Villages have clear social boundaries, they tend to be inward looking, and cautious relations with outsiders are regulated by ideologies of patronage that define reasonable levels of surplus extraction in good times and appropriate forms of assistance in times of need. When moral regulation fails, everyday forms of resistance, subversion, and evasion, combined with the administrative illegality of communal arrangements, can help put a brake on the subsistence-threatening predations of overlords and tax collectors. At its most extreme, the breaching of the subsistence ethic by elites can prompt rebellion or even revolution. The normative roots of peasant politics lie in a defensive reaction against the subsistence threats posed by external economic and political forces. These are the foundational terms in which peasant political behavior has come to be understood in Southeast Asia.

For the peasants of Ban Tiam, and for most other rural dwellers in Thailand, the socioeconomic assumptions that underpin this influential political

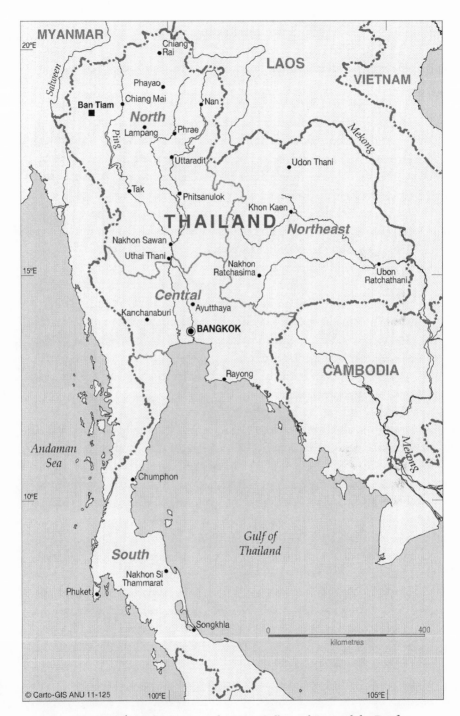

MAP 1. Thailand. (Map by Cartography Unit, College of Asia and the Pacific, Australian National University.)

narrative are no longer useful. Four interrelated transformations have created a new environment for political action.

First, *peasants in Thailand are, for the most part, no longer poor.* They are
now middle-income peasants. They are not necessarily well-off, nor do they
enjoy the consumer comforts of the urban middle class, but dramatic improvements in the rural standard of living have raised most of them well
above the water level of outright livelihood failure. In most areas of rural
Thailand, the primary livelihood challenges have moved away from the classic low-income challenges of food security and subsistence survival to the
middle-income challenges of diversification and productivity improvement.

Second, *Thailand's middle-income peasants have a diversified economy.* Subsistence cultivation is now only a modest component of agricultural activity. There has been a dramatic increase in cash crop production for local and
international markets. Even more important is the fact that nonagricultural
sources of income have proliferated and they are now more significant than
farming for a great many rural households. Only about one in five peasant
households rely solely on agricultural income. Agriculture is still important,
but peasant livelihoods are no longer predominantly agricultural livelihoods.
Peasants are no longer just farmers.

Third, *peasants in Thailand confront a new form of economic disparity.* Thailand has been remarkably successful in tackling absolute poverty, but its
performance on relative poverty (inequality) has been much worse. This
inequality is not the product of surplus extraction by dominating elites; it is
a product of uneven economic development. Disparity is caused by the
relatively low productivity of the rural economy, especially the agricultural
sector. Incomes in rural areas have certainly improved, but not as fast as
incomes in other parts of the economy. In this context, the political challenge
for middle-income peasants is not to avoid subsistence-disrupting extractions but to attract productivity-enhancing inputs.

Fourth, *the Thai state now plays a central role in supporting the peasant economy.* As countries develop, their governments often try to address economic
disparity by subsidizing the rural economy. The Thai government has enthusiastically taken up this challenge, especially since the mid-1970s. Recognizing
the implications of this fiscal shift requires a radical conceptual reorientation.
The peasantry has conventionally been defined in terms of its subordinate
relationship with external power. An enormous amount of scholarly attention has been placed on the political tussle between state extraction and local
resistance. However, in Thailand a new relationship has developed between

the state and the rural economy, characterized not by taxation but by subsidy. Thaksin Shinawatra's government epitomized this new arrangement, but it did not create it: Thaksin's rural populism was the product of a long-term shift in the structural dynamics of Thailand's political economy. The contemporary moral reckoning of the middle-income peasant is not concerned with limiting the state's impositions but with maximizing its largesse.

Some readers may find it disconcerting to talk about middle-income peasants, given the long tradition, and alliterative allure, of coupling peasants with poverty. Let me emphasize that in writing about Thailand's middle-income peasants, I do not intend to deny that unacceptable levels of rural poverty persist in some places, nor do I want to gloss over the livelihood risks confronted by even relatively affluent rural households. Statistical and ethnographic data in the chapters that follow will show that these rural challenges are very real. The middle-income peasantry is a socioeconomic work in progress, and plenty of hazards lie ahead. Nevertheless, there is now an established momentum in rural society toward higher incomes, occupationally diverse livelihoods, and, in a context of national inequality, increasing support from the state. Political identities are now formed by the productive intersection between external power and local livelihoods. This middle-income condition is the essence of political society in contemporary rural Thailand.

But are middle-income peasants really peasants? Classic definitions of peasants focus on a number of criteria: the household is the site of both production and consumption, production is oriented toward subsistence rather than profit, the local community is an important point of social and cultural reference, and the peasant economy is subordinate to the wider political system.[5] Overall, despite very substantial change in recent decades, Thailand's middle-income peasants stand up well against this definition. Household production, in the form of farming and handicrafts, plays a much less dominant role than it once did, because a substantial proportion of income is now earned off-farm from private sector and government employment. Nevertheless, even though livelihood strategies are often multisited, the household remains a principle unit for coordinating the allocation of labor and other resources between various income-earning activities, and, for the substantial majority who own or regularly rent land, the "farm" is still an important source of economic and cultural identity. Regardless of how much income they earn off-farm, rural people in Thailand are still inclined to refer to themselves as farmers (*chao na, chao rai*) or villagers (*chao ban*). Subsistence rice cultivation now makes up only a modest share of most rural households' income, but the aim of other market-oriented economic activities is the maintenance, improvement, and reproduction of the household rather than capital accumulation. *Profit* is not a meaningful term in the vast majority of middle-income rural households. The local community also continues to play an important role in many areas of Thailand, though now less as a source of subsistence security and social insurance than as a foundation for engaging with the state and its development programs. The peasant community has been refashioned, but certainly not dissolved. The most fundamental change in the character of the peasantry has been in the relation between rural people and the wider political system. Surplus extraction has given way to subsidization. This is a very important change in the balance of exchange between the peasantry and the state, but the relationship with the state system remains a central component of rural political identity. For these various reasons, I am comfortable with referring to members of the majority of rural households in Thailand as "middle-income peasants," and the term is certainly preferable to some of the other clumsy labels—*post-peasant* or even *polybian*!—that have been proposed to describe rural people in modern economic and political systems.[6]

POWER IN RURAL THAILAND

Studies of power relations in rural Thailand have emphasized three different dimensions: (1) vertical linkages between people of different social status, (2) horizontal class or community solidarities, and (3) dispersed networks of power and potency. The first two approaches tell us a lot about the politics, or lack of it, of Thailand's poor peasantry—and they provide some useful insights into recent political developments—but they struggle to account for the ambitions and strategies of the new middle-income peasantry. The third, though seemingly somewhat tangential in its attention to supernatural affairs, points in some useful new directions.

Vertical Linkages

During the 1960s and early 1970s, discussions of politics in rural Thailand were dominated by the "patron-client" model. American anthropological research, much of it conducted in the village of Bang Chan on the outskirts of Bangkok, played a crucial role in introducing this idea to Thai studies. In two influential articles, Lucien M. Hanks, one of the principle researchers at Bang Chan, argued that social hierarchies in Thailand were based on the differential accumulation of Buddhist merit and, secondarily, inequalities in power and material resources.[7] These pervasive hierarchies provided a framework for the development of reciprocal relationships in which those of higher status provided protection and other benefits to those below them in return for tribute, loyalty, and personal service. Patron-client ties extended from the poor peasant household to the king himself, organizing Thai society into numerous overlapping "entourages" that cut across status divisions. Within these entourages, relations between patrons and clients were multistranded, drawing together economic, social, religious, and legal connections. Yet, despite this intertwining of roles, patron-client relationships were flexible, both because of movement up and down the hierarchy as merit and status were accumulated and lost and because the relationships were easily terminated if they failed to satisfy either party. "The system has the familiar shape of Adam Smith's free enterprise," a major study of Bang Chan pointed out, as "each person bargains in the open market for the best arrangement he can make, and if this is not satisfactory, he may move elsewhere."[8]

In the Cold War context of communist rebellion in Indochina, the idea that the gap between rich and poor in Thailand was mediated by amiable and flexible relations of patronage was reassuring to Thailand's powerful backers. The American government, which was pouring aid and counterinsurgency funds into Thailand, hoped that its investments would create an effective bulwark against communism. American social science provided the perfect rationale, portraying Thailand as a country where a peasant uprising was unlikely due to the lack of horizontal classlike affiliations: "There are no publics, no masses, nor even a proletariat; instead of these, segments of the population are provided for more or less adequately according to the circle of their affiliation."[9] In a study of "peasant personality" in Bang Chan, Herbert P. Phillips found that there was a strong emphasis on the "munificence, security and benevolence of the authority figure." This political outlook contributed to a "placid community" characterized by "gentleness, affability, and politeness ... in most face-to-face relationships."[10] Writing about the 1957 national election, Phillips argued that those who voted for the prime minister did so because "he is our Master. He has been very good and kind to us. He is like our father, and we are like his children."[11] A similar study in the remote northeast of Thailand by Stephen B. Young described a "non-participatory democracy" based on peasant expectations that their involvement with government should be minimal, powerful people should be obeyed, and duties were unquestioned obligations imposed by the conditions of life.[12]

Given the apparent passivity and disengagement of the peasantry, the search was on for local luminaries who could provide political leadership and form a vanguard for rural advancement. Likely candidates included village headmen, monks, teachers, health workers, irrigation group leaders, crop traders, rich landowners, and merchants. Based on research in three northern Thai villages, the political scientist Clark D. Neher proposed that village leaders operated as a "bridge between the great masses of villagers and the minority group of authorities."[13] These leaders comprised a narrow "political" stratum that was actively involved in dealings with government officials and in implementing development projects. They stood in contrast to the "apoliticals" who comprised the vast majority of rural households for whom "the political system bears no meaningful relationship to daily activities."[14] These apolitical villagers expressed their needs not on the basis of their own livelihood challenges but according to the specific development agenda of the village leadership.[15] In another important study from northern Thailand, Michael Moerman suggested that village headmen were "synaptic" leaders who managed transactions between villagers and the national bureaucracy and, perhaps even more important, prevented state officials from meddling in village affairs.[16]

Although the role of local leaders has continued to be a core preoccupation of studies of rural politics in Thailand, in the 1980s and 1990s the reputation of such leaders shifted sharply. In a national economy experiencing extraordinarily rapid economic growth, accounts of benevolent patrons and village notables pursuing rural improvement were pushed aside by more confronting profiles of "godfathers" (*jaw pho*) who used charisma, money, and strong-arm tactics to create local and provincial fiefdoms.[17] These godfathers embodied an unpleasant combination of business and politics. They used money from provincial enterprises, many of them illegal, to mobilize electoral support, and they used the power of political office to convert public resources into private wealth. In this context, a new paradigm emerged to explain the political behavior of the peasantry: vote buying. The exchange of votes for money was said to be coordinated by provincial power brokers and implemented by teams of cashed-up canvassers who operated at the district and village levels. In studies of political behavior this electoral corruption was described as a typically rural phenomenon, arising out of poverty, parochialism, low levels of education, and a lack of civic morality. Whereas members of the urban middle class made political decisions on the basis of policies and public interest, gullible and grateful voters in the countryside were readily persuaded to exchange their votes for cash, development projects, or protection. This division in political culture was famously described by the political scientist Anek Laothamatas as a "tale of two democracies" that could only be united when rural development transformed "patronage-ridden villages into small towns of middle-class farmers or well-paid workers."[18] Most studies of modern patronage and vote buying describe the political influence of local leaders in morally negative terms, although some have pointed out that provincial godfathers emerged out of a quite specific cultural milieu and often derived legitimacy from old-style idioms of patronage, generosity, and local identity.[19] Some accounts pointed out that vote buying itself was embedded in local systems of evaluation and exchange, belatedly granting the beleaguered peasant a modicum of agency within the overarching patron-client framework.[20]

Horizontal Alliances

The political tumult of the 1970s—which included an unusually open period of government bracketed by bloody Bangkok massacres in 1973 and 1976—prompted some radically different interpretations of rural Thai politics. The contentious and divisive politics of this period encouraged some scholars of rural Thailand to adopt a Marxist framework that focused on class struggle. This new paradigm replaced the reassuring patron-client idioms of reciprocity with the rhetoric of exploitation. Left-leaning observers of rural politics explicitly rejected the "culturalist" assertion that benign patron-client relationships produced political passivity. They argued that the Western academic view of Thailand as "a tranquil peasant society, untouched by the currents of left ideology" was the product of the Thai government's successful oppression of alternative political voices.[21] A new body of historically informed research challenged the relevance of the patron-client model, pointing to earlier cases of peasant struggle against elite oppression and the intrusion of capitalist relations of production. The deepening penetration of capitalism into the countryside since the 1950s, combined with population growth and resource constraints, sharpened social divisions, creating a potentially revolutionary class of marginal peasants and impoverished rural laborers. The commercialization of agriculture undermined subsistence production, increased landlessness and indebtedness, and created many new opportunities for landlords, traders, moneylenders, and corrupt officials to exploit the land and labor of peasant producers. Class division brought about by the dual process of capital accumulation and impoverishment was compounded by the fact that the government's rural development efforts primarily benefited richer peasants.

In an influential account of "the current situation in the Thai countryside," the anthropologist Andrew Turton argued that these socioeconomic developments came to a head in the 1970s, creating a "new historical conjuncture" for Thailand's peasantry, characterized by "new forms of organization and consciousness."[22] Hundreds of local peasant unions were formed throughout Thailand, and peasants assembled in Bangkok and provincial centers to protest about rents, interest rates, and foreclosures. The most important manifestation of this new rural politics was the formation of the Peasants' Federation of Thailand (PFT) in November 1974. The PFT grew rapidly, establishing branches in many provinces and linking up with many isolated farmers' organizations. The support for the PFT was regarded as a clear expression of class tension, with membership strongest in areas where landlessness and tenancy was common. PFT organizers played an active role in promoting newly enacted rental controls, educating farmers about their rights, distributing progressive pamphlets and newspapers, and denouncing corrupt officials and other exploitative village leaders. According to Turton, the effect of this period of rural activism was that "a great many of the rural population were beginning to understand their situation and to formulate political and economic expectations, of at least democratic participation, reforms and greater economic and social justice."[23]

Ultimately, the hopes that rising rural consciousness would bring about radical social change—perhaps even revolution—were unfulfilled. The brutal reimposition of military rule in 1976 witnessed a widespread crackdown on political agitation and the banning of most farmers' organizations. By 1984 even the Communist Party of Thailand had abandoned its rural insurgency and settled for amnesties and social reintegration. This dramatic reversal forced left-leaning scholars to explore the reasons for the failure of agrarian mobilization. One of the principle explanations was the successful use of violence by the Thai state and its allies in the rural elite. Soon after the PFT's formation, a murderous campaign was launched against its leaders. The assassination of many of its leading figures, and a concerted campaign of rural harassment, meant that within nine months of its formation the PFT "had suffered a serious defeat before it had a chance to organize intensively and extensively beyond a few areas in a minority of the country's provinces."[24] Critical academic attention was also directed toward the ideological constraints on peasant mobilization. Katherine A. Bowie produced an extraordinary firsthand account of the right-wing Village Scouts, who counteracted the rhetoric of class divisions by indoctrinating villagers with nationalist and royalist images of Thailand as a united family under the benevolent leadership of the king.[25] Andrew Turton argued that more diffuse ideological forces, such as an increasing culture of consumerism and the pervasive commodification of social relationships, also stunted the development of class sentiments.[26] Picking up on strong academic and applied interest in rural leaders, Turton highlighted the state's success in cultivating village elites who became a rural vanguard in promoting its bureaucratic and capitalist agenda.[27] One of Turton's students, Philip Hirsch, identified rural development schemes as playing a pivotal role in supporting this new array of forces by implanting state power in villages and conscripting villagers to the cause of economic growth and commercialization.[28]

An alternative to this rather bleak imagery of state domination is provided by the conceptual language of resistance. This influential idea was popularized by James C. Scott to argue that peasants were not only political on the rare occasions when they actually rebelled. Drawing on fieldwork in a village in northern Malaysia, Scott vigorously rejected the idea that nonrevolutionary peasants were subject to the ideological hegemony of the state and its allies in the rural elite.[29] He demonstrated that the "everyday politics" of the peasantry was full of evasion, dissent, gossip, foot-dragging, theft, and sabotage. These "weapons of the weak" comprised an active, but nonrevolutionary, domain of peasant politics. In Thailand there have been few explicit studies of these everyday forms of peasant protest, but the concept of rural resistance fell on fertile ground in an activist and academic context where the modern state and the capitalist market were often regarded as corrosive of peasant livelihoods. The idea of nonrevolutionary resistance to the ideological and practical domination of the state has provided a reassuring diversion since the revolutionary hopes of the 1970s were so cruelly dashed.

As in many other countries, one important aspect of this reformulation involved attention to new social movements. During the 1980s and 1990s there was rapid growth in the number of nongovernmental organizations (NGOs) working in rural areas, taking advantage of the opening created by the state-led push for rural development. This new organizational infrastructure contributed to a "new round of political mobilisation" focused on civil society organizations.[30] In a new phase of rural assertiveness, farmers protested about low crop prices, high fertilizer costs, the failure of government-promoted agricultural schemes, indebtedness, the favorable treatment of

agribusinesses, and, most spectacular of all, army-led plans to relocate mil-
lions of farmers out of forest areas. According to Chris Baker's historical
overview, this rural activism gradually divided into two streams.[31] Commercially oriented and secure farmers pursued market-based concerns about
pricing, subsidies, and credit. They negotiated with state agencies and political parties to provide financial relief to farmers who were hurt by climatic
fluctuations, market instability, and government mismanagement. A less
collaborative approach was adopted by marginal farmers—many of whom
lacked tenure security—who faced displacement as a result of dam building, forest conservation schemes, and resource concessions provided to
investors. They were much more cautious in their dealings with state agencies and politicians. Groups representing these poorer farmers eventually
coalesced into the famous Assembly of the Poor, which staged a high-profile
ninety-nine-day rally in Bangkok in 1997 and succeeded in extracting important concessions from the government.[32] Although there is ongoing debate
about the political effectiveness of these social movements, their supporters
argue that they give rural people an alternative to the money politics and
patronage of the electoral system: "The masses, especially in the countryside, have no chance to engage in other democratic activities. However,
when they join grassroots organizations, they are able to learn how the democratic system works, and how to act democratically."[33]

A related approach to rural politics focused attention on issues of local
identity, especially in the north and northeast where there are many distinct cultural and linguistic traditions. In this approach to rural politics, the
Western-tainted language of class slipped away and was replaced by the more
locally palatable language of community (*chumchon*). Academics and leaders
of NGOs argued that the interests of poor and marginal farmers were best
served not by conventional forms of political engagement but by empower-
ing culture, knowledge, and institutions within rural villages. The Thai economic historian Chatthip Nartsupha championed the famous "community
culture" school of thought, drawing inspiration from his extensive interviews
with rural people about rice production, village institutions, rituals, and local
technology.[34] For Chatthip and his followers, the most important line of
political division was not between social classes but between rural communities and the state. Rural communities stood for sustainable economic practice and cultural authenticity whereas the state had become an agent for
Western-dominated globalization and capitalist accumulation. The rich body
of research and activism inspired by the community culture idea was very

successful in documenting genuinely alternative forms of community culture in poor and remote ethnic minority villages where distinctive forms of agricultural practice, resource management, and "local wisdom" (*phum panya*) could be easily identified. However, among what might be called "mainstream" peasants, it was much tougher going as many of them seemed rather happy to abandon their traditions and embrace the benefits, and risks, of commercialization. Faced with the adulterated culture of the peasantry in Thailand, communitarian researchers extended their quest into Laos, Burma, and China to find more authentic versions of traditional "Thai" community.[35]

Despite their origins in the ideological struggles of the Cold War, the "vertical" and "horizontal" approaches to rural politics in Thailand provide some useful insights into the situation of the middle-income peasantry. Debate about the contemporary morality of patronage, leadership, and money politics remains an important preoccupation in Thailand's political culture. Some argue that Thaksin Shinawatra is the ultimate patron gone bad, using his vast financial resources to secure political and economic power. Others view his patronage in a much more benevolent light, suggesting that his economic support for rural people outweighs any faults in his financial or political dealings. More generally, in contemporary rural Thailand, peasants continue to draw on patron-client idioms to express their expectations in dealings with both private enterprise and the state. There is often a degree of nostalgia in these appeals, but they are also part of an assertively modernist, and even experimental, call for fair access to the benefits of economic development. Judgments about old-style values of benevolence and reciprocity are increasingly tangled up with discussions about equity, transparency, and the appropriate balance that leaders strike between private benefit and public good. Understanding the values and idioms of patronage can still help us to understand contemporary rural politics.

Alternative analyses of horizontal alliances also have continuing relevance. Most important, accounts of peasant assertiveness since the 1970s help to explain why the state has been so preoccupied with the economic development of rural Thailand. From the 1960s to the 1980s there was real fear of a communist-led rural rebellion in parts of Thailand. In part, the response to this was military and ideological, but the most enduring strategy has involved extensive state investment in rural development in an attempt to reduce rural poverty and create a politically stable class of middle-income farmers. Elite anxieties about rural rebellion have reemerged in recent years, with some

military and political leaders drawing direct links between the rural activism
of Thaksin's red-shirt supporters and the communist insurgency of earlier
decades.[36] Once again, the government has responded with a strong policy and
budgetary commitment to rural development and social welfare. Some scholars have also painted the recent political turmoil in Thailand as a renewed
phase of the class struggle that was violently repressed in the 1970s.[37] Red-
shirt leaders themselves have promoted their campaign as a struggle between
the rural "serfs" (*phrai*) and the urban "aristocracy" (*amat*). The important
issue is not how sociologically accurate these various claims are but the fact
that idioms of class struggle, and anxieties about social inequality, continue
to influence the political relationship between the peasantry and the state.

However, even though established approaches to rural politics have continuing relevance, it is important to recognize how much rural Thailand has
changed since many of the foundational studies were written. The economic
diversification of the countryside has reconfigured old patron-client ties.
The spatially and economically dispersed livelihood strategies pursued by
most peasant households mean that multistranded ties with a single patron
are much less common. Connections with economically influential figures
remain important, but the modern proliferation of economic and administrative power means that such linkages are now components in a much more
complex network of livelihood security. This diversification of power has also
made class solidarities much less compelling. In the modern rural economy,
connections with various arms of the bureaucracy are often more important
for economic security than relationships with those of similar socioeconomic
status. Community is still an important point of reference, but now as a basis
for engaging with the state rather than seeking autonomy from it. In a highly
commercialized rural economy, the communitarian pitch of many civil society organizations only has niche appeal and is most compelling in specific
cases of intense resource conflict such as dam displacement. All in all, rural
Thailand's modern circumstances have brought about a new form of rural
"political society" that requires new ways of thinking about active and productive relationships with sources of power.

Before examining this new political society, I want to briefly consider a
third approach to power and politics in rural Thailand.

Dispersed Nodes of Power

Most discussions of rural power in Thailand have been premised on the
common sociological view that power amounts to the ability to influence the

behavior of others. Within the patron-client paradigm this power is expressed most clearly through the leadership of the patron, while in alternative approaches based on class, social movements, and community the attempts by local and national leaders to shape the behavior of the peasantry are contested by rebellion, resistance, and withdrawal. However there is a third approach, which adopts a rather different perspective on power, linking it to ideas about sacredness and potency. The anthropologist Neils Mulder provides a very useful summary.

> Power is primarily vested in *sing saksit* (holy objects), such as Buddha images, . . . temple buildings, amulets, holy words, holy water, the spirits and the gods . . . , and in the shrines that they animate, sometimes in strange natural manifestations . . . , very abstractly in the position of the King . . . and as a matter of principle in everything that has mysterious qualities. This power is potentially protective and potentially harmful; it lies all around us like the atmosphere, is everywhere, and when it concentrates in places it results in *sing saksit*. . . . The power of *sing saksit* can be tapped for personal purposes, its protection may be sought and its vengeful manifestations can be neutralized.[38]

Three separate elements in Mulder's summary provide valuable insight into the character of power and politics in rural Thailand. First, power is dispersed; it is a generalized force that can promote security and prosperity. It runs throughout the cosmos and finds potent expression in a wide range of objects, individuals, and actions. Writing about Indonesia, Benedict R. O'G. Anderson famously observed that power is an "intangible, mysterious, and divine energy which animates the universe."[39] Power coalesces in people, spirits, places, objects, words, images, and sounds. It is a pervasive force that can become apparent in a great many different contexts. This may all seem rather arcane, but these ideas about power are fundamentally subversive of prominent political perspectives. Within Thai culture, ideas about potency, magic, and the efficacy of supernatural entities challenge the monopoly of Buddhist merit as an indicator of sacredness. Neat hierarchies of patronage are subverted by untidy and unpredictable networks of power and potency. Within this dispersed framework, the Thai king is clearly one important node of power, but rather than sitting at the pinnacle of the social system, he occupies just one position within it. At the same time, relationships based on class position or community are potentially useful for harnessing power, but they have no particular precedence or any exceptional ideological value. Dispersed power congeals in many different ways, and if the connections that are established within one network of power prove inauspicious, new configurations can be explored.

A second important point highlighted by Mulder is that power can be "tapped into for personal purposes." To use sociological jargon, power is amenable to human agency. Anthropological studies in Thailand, and other parts of Southeast Asia, have shown that there are many ways in which those who want to enhance their prospects for security, health, and prosperity can attach themselves to nodes of power and draw them into highly localized fields of auspiciousness. In rural Thailand, villagers house and feed the spirits that populate the environment; they wear clothes marked with the colors and symbols of power; they carry amulets that have been charged with sacred potency; they tattoo protective charms onto their skin; they hang images of royalty, Buddhism, politics, and commerce in their houses; and their motor vehicles include an array of supernatural accessories to compensate for poor roads and worse driving. The anthropologist Nicola Beth Tannenbaum has written a detailed account of how the dual force of power protection is cultivated through village festivals and private life-cycle rituals.[40] Individuals can enhance their own capacity for power, and their ability to provide protection, by acts of virtuous restraint such as abstaining from sex, alcohol, and certain types of food. Alternatively, they can tap into power more directly by acquiring amulets and tattoos. Power is ubiquitous, but it requires appropriate words and deeds to concentrate it and draw it into intimate domains. In Western sociological traditions, power is often seen as being productive of behavior, but in these cases appropriate behavior and skillful technique are productive of power.

The third important element in Mulder's description relates to the ambivalence of power—it can be "potentially protective and potentially harmful." Tannenbaum notes, "Power is morally neutral. It is inherently neither good nor bad. Beings who have power decide how they will use it."[41] In this sense, power is both unpredictable and malleable. Its ideal representation is neither the virtuous patron nor the predatory capitalist; the uneven distribution of power need not result in either benevolence or exploitation. The form that power takes depends a great deal on how it is treated. In dealings with the spirit world, proper treatment can be understood as a process of domestication through which forms of power that are potentially malevolent are rendered genial and protective as a result of hospitality, generous gifts, and carefully chosen words. The anthropologist Nancy Eberhardt nicely captures the malleability of power by pointing out that villagers consider the domestication of powerful spirits to be similar to the process of child rearing, because both children and spirits are vulnerable to manipulation.[42] The point of the analogy is not that power is weak or innocent but that it can be molded, developed, and socialized in order to meet desirable ends. Once again, this is a subversive perspective on power, given the tendency for discussions of politics in Thailand to draw sharp distinctions between good and able leaders (such as the king) on the one hand and corrupt and unworthy leaders (such as Thaksin) on the other. In fact, power is much too ambivalent to be so neatly categorized, and even the potency of a bad man can be molded and channeled to meet honorable objectives. This moral ambivalence is a persistent motif in rural Thailand's new political society.

MIDDLE-INCOME PEASANTS AND POLITICAL SOCIETY

In order to understand the political dimensions of Thailand's modern rural economy—in which the state plays a central role—I find it useful to draw on the growing body of scholarly work that explores the synergies and productive intersection between the modern state and local livelihoods. In general terms, this work places much less emphasis on administrative and ideological incorporation and more on the collaborative construction of locally specific forms of state practice.[43] It shifts the focus away from the axis of domination and resistance toward an understanding of how power is domesticated and mingled with local aspirations for security and prosperity. Within this body of literature, a particularly useful conceptual guide to what is emerging in Thailand is provided by Partha Chatterjee in his discussions of the changing political culture of the Asian peasantry.[44]

Chatterjee argues that a new form of "political society" has emerged based on the productive interaction between peasant culture and the governing practices of the modern state.[45] Within this political society, local political identities are not remnants from a pre-state era, nor do they emerge in opposition to the state; rather they are the product of engagement with the array of livelihood and welfare programs that the modern state provides. The state now contributes to the "preservation of peasant production and peasant cultures, but under completely altered conditions."[46] The governmental urge to maintain and improve the welfare of rural populations is motivated by norms of benevolence, the expectations of international aid donors, the state's need to mitigate social disruption, the growing electoral power of rural voters, and recognition that the capital-intensive industrial sector cannot absorb the large numbers of people who could be displaced from economically unviable rural communities. Livelihood and welfare support is provided in the form of poverty alleviation programs, employment guarantees, microcredit schemes, and subsistence support. These various programs help to sustain agricultural commercialization and livelihood diversification, but they are usually oriented toward guaranteeing livelihood security rather than promoting capital accumulation. In this sense, state support tends to preserve the peasantry rather than fundamentally transform it.

The politics of rural political society is quite different from the old-style politics of the subsistence-oriented peasantry. In his discussion of twenty-first-century peasant cultures in Asia, Chatterjee makes a very important point when he writes that modern complaints against the state are motivated by concerns about discrimination rather than exploitation.[47] The new rural economy is one in which both the state and the market are "internal" to peasant society, the feudal power of exploiting classes has been eroded, the burden of state taxation is much lighter than it used to be, and there are numerous opportunities for nonfarm employment. In this context, the most important peasant concern is to ensure a nondiscriminatory share of the support and protection that the state provides rather than attempting to avoid the subsistence-undermining threats of onerous taxes and rents. Even violent peasant protests, Chatterjee argues, are a calculated attempt to "draw attention to specific grievances with a view to seeking appropriate governmental benefits" rather than a direct revolt against exploitation. This preoccupation with government benefits "has given a completely new quality to peasant politics, one that was completely missing in the classical understandings of peasant society."[48]

The relationships that develop within rural political society are quite different from those envisaged in the modernist narratives of national citizenship and liberal democracy, which emphasize universal rights, the formal rule of law, civic virtue, and bureaucratic rationality. For Chatterjee, these are the modernist dreams of civil society, which is demographically restricted to "a small section of culturally equipped citizens" within the urban elite.[49] Political society challenges modernist virtues of universality and comes with quite specific strings attached. It is characterized by special interests, personal ties, a plethora of programs serving specific population groups, charismatic and controversial personalities, and recipients who are skilled in negotiating access to the state's resources. It is the politics of diversity and complexity. It resembles what, in China, the anthropologist Mayfair Mei-Hui Yang called a

"gift economy" in which "social relationships and obligations . . . are immediate and revisable, contingent upon personal circumstances and specific
power situations."[50] In the world of political society, benefits flow primarily
from connections, manipulation, calculation, and expediency, not from the
universal rights of modern citizenship.

As a result of its reliance on idiosyncratic and personal ties, political society is often derided as being backward, irrational, and even illegal. It is portrayed as the world of patronage gone bad. This vilification of cronyism and
particularism often gains momentum when the perception develops that
the untidy connections of political society are giving rural populations undue
political influence. Chatterjee writes that "the complaint is widespread in
middle-class circles today that politics has been taken over by mobs and
criminals . . . [by] the importation of the disorderly, corrupt, and irrational
practices of unreformed popular culture into the very hallways and chambers
of civic life, all because of the calculations of electoral expediency. The noble
pursuit of modernity appears to have been seriously compromised because
of the compulsions of parliamentary democracy."[51]

Observers of Thai politics will recognize these as exactly the complaints
that have been leveled against Thaksin's electorally successful populism. Following the coup of September 2006, there was a rush by Thailand's elite to
condemn the political and economic immorality of Thaksin's government
and the electorate that had voted it into power. Bangkok's power brokers
were deeply concerned that new political alignments had emerged characterized by direct transactions between political agents of the state and their rural
beneficiaries. Active attempts were made to delegitimize this new political
society with regular disparaging talk of local strongmen, parochial electors,
and rampant vote buying. The old language of patronage and political passivity was rolled out to explain, and dismiss, Thaksin's electoral success. A
grotesque stereotype of political society was created in which complex political relationships were reduced to one-dimensional transactions between
compliant peasants and manipulative elites. This was not just propaganda
from a military-appointed government. Progressive forces within Thailand's
civil society, seemingly alarmed by the peasantry's abandonment of class
consciousness and communal values, provided plenty of ammunition for
those who wished to condemn Thailand's new "electocracy." As one of Thailand's leading leftist intellectuals wrote, "At the base of the electocracy lay
the 40 million voters, the majority of whom were poor, ill-educated and rural-
based. With most of their constitutional rights routinely trampled by arrogant

officials, local mafia bosses and politicians, they had to take advantage of the one that remained: to sell their votes to their local political patrons for money, jobs, protection or informal welfare benefits. Their interests long ignored by urban policy-makers, their local resources depleted by both state and private sectors, these voters perforce became willing accomplices of the electocrats in the systematic corruption of electoral 'democracy.'"[52]

POLITICAL SOCIETY IN BAN TIAM

If we are to understand the contemporary politics of rural Thailand we need to do much better than hackneyed images of poor, uneducated, and compliant peasants who are only legitimately political when they actively oppose external power. The concept of political society provides a useful way forward, especially when combined with anthropological insights into the diversity and malleability of power. Chatterjee's interest in the informal and unorthodox connections that people create with sources of power usefully extends the boundaries of what is considered to be political behavior. This approach alerts us to the reality that political activities are often illegible, especially when placed alongside the more formal vocabulary of patronage, leadership, class consciousness, and social movements. In adopting and adapting this approach to examine the northern Thai village of Ban Tiam, I consider political society to comprise the overlapping networks of relationships that link people and entities of differential power. The residents of Ban Tiam create these networks through day-to-day acts of sociality, ritual, language, and labor in an attempt to enhance their security and prosperity. In creating, maintaining, and evaluating these connections, the residents of Ban Tiam are informed by an evolving set of values that regulate the performance of power and define how more socially distant relationships should be drawn into local circuits of political exchange. I examine these processes in four different domains: the spirit world, the state, the market, and the community.

Malleable Spirits

Ban Tiam's sprawling political society is populated by a vast number of spirits (fig. 1). They occupy trees, rivers, mountains, paddy fields, rocks, natural springs, and buildings. There are spirits that watch over the temple, the irrigation dams, the community rice mill, and each house in the village. Social groups, whether they are families, lineages, hamlets, or the entire village, have relationships with particular spirits. Some of Ban Tiam's spirits are highly localized, exercising their authority over only a single building or just one small plot of land. Others are great lords whose vast networks of influence extend throughout northern Thailand. Many of them are unnamed, but those with greater powers usually have impressive aristocratic titles. In this spiritually fertile landscape, new spirits can be discovered, given names, and solicited for advice and protection. Ambitious claims about the lordly status of spirit guardians can be made by erecting a shrine, passing on their advice and guidance to other villagers, or even, as one woman occasionally did, sitting painlessly on a bed of nails to demonstrate her supernatural master's protective skills.

Given Thai society's pervasive enchantment with the supernatural, the spirit world is a useful place to start when exploring the peasantry's orientation to power. As John Holt, a scholar of Buddhism, argues in his recent study of Lao religion, spirits have a distinct "ontology of power."[53] Spirits are concentrated nodes of the generalized and intangible forces that run throughout the cosmos. More specifically, they are coagulations of the forces of nature— it is no accident that many sprits are associated with large trees—and of the

FIGURE 1. Forest spirits at a festival in Ban Tiam, Thailand. (Photo by the author.)

enduring influence of former occupants, especially the founding ancestors who established the first human settlements. Spirits are spatially and socially dispersed and can be readily mobilized through local ritual action. This model of "fragmentary, disorganized and unsystematic" power has long been unattractive to ruling elites, who have sought to centralize power and promote the royal or bureaucratic virtue of the capital.[54] Rulers have variously sought to restrict, or disparage, the population's dealings with spirits; to promote more orthodox forms of religious belief; to draw the most powerful spirits into their central domain; or to make themselves the object of local devotion. However, the landscape is simply too productive of spiritual power for these efforts to achieve long-term success. A supernatural counterpart of Chatterjee's political society flourishes, in which villagers can negotiate mutually beneficial arrangements with an unpredictable array of lords and masters. Photos of Thailand's king are displayed in most homes in Ban Tiam, but he is just one among many sources of divine authority.

Spirits are highly malleable entities, and, if they are treated correctly, they are generous in their provision of health, good fortune, and protection. They can watch over crops, help in the selection of winning lottery numbers, ensure safe return from journeys, and even help young men to avoid military conscription. Lineage spirits can bless a marriage, help a couple to live together in harmony, and bring good fortune to their enterprises. However, if spirits are neglected or offended they can bring bad weather, crop failure, illness, accidents, and domestic disharmony. So what does it mean to treat spirits correctly? Spirits do not necessarily respond positively to behavior that is regarded as ethically good; their politics is based on the pragmatic exchange of favors.[55] In the secular world, some observers may be inclined to call this corruption. Typically, these exchanges involve acts of domestication that draw spirits into the human realm and bind them, with offerings, into mutually beneficial relationships. Some acts of domestication are very mundane: before a meal is eaten in a natural setting it is common for one of the party to honor the lord of the place by putting a small ball of sticky rice on the ground and pouring a tiny shot of whisky into the soil. More long-lasting interactions with spirits are marked by building a small house for the spirit and inviting it to live there. These spirit shrines are a common feature of the village landscape. Most are small and unremarkable structures, usually unobtrusive amid the shrubbery and domestic detritus that marks household compounds. Others, especially those belonging to the protective lords, are more substantial, resembling small houses. Offerings to spirits, whether they are capricious tree spirits or great lords, usually take the form of food and drink. Hungry spirits, like hungry people, can become fractious and cause trouble, so they must be fed with rice, curries, fruit, and drinks. On exceptional occasions, the spirits are honored with a pig's head. Spirits are also kept in good temper with inducements of incense, flowers, candles, tobacco, betel nuts, puffed rice, and, occasionally, music.

Attitudes toward spirits reflect orientations to power that are both highly parochial and much more wide ranging. The authority of some of the most important spirits in Ban Tiam derives from their intimate relationship with local descent groups. This is a highly localist version of power and potency, linked to ancestors, domesticity, and, in particular, maternal relationships, which are traced back matrilineally to ancestral "origin houses" within the village. These are northern Thailand's famous *pu nya* (ancestor) spirits, and in Ban Tiam they remain an important point of moral reference and source of security for many residents. Other spirits, by contrast, are much more cosmopolitan, forming part of an administrative hierarchy that connects Ban Tiam with other places and other layers of supernatural authority. For these spirits, power is a matter of lordship and territorial incorporation. There are certainly points of tension between these two types of power, but one of the striking features of spirit practice in Ban Tiam is the strength of the connection that has been established between them. Ban Tiam is a small village, but it has forged supernatural connections with some of the most powerful lords in the land.

The Desirable State

If you sit down to eat at any social gathering in Ban Tiam, the chances are that you will be sitting with an agent of the state (fig. 2). As the Thai state has consolidated its administrative reach, expanded its support for rural communities, and decentralized many of its functions, the line between bureaucracy and community has become very blurred. At the lowest levels of administration, the workplaces, personal lives, and administrative practices of state officials are often comprehensively entangled with the lives of those they are charged with governing. In Ban Tiam about 30 villagers (out of 130 households) hold regular positions in various arms of the vast Thai bureaucracy. About a dozen currently hold, or have held, various types of political office, either by election or by appointment. Many others find temporary employment in state-initiated construction projects, environmental programs, and economic development schemes. On top of this direct engagement, the standard bureaucratic markers of statecraft—house numbers, surnames, land-tenure documents, compulsory schooling, a national currency, and keenly contested elections—have become unremarkable aspects of village social life. State practice now plays a central role in maintaining the economic via-bility of Ban Tiam's middle-income peasants, and in shaping their political and cultural orientations.

This social and cultural embeddedness is reflected in the way people talk about the state. Anthropological research on localized practices of state mak-ing has shown that the tendency of the state to present itself in standardized and autonomous terms is often countered by the entanglement of its officials in local networks of meaning. In Ban Tiam I cannot recall people using the formal Thai word for the state (*rat*), nor is there any obvious northern Thai counterpart. The use of the general word for government (*rataban*) is more common, although people are much more likely to refer to specific govern-ments by using the name of the prime minister who led them. Most common is for the state to be talked about in terms of the various agencies and officials

FIGURE 2. Sharing a meal with the head of the National Park Office, Ban Tiam, Thailand. (Photo by the author.)

with which villagers have regular dealings, often using acronyms, abbreviations, or locational markers for agencies and kin terms combined with nicknames for individual officials. So, the Royal Forest Department is simply *pa may* (forest) in which *ai pong* (older brother Pong)—or, more disrespectfully, *ki maw pong* (drunken Pong)—is the senior local official. These are unremarkable practices, but they provide some indication of how the modern state is conceptually disaggregated and personalized so that it can be subjected to the regulatory force of local value systems.

In Ban Tiam, multistranded relations with the state are regulated by a set of values that I refer to as a "rural constitution." I use this term to emphasize that it is not just formal written constitutions that regulate and channel the power of the state in Thailand. The regulatory object of the rural constitution is not the formal political system but the extensive network of relationships that makes up political society. The rural constitution is an uncodified set of values that is based on the desirability of embedding political and administrative power into local networks of exchange and evaluation. Agents of the state, like spirits, need to be domesticated. The rural constitution is not one that seeks to limit the state's reach, so as to preserve local sources of power. Rather it is premised on the view that the state can enhance local power by providing new modes of authority, additional resources, and innovative forms of symbolic capital that can all be selectively drawn on to pursue security, status, and livelihood enhancement. Of course, the state often fails to meet the expectations embodied within the rural constitution, and this generates responses that range from idle gossip to slander, open dissent, and protest at the ballot box. These responses may look like classic forms of peasant resistance, but it is important to remember that they are now motivated primarily by the state's failure to deliver expected benefits rather than by its disruptive intrusion. The middle-income peasant's political responses are very different from the subsistence-protecting resistance of farmers who lived with the ever-present threat of livelihood catastrophe.

In Ban Tiam, the development of political society has taken a particular institutional form: the project (*khrongkan*). Projects are local initiatives, usually funded by the state but sometimes supplemented by private donations, that are aimed at supporting livelihoods and promoting development. At a village level these have become a central manifestation of the new fiscal relationship between the peasantry and the state. The beauty of projects is that they provide a clearly defined institutional framework for concentrating and domesticating diffuse forms of state power. They can be thought of as spirit shrines for the state. They are auspicious sites of development, where the forces of the state are productively bound with local livelihoods and the moral appeal of community.

The Hollow Market

For the residents of Ban Tiam, "the market" (*kad* in northern Thai, *talat* in central Thai) is a place where you go to buy and sell things. There is the regular market in the district center, where a number of Ban Tiam's residents work selling vegetables, cooked food, and clothing. The district market is a place where you can get a quick meal and a shot of whiskey, buy freshly slaughtered pork and beef, visit a beautician, sell bunches of coriander collected in the paddy fields, or get a document photocopied. The district market swells dramatically every Monday when it hosts the weekly market, attended by a mass of traveling merchants selling rice, clothing, household utensils, and electrical appliances. In this chaos of commodities, agricultural tools are laid out alongside brassieres, alarm clocks, Buddhist amulets, DVDs, tracksuits, and pungent piles of red chilies. Surrounding the market is a cluster of shops, restaurants, and banks, which comprise the commercial hub of the district. A few kilometers to the west, on the outskirts of the district center, there is the "Chinese market." It is really just a couple of shops and a petrol station, but it was once an important site of local commerce established by a Chinese merchant family. It is now a good place to buy a motorbike, a handheld tractor, a karaoke player, or a mobile phone. Some Ban Tiam villagers make regular trips to the large markets in Chiang Mai to buy stock for their shops and market stalls or, in the case of the village's traders, to sell the agricultural produce they have purchased from neighbors. These are the various places that residents of Ban Tiam refer to when they talk about the market: they are physical sites of exchange where, much like spirit shrines and development projects, impersonal and invisible forces are congealed and drawn into specific interpersonal transactions.

The terms *kad* or *talat* are rarely, if ever, used to describe the market in more abstract terms. I sometimes heard people talking about the government's attempt to promote a "free market" (*talat seri*) through its agricultural trade agreement with China. That this term was picked up in Ban Tiam is hardly surprising: garlic has been the village's most important cash crop, and there was widespread concern about the impact of Chinese garlic imports on Thai producers. However, it is much more common to hear people talk about economic forces in terms of prices (*rakha*). Ban Tiam's farmers have particular reason to be preoccupied with prices because of the roller-coaster fluctuations that have occurred in the price of garlic over the past few decades. High garlic prices have made farmers wealthy, but low prices have also plunged many of them into debt. In Ban Tiam the vagaries of the market are simplified into the standard complaint of agriculturalists that commodity prices are inclined to fall while input costs can be relied upon to rise. These complaints frequently crop up in discussions of another abstract concept: the economy (*setthakhit*). The economy is almost always described in negative terms except when nostalgically, and selectively, recalling the good old days of the garlic boom. As one farmer commented, parodying the local administration's new tourism slogan, "Ban Tiam has the atmosphere of Switzerland but the economy of Ethiopia." A common self-deprecating response when I greeted people each time I arrived in the village was that they were keeping well but lacked only one thing—money.

These local expressions of economic deficiency have a sound basis in the fact that the local economy is a rather hollow one. Whereas agents of the state and the supernatural world are thick on the ground, private capital is conspicuously underrepresented in Ban Tiam's political society. In the past there were timber companies, a mine, and a tobacco factory in the district, but they have now disappeared and are represented only by malevolent spirits that haunt some of the old timber camps. Over the past thirty years the private sector has expanded in size but, apart from the heavily government-supported construction sector, it remains dominated by shopkeeping and household-based handicrafts. There is very little evidence of local capital accumulation and a dearth of domestic or foreign investment in local enterprise. Government attempts to promote rural enterprise have been largely ineffectual, beyond the widespread promotion of low-value handicraft activity. This takes us back to the important point made by Chatterjee in his discussion of political society: the state resources that flow through political society tend to preserve, rather than transform, the basic structures of the rural economy. State programs are directed primarily toward livelihood support rather than promoting capital accumulation.

The marginal role of private capital in the local economy informs a particular orientation toward it. I describe this as an "experimental" orientation. This involves an open-minded willingness to enter into new kinds of commercial relationships in order to draw private capital more fully into the clearly deficient local economy. At present in Ban Tiam, this is most evident in the agricultural sector where contract farming arrangements with agribusinesses in Chiang Mai have been used to try out new cash crops, agricultural inputs, and cultivation techniques. Farmers explicitly refer to the advent of contract farming as a process of experimentation, often stating that they are uncertain about what results they can expect and that they are just "trying out" a new crop or agricultural input. Some even talk of "playing" with alternatives, conveying a sense that engagement with private capital involves a significant element of risk taking, perhaps even gambling. This is not the sort of language that is used in relation to subsistence rice production, nor would more fundamental relationships with the spirit world or the state be framed in such speculative terms. Of course, an open-minded experimental orientation does not rule out critique. Experiments often fail, and agents of private capital do not always fulfill expectations. It is unsurprising that these inevitable disappointments give rise to frustration, anger, and attempts to manipulate the system to minimize losses. Again, these acts may appear to be typical examples of peasant discontent with capitalist intrusion, but to describe them in these terms is to resort to an ethnographically thin account that dis-embeds acts of discontent from their broader context of experimental engagement.

The Lure of Community

The peasant community is often viewed as an important site of opposition to both the bureaucratic state and the capitalist market. For followers of Thailand's community culture school, communal institutions mark a clear boundary between insiders and outsiders and enforce internal norms of reciprocity, assistance, and redistribution. However, communal practices in Ban Tiam are now only peripherally and nostalgically concerned with guaranteeing basic subsistence. The central concern of communal practice is now to ensure that the village is favorably positioned as an appropriate site for subsidy and investment. Community is a powerful lure that can draw external sources of power into local circuits of exchange. This shift has not brought about the demise of community, nor has it produced a simple transition from communities that are "inwardly oriented" to communities that "look upward and outward."[56] The transformation is more subtle than that. In rural Thailand's new political society, community has become a morally valued strategy for pursuing local security, prosperity, and good health through interaction with the state, the market, and the spirit world.

The virtuous interaction between communal solidarity and economic development is achieved through the manipulation of symbols. Following Anthony P. Cohen, I take the view that community is based on "attachment or commitment to a common body of symbols."[57] These symbols are usually rather vague, simple, superficial, and unelaborated because this enables them to accommodate a range of different interpretations and avoids dispute over specifics. In Ban Tiam these aggregating symbols cluster around the term *suan huam* rather than the recently coined Thai word for community, *chumchon*. The term *suan huam*, which can be translated as "the group as a whole" or "collective," refers to a morally desirable domain of common endeavor. The *suan huam* is concerned with village activities, public festivals, shared infrastructure, community projects, and common worship. These are morally desirable domains of activity because they typically involve personal sacrifice: they divert time, labor, or resources from the individual domain to the broader collective.

What role does the *suan huam*/community play in the constellations of power that I have been considering? Put simply, community adds potency in the form of visibility and moral authority. Chatterjee's discussion of political society is particularly helpful on this point. In his discussion of a squatter colony in Calcutta, he shows how community-based welfare organizations help the residents to "get themselves identified as a distinct population group that could receive the benefits of governmental programs."[58] Among scholars of development it has become commonplace to observe that the modern state uses categories of community to render populations legible to administrative practice. But in Chatterjee's observations we see the flip side of this process: the institutions and imagery of community are used by the population to render themselves eligible for government support. In this sense, community is the mutual construction of both legibility and eligibility. Aspirations for socioeconomic improvement and claims for livelihood support from the state are turbocharged when they are embedded in the sacred context of collective endeavor. In rural Thailand's new political society, community is a site where external power is domesticated and bound to local livelihoods.

1

Thailand's Persistent Peasantry

For more than one hundred years there have been claims from many parts of the world that the peasantry is disappearing. Writing at the end of the nineteenth century, Vladimir Lenin famously argued that "commodity exchange and capitalist production" in rural Russia meant that the peasantry was "being completely dissolved" and replaced with classes of bourgeois commodity producers and proletarian wage laborers.[1] A hundred years later the historian Eric Hobsbawm declared that the work of international capitalism was done, writing that "the most dramatic and far-reaching social change of the second half of the twentieth century, and the one which cuts us off for ever from the world of the past, is the death of the peasantry."[2] Soon after, Michael Kearny criticized his fellow anthropologists' nostalgic preoccupations with the peasantry, arguing that "peasants are mostly gone and . . . global conditions do not favour the perpetuation of those who remain."[3] Closer to home, another nail in the coffin was provided by Robert Elson's *The End of the Peasantry in Southeast Asia*: "There can be no mistaking the romanticized shadow for the substance, which is that the peasantry, gradually from the early twentieth century, and from the mid-century on at an accelerating rate, has been radically reconstituted, through its own agency and that of broader forces of change, into a series of more modern categories of social formation. The world of Southeast Asia is no longer a world dominated by peasants and peasant modes of life."[4]

In recent years, rural commentators have been particularly preoccupied with the role of "neoliberal" policies in accelerating this process of "depeasantization."[5] In the rural context, neoliberalism refers to free-market policies

34

such as reducing tariffs on agricultural imports, encouraging exports, reducing farm subsidies, dismantling government marketing boards, halting land reform, making it easier to buy and sell land, and encouraging agribusinesses to get involved in farming. Many developing countries have adopted these policies in response to structural adjustment pressures from international financial institutions. Writing about African peasantries, Deborah Fahy Bryceson describes a series of neoliberal "turning point policies" that undercut the prosperity rural producers had achieved during the 1950s and 1960s. These policies have reduced the profitability of farming, promoted the fragmentation and individuation of livelihoods, undermined social cohesion, and prompted many rural households to revert to low-value subsistence cultivation.[6] Echoing Lenin's prognosis for Russia in the 1890s, Bryceson writes, "Agricultural restructuring has struck at the heart of the middle peasantries' agrarian base.... As the middle peasantries' productive base gives way, strong centrifugal forces of economic polarization and class differentiation set in ... and the middle peasantry starts pulling apart at the seams."[7] Similar scholarship has also emerged from Latin America where the abandonment of agrarian reform and social welfare policies means that "Increasingly ... peasant livelihoods and rural community trajectories will be determined by powerful global forces, resulting in dependency for those who survive as peasants and proletarianization for those who do not."[8]

If these pessimistic assessments are correct, then the political society of the peasantry would best be interpreted as a rearguard attempt by an ever-diminishing population to hold onto the last remnants of social identity and state support and to resist the incursion of market forces for as long as possible. The apparent threat of neoliberalism has provided fertile ground for a new generation of studies on resistance and the mobilization of transnational social movements to defend the rights and livelihoods of ever more marginal peasant farmers. Partha Chatterjee's account of political society in India has been criticized for failing to recognize that state support for marginal population groups is tenuous and likely to be swept away by the rising tide of neoliberal policies. One critic argues that Chatterjee "seems to be curiously oblivious of the neoliberal turn in the global economy" and that contemporary India has witnessed the "withdrawal of the state from the economy and social sectors, not its intervention in favour of the dispossessed."[9] Another reviewer of Chatterjee's work describes political society as "already part of an older world order" and a "social compromise which capital and the state have abandoned for aggressive neoliberal policies."[10]

I don't accept these predictions about the disappearance of the peasantry and the triumph of neoliberalism. Recent rural sociology has shown us that peasant societies encountering capitalist development do not follow any clear trajectory toward social bifurcation, proletarianization, or impoverishment. Peasantries have proven to be remarkably resilient. One of the principle reasons for this is that rural households are often very efficient managers of agricultural land and labor—especially in sectors such as rice farming where economies of scale are elusive—and they are also very good at combining farm and nonfarm sources of income. Peasant households are certainly changing, but it is wrong to assume that they are disappearing. It is also important to note that these adaptive households are not confronting an internationally standard set of neoliberal policies. The catchall label "neoliberalism" conceals the reality that economic policy has been diverse in its implementation and its impact on the peasantry. In Thailand, a range of policies commonly identified as neoliberal have been adopted, especially in response to the Asian financial crisis of the late 1990s. Thaksin Shinawatra's rural neoliberalism included the negotiation of free trade agreements with China, India, and Australia; the continued promotion of agribusiness; and the extension of land tenure to promote asset capitalization. These policies created concerns among some rural producers, but they were not accompanied by the withdrawal of state support for the rural sector. The policy record in Thailand is not consistent with the negative picture emerging out of Africa and Latin America. In Thailand, state support over the past forty years has helped to lift the peasantry out of poverty and consolidate its middle-income position.

The Rise of the Middle-Income Peasantry

The majority of rural households in Thailand are composed of middle-income peasants in a middle-income country. Thailand's gross domestic product (GDP) per capita of US$3,894 places it firmly within the World Bank's middle-income range, along with regional neighbors China (US$3,744), Indonesia (US$2,349), and the Philippines (US$1,745).[11] It is substantially more affluent than low-income Vietnam (US$1,052), Laos (US$940), and Cambodia (US$677) but well behind upper-middle-income Malaysia (US$6,975) and high-income South Korea (US$17,078). Thailand's current economic position is the result of sustained economic growth since the 1960s (chart 1). From 1960 until the mid-1980s there was an average annual growth in GDP of about 7 percent, driven first by a 70 percent increase in the area of agricultural cultivation, followed by a phase of import-substituting industrialization.[12] Since the mid-1980s strong foreign investment in Thai industry has produced a surge in manufactured exports. From 1987 until the economic crash that occurred ten years later, the size of Thailand's economy more than tripled, with annual growth averaging 9.5 percent. This was the most rapid economic growth in the world. There was a sharp contraction of 11 percent in 1998 as a result of the Asian financial crisis but a resumption of more modest growth the following year. After 2000 the average growth rate was around 5 percent per year, until the global financial crisis briefly put the economy into reverse in 2009.

Despite very considerable geographic and sectoral unevenness, which will be considered in detail in the following section, sustained economic growth has occurred in all regions of Thailand. This is clear from data on gross regional product (GRP) per capita.[13] Overall, between 1981 and 2008, Thailand's GDP per capita increased by 224 percent in real terms. The most extraordinary regional success story was the central region (not including Bangkok) where urbanization, industrialization, and agricultural commercialization lifted GRP per capita by a phenomenal 452 percent. Growth in other regions was considerably slower, but still substantial. In the northeast,

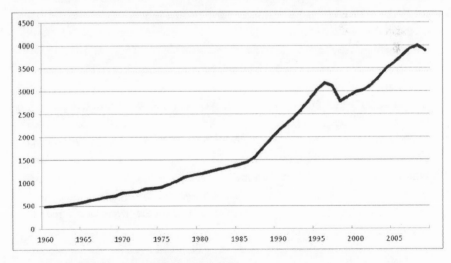

CHART 1. GDP per capita in Thailand from 1960 to 2009, constant 2009 US$. (Data from the World Bank's World Development Indicators Online, accessed 23 June 2010.)

regarded as Thailand's most economically backward region, GRP per capita increased by 143 percent over the same period. A recent study of agricultural development noted that "during the last 35 years, the Northeast was one of the fastest growing economies in the world. The Northeast's long-run growth rate of annual real GDP during 1970 to 2004 was 3.1%, rival[ing] that of Latin America, South Asia or of high-income countries."[14] Since 1981, the increase in GRP per capita has been equally impressive in the north (136 percent) and the south (155 percent). These regional rates of per capita increase are only slightly lower than the increase in Bangkok itself (164 percent), although, of course, GRP per capita in Bangkok started from a much higher base.

This sustained economic growth has been accompanied by considerable diversification in Thailand's economy. Thailand has "successfully transformed itself from an agrarian economy, heavily dependent on rice and land-intensive production, to an export-led economy that combines agriculture, agro-industry, manufacturing and services."[15] The industrial sector has grown from 19 percent of the economy in the early 1960s to about 44 percent of a much larger economy in 2008. A sevenfold increase in industrial output since the early 1980s has created more than 5 million new jobs. Thailand has emerged as a major producer and exporter of clothing and footwear, electronic appliances, and automobiles. Rapid growth in tourism, retailing, and food services has created more than 10 million new jobs in the service sector.[16] Diversification has also taken place in the agricultural sector, with a considerable increase in the importance of nonsubsistence crops. Thailand has become a very successful and highly diverse agricultural exporter. In the early 1960s, rice made up about 43 percent of Thailand's agricultural exports, and there were only seven commodities that contributed more than 1 percent of agricultural exports. By 2007, rice contributed only about 20 percent to agricultural exports, and there were fifteen commodities that contributed more than 1 percent each.[17] A good number of Thailand's newer agricultural exports are the product of value-added domestic processing: canned chicken, refined sugar, pet food, canned pineapples, and beverages. Thailand's agricultural work force has declined—although, as we will see, not as much as in many other middle-income countries—but the range of livelihood activities has increased considerably.

In absolute terms, the social impacts of Thailand's rapid growth and economic diversification have been very positive indeed. Livelihoods in rural Thailand are now much more secure than they were when many of the foundational studies of peasant politics were written in the 1960s and 1970s. The most striking change is the dramatic reduction in rural poverty. In the 1960s about 96 percent of rural household were living below the poverty line. Almost every peasant household was poor. The rate of rural poverty fell steadily during the 1960s and 1970s, increased as a result of the economic slowdown in the early 1980s, and then continued its downward trend until the middle of the 1990s, when it reached 14 percent. As a result of the Asian financial crisis, rural poverty climbed sharply to 22 percent in 1999, but it has declined rapidly since the early 2000s, falling to 10 percent in 2007.[18] Thailand's poverty reduction is part of an East Asian regional trend that is "unprecedented in world history."[19] Thailand's recent performance is all the more remarkable because since 2002 the poverty rate has been based on an increased poverty line that better reflects household consumption patterns.[20] Thailand's performance on other indicators has been equally impressive: since the 1960s life expectancy at birth has risen from age 54 to 69; the infant mortality rate has dropped from 10 percent to about 1 percent; and primary school completion has increased from 36 to 87 percent.[21] The United Nations' Millennium Development Goals have been "effectively achieved" well in advance of the 2015 target.[22] For most people in rural Thailand economic growth and diversification have meant that subsistence-threatening absolute poverty is no longer a predominant concern, although there are areas of persistent hardship in the least-developed provinces of the northeast and north.

National income data coming out of Thailand's regular household socioeconomic survey provide a broad indication of the condition of Thailand's contemporary peasantry (table 1). The average income of all households in Thailand is 224,000 baht per year. Unsurprisingly, in rural areas the average is somewhat lower at 172,000. There is some regional variation in average rural incomes: household incomes are highest in central Thailand (187,000 baht) followed by southern Thailand (175,000), northeast Thailand (166,000), and northern Thailand (156,000). Of course, not all rural people are peasants, and these rural averages also include the household incomes of shopkeepers, business operators, and civil servants. Fortunately, the household socioeconomic survey includes data for broad occupational groups, although these are not disaggregated by region. For landowning farmers (about 20 percent of the national population) the average household income is 150,000 baht; for tenants (4 percent) household income is 145,000. Agricultural workers (7 percent) are the worst off with average household incomes of 117,000.[23]

TABLE 1. Average income and the poverty line in Thailand by region and population group.

	Thailand	Bangkok	Central (rural)	North (rural)	Northeast (rural)	South (rural)	Municipal	Non-municipal	Landowning Farmers	Tenant Farmers	Agricultural Workers
Average monthly household income (baht)	18,660	35,007	15,586	12,977	13,828	14,593	28,005	14,307	12,488	12,046	9,759
Average annual household income (baht)	223,920	420,084	187,026	155,719	165,940	175,121	336,060	171,684	149,856	144,552	117,108
Poverty line per person per month (baht)	1,443	2,065	1,554	1,437	1,452	1,496	1,443	1,333	1,333	1,333	1,333
Average household size (persons)	3.3	3.2	3.2	3.1	3.6	3.5	3.2	3.4	3.4	3.4	3.4
Annual household poverty line (baht)	57,143	79,296	59,674	53,456	62,726	62,832	65,472	54,386	54,386	54,386	54,386
Average annual household income as percentage of annual household poverty line (percent)	392	530	313	291	265	279	513	316	276	266	215

SOURCES: National Statistics Office, *Report of the 2007 Household Socio-economic Survey*, tables 1 and 2; Department of Community Development, *Report of Thai People's Quality of Life in 2008*. Poverty line data are from National Statistics Office, *Sathiti Khomun Khwam Yakchon lae Kan Krachai Raidai, 2531–2552* [Data on poverty and income distribution, 1998–2009], table 1. Household size data are from United Nations Development Program, *Human Security*, table A1.0.

NOTE: The household poverty line is the poverty line per person per month multiplied by twelve and by average household size. For the agricultural occupation groups I have assumed the poverty line to be the nonmunicipal poverty line. Regional (rural) data are from 2008; all other income data are from 2007.

Absolute figures like this don't necessarily mean a lot, especially when one is trying to make some assessment about livelihood security or middle-income status. One way of making them a little more meaningful is by comparing them to the poverty line, which in 2007 was about 57,000 baht per household per year, although it varies from region to region (table 1, fifth row). This poverty line is based on the costs of a bundle of food and nonfood items. It was raised by 26 percent for rural Thailand in 2002 in response to concerns that it did not adequately reflect contemporary consumption patterns.[24] For Thailand as a whole, the average income in 2007 was 3.9 times the poverty line (table 1, final row). For rural Thailand the ratio was almost 3.2, for landowning farmers it was 2.8, for tenants it was 2.7, and for agricultural workers it was 2.2. Given that in the 1960s almost all rural people lay below the poverty line, these ratios are clear indications of a very significant increase in the living standards of peasant households. With an average income of two to three times the poverty line, the Thai peasantry is certainly not affluent, but for the average rural household there is now a substantial buffer against outright livelihood failure.

Of course, averages conceal internal variation. What do the national statistics tell us about income variation in rural Thailand? Table 2 provides a broad illustration. It is based on average per capita income data for population deciles, from the poorest 10 percent of households in Thailand to the richest 10 percent. Unfortunately, these specific data are only provided on a regional basis and not for occupational groups. The percentage figure provided for each decile is the relationship between the average income and the poverty line. In the north, for example, the average income of the poorest decile is 66 percent of the poverty line, while the average income of the second decile is 112 percent of the poverty line. The table shows that in the center, north, northeast, and south the average income of the bottom 10 percent of the population is below the poverty line. For the second decile, the average income is below the poverty line only in the northeast, although in the north it is only marginally above it. In the northeast the third decile is only 22 percent above the poverty line.

A different set of data is available for agricultural income groups (not disaggregated by region). According to the National Statistics Office (personal communication), these groups are made up of households in which agricultural activities take up a majority of their members' time and, as such, they are likely to be a somewhat poorer cohort than peasant households in which nonfarm income is more important. Table 3 shows that only a very small

TABLE 2. Average income as a percentage of the poverty line by income decile and region.

	Central	North	Northeast	South
1	91	66	61	77
2	149	112	95	136
3	192	143	122	180
4	233	173	147	227
5	278	207	176	281
6	335	248	211	351
7	407	303	257	433
8	502	393	328	560
9	678	552	487	785
10	1,471	1,355	1,154	1,685

SOURCE: National Statistics Office, *Report of the 2007 Household Socio-economic Survey*, table 5.
NOTE: The shaded area is a rough representation of the location of the middle-income peasantry (based on at least 150 percent of the poverty line).

percentage of farmers or agricultural workers are located in the bottommost income group, where income levels are well below the poverty line. A little over 20 percent are located in the second-lowest group, which extends to about 12 percent above the nonmunicipal poverty line. The next income category, which includes the largest number of households, is frustrating from an analytical point of view. It includes households that are only marginally above the poverty line up to households whose income is double the poverty line. If an income threshold was to be drawn for the middle-income peasant, I would be inclined to draw it within this income category, at a point around 50 percent above the poverty line. Exactly how many households fall into the near-poor category (100 to 150 percent of the poverty line) is a matter for conjecture, although table 2 makes it clear that there would be considerably more of them in the northeast and the north than in the center and the south.

What is the big picture of income distribution that emerges from these various data sources? Obviously precise judgments are not possible given the nature of the data and the broad categories used. In terms of the percentage of peasant households that could be considered to be poor, it is very much a matter of definition. As noted above, national data put the rural poverty rate—based on the official poverty line—at about 10 percent (4.7 million people). However, data for agricultural households (table 3) suggest

TABLE 3. Percentage of households in income cohorts by occupational group.

Monthly Income per Capita	Landowning Farmers	Tenant Farmers	Agricultural Workers
0–500	1.3	2.4	0.4
500–1,500	23.6	23.3	18.3
1,500–3,000	36.8	34.5	41.6
3,000–5,000	18.8	21.9	23.9
5,000–10,000	13.3	13.8	14.1
10,000–15,000	3.8	2.1	1.6
15,000–30,000	2.0	1.6	—
30,000–50,000	0.4	0.3	—
50,000–100,000	0.1	—	—
100,000 plus	—	—	—

SOURCE: National Statistics Office, *Report of the 2007 Household Socio-economic Survey*, table 4.
NOTE: The dotted line represents the approximate location of the poverty line.

a higher rate, with more than 20 percent below the poverty line or very close to it. Overall, my estimate is that 20 to 30 percent of households in rural Thailand could be classified as poor or near poor. Many of these peasants are likely to be tenants or have very small landholdings, often on marginal land that lacks irrigation facilities and, in some cases, tenure security. Their numbers are highest in remote areas where transport connections are poor, good agricultural land is scarce, and off-farm employment opportunities are hard to come by. A good number of the poorest peasants are landless laborers, although given the increasing importance of nonfarm income, there is no longer a clear correlation between landlessness and poverty.

However, without understating the importance of this poverty, it is also clear that what I refer to as middle-income peasants have become the largest group in rural Thailand. In all regions outside Bangkok, the majority of the population is at least 50 percent above the poverty line. The percentage of these middle-income households ranges from at least 80 percent in central Thailand to 70 percent in southern and northern Thailand and 60 percent in northeastern Thailand.[25] Clearly a good number of these have a relatively narrow buffer against poverty, and I am not suggesting that they are comfortably well off. But to categorize them as poor starts to stretch the analytical usefulness of the category. Even if the middle-income peasant threshold is set conservatively at double the official poverty line, around 60 percent of the population outside Bangkok sits above it. Middle-income peasant households are enormously diverse—indeed, this diversity is one of the underpinnings of their middle-income status—but their typical profile is likely to involve a combination of subsistence and cash-crop agriculture with various sources of off-farm income. At the upper end of the middle-income spectrum, and among rich peasants, profitable cash cropping is likely to be combined with rural enterprises such as shopkeeping, crop trading, construction, and moneylending.

Income categories and thresholds are always going to be contentious, and I want to avoid getting bogged down in a definitional dispute. My purpose in presenting these income data is to underline the very significant improvements in standards of living that have occurred in rural Thailand over the past half century. Despite the setbacks caused by the financial crisis of the late 1990s, the long-term trajectory is not toward rural impoverishment but toward a middle-income peasantry. This trajectory is continuing: those who have already achieved middle-income status are consolidating their position, and their numbers are increasing as more households move out of absolute poverty. In 1988 there were more than 18 million rural people living below the poverty line; now there are less than 5 million. The majority of poor and near-poor households are in northeastern Thailand, and the rate of poverty in this region has been declining very quickly over the past decade. Between 2000 and 2009, poverty incidence in the northeast was cut by almost two-thirds, pushing more than 4 million people above the poverty line.[26]

Snapshots of income data provide only a small part of the story. More important are the ongoing processes shaping the middle-income peasantry and its political orientation. Chief among these is the interaction among low agricultural productivity, economic disparity, and state support for the rural economy.

AGRICULTURAL DEVELOPMENT AND INEQUALITY

Thailand has been very successful in addressing the problem of absolute poverty in rural areas. Now the primary social challenge is relative poverty. There are stark disparities in income and living standards between rural and urban populations. Many developing countries face the challenge of a widening gap between rich and poor, but Thailand's performance is particularly bad and shows little sign of improving. Since the mid-1980s, Thailand has been more unequal than its main regional neighbors.[27] National statistics, which understate the affluence of the survey-avoiding rich, show that Thailand's inequality has steadily worsened, dipping only temporarily after the Asian economic crisis of the late 1990s. In the mid-1970s the richest 20 percent of the population earned about 8 times as much as the poorest 20 percent, whereas in the 2000s this ratio has climbed to between 12 and 14.[28] The recent *Human Development Report* for Thailand highlights the regional dimensions of this inequality, which extends well beyond income.[29] According to a range of human development indicators of income, health, education, and housing, Bangkok and its hinterland perform very strongly whereas the worst performers are predominantly rural provinces in the northeast, north, and far south. Average household income in Bangkok is about three times higher than in the rural north and northeast. The *Human Development Report* shows that, compared to those in and around Bangkok, residents of rural provinces are significantly more likely to be sick or disabled, have much less access to health services, attend school for about three years less, have lower standards of housing, and have less access to mobile phones and the Internet. Although the national (and rural) poverty rate has declined dramatically, poverty is still about ten times more prevalent in the north and northeast than it is in Bangkok.

Important insight into the nature of Thailand's inequality, and some of the related challenges of its middle-income status, can be gained by examining the position of agriculture within the overall economy. As Thailand's economy has diversified and grown, the contribution of agriculture to GDP has declined. In 1960, agriculture contributed 36 percent of Thailand's GDP.[30] This share declined steadily over the next three decades and reached a low of only 9 percent in 1993. This declining share has stabilized since then, helped by the sharp blow to manufacturing and services caused by the financial crisis of 1997 and healthy crop prices in recent years. In 2008, agriculture made up 12 percent of Thailand's GDP, somewhat higher than the average for middle-income countries throughout the world (9 percent) but still much lower than it had been in Thailand in the 1960s and 1970s.

However, the change in the structure of Thailand's economy has not been fully matched by workforce transformation. Thailand is typical of other countries that make the transition from low-income to middle-income status in having a pronounced lag in the movement of labor out of agriculture and into industry and services. Many rural households have diversified their livelihoods—and this has made an important contribution to increasing rural incomes—but the overall movement out of agriculture has been rather slow. In the early 1960s, agricultural workers made up 83 percent of the labor force while in 2008 their percentage had fallen to 42 percent.[31] This is a significant reduction, but it is considerably less than the reduction in agriculture's share of GDP and it has occurred from a much higher base. By one account, labor movement out of agriculture has practically ceased since the economic crisis of the late 1990s.[32] There may be a degree of overestimation in agricultural workforce statistics—with many farmers combining on-farm and off-farm labor—but it is clear that with more than one-third of the workforce producing only about one-tenth of Thailand's total output, labor productivity in agriculture is low in comparison to other sectors. In other words, the main challenge for Thailand's agriculture—its relatively low labor productivity—arises from the persistence of an agricultural peasantry, not its disappearance.

The lower productivity of agriculture compared to that of other sectors lies at the heart of what the agricultural economist Yujiro Hayami calls the "disparity problem" faced by many middle-income countries.[33] In poor countries—as in poor households—the core concern is food security, and governments are anxious to secure affordable food for potentially fractious urban populations where their political base often lies. Cheap food is also important to ensure the low wages that can facilitate the early stage of industrial expansion. Except in the most extreme circumstances, when direct appropriations of foodstuffs from rural areas may be necessary, governments achieve their objective more subtly, by suppressing crop prices and, as such, indirectly taxing rural producers. However, as poor countries develop into middle-income countries, a different challenge emerges. Hayami argues that as countries industrialize, productivity growth in the manufacturing sector tends to outstrip productivity growth in agriculture. Manufacturing industry benefits from technology transfer, whereas the biological and environmental specificities of agriculture make it less amenable to technological innovation.[34] Industry is also more likely than agriculture to benefit from economies of scale, especially in countries where small-holder farming predominates. In this new situation, disparity, rather than food security, becomes the core preoccupation.

In Thailand, the main ingredients of this disparity problem are clearly evident. Thailand's very rapid industrialization and economic growth has been accompanied by some land and labor productivity growth in agriculture but it has been uneven within the country and in some important respects has been modest by the standards of its regional neighbors. Thai rice yields, for example, are among the lowest in the world.[35] In the 1960s, Thailand had rice yields comparable to those of Indonesia and Vietnam, but since 1990 yields in these two countries have been 60 to 70 percent higher than those in Thailand. Rice yields in underdeveloped Laos rose above Thai yields in the mid-1980s and are now around 15 percent higher. There has been labor productivity growth in Thai agriculture as a result of mechanization and other labor-saving cultivation techniques, but it has been relatively low in regions of Thailand, such as the north, where labor-intensive cultivation on small plots is the norm. According to Richard F. Doner's account of Thailand's uneven development, "[T]he seed-fertilizer technology (embodied in the Green Revolution) that has been so important for agricultural growth elsewhere in East Asia played a relatively small role in Thailand."[36] The most substantial contribution agriculture has made to national productivity is releasing labor to work in manufacturing and services.[37]

The disparity between agriculture and industry becomes very clear when examining national accounts data. Chart 2 sets out the productivity of labor

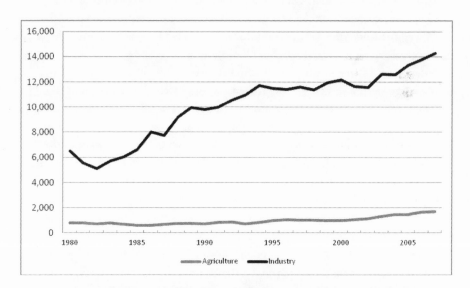

CHART 2. Thailand's labor productivity in agriculture and industry, 1980–2007, constant 2008 US$. Labor productivity is calculated by dividing sectoral GDP by the number of workers in the sector. (Data from the World Bank's World Development Indicators Online, accessed 23 June, 2010.)

(expressed in terms of GDP per worker) in the agricultural and industrial sectors.[38] There has certainly been productivity growth in the agricultural sector—with GDP per worker more than doubling between 1980 and 2007—and this has made an important contribution to Thailand's dramatic reduction in rural poverty. But the data also make it clear that productivity in industry not only started from a considerably higher base but increased more rapidly, especially during the economic boom from the mid-1980s to the mid-1990s. In 1980, labor in industry was about 8 times as productive as labor in agriculture, and by 1993 this had increased to 16 times. The gap has closed to 8.5 times in recent years, as a result of the economic crisis of the late 1990s and healthy agricultural prices, but it is still higher than the gap in Indonesia (7.5 times), the Philippines (5.3 times), and Malaysia (2.4 times). This productivity gap has a direct bearing on the wages paid in the agricultural and industrial sectors. In 2006, Thailand's average agricultural wages were only 44 percent of wages in the manufacturing sector.[39]

The wide productivity and income gap between urban and rural areas in middle-income countries creates an important axis of political desire and gives rural political society a distinctive character. As Hayami puts it, albeit somewhat crudely, "[F]armers become envious and eventually develop [a] grudge against the social system."[40] In Chatterjee's terms, farmers are concerned that a discriminatory (rather than exploitative) social system is failing to deliver them a fair share of the benefits of economic development. The political potency of disparity in middle-income countries derives from the fact that it emerges at the same time as rural education, communication, and mobility improve. Rural-urban interconnection supports livelihood diversification, promotes new forms of consumption, and blurs spatial distinctions, but it also means that those who perform less well become all too aware of their comparative disadvantage due to their direct experiences of affluent urban areas. This heightened awareness of inequality can easily undermine some of the satisfaction gained from improved quality of life. Movement into middle-income status also often involves a decrease in authoritarian controls over rural political organization, meaning that concerns about relative poverty can be freely expressed by farmers' organizations, NGOs, and voters at the ballot box. The forces of socioeconomic modernization that increase disparity also increase the power and eloquence of rural political opinion.

According to Hayami's model, governments respond to this rural discontent by attempting to subsidize rural livelihoods. But their ability to do this is constrained by the country's middle-income status: there is simply not enough government revenue available to close the income gap. Limits to rural subsidies are also imposed by the need to avoid excessive trade distortions, political opposition from the urban population, and the corrupt diversion of funds directed to rural development. Overall, the tendency is for governments to "muddle around in search of ways and means to protect farmers," and, without effective resolution, there is the possibility of "social instability or even disruption."[41]

FROM TAXATION TO SUBSIDY

So how has Thailand muddled through the challenge of disparity? Like many other countries in the world, it has moved from taxing agriculture to subsidizing it.[42] In the past, Thailand had a "rice premium," which taxed rice exports to generate government revenue and reduce domestic rice prices. This was a classic example of what the development economist Michael Lipton referred to as "urban bias" because it lowered farming incomes in order to subsidize the early stages of industrialization and deliver low-cost food to the rapidly expanding population in Bangkok.[43] The rice premium was established during a time of authoritarian government when there was relatively little concern with wooing the political support of the rural masses. This "deliberate taxation of the poorest part of the population" contributed around 20 percent of total government revenue during the 1950s and about 10 percent in the 1960s.[44] Other policies, such as a duty on fertilizer imports to protect state-owned producers, compounded the impost on agricultural producers.[45] In the early 1970s, the ratio between the fertilizer price and the rice price in Thailand was the highest of any country in Asia.[46] By one estimate, income earned by farmers during the 1970s was 17 percent lower than it would have been if sector-neutral government policies were in place.[47] Another study found that in the 1960s and 1970s about 4 percent of GDP was transferred out of the agricultural sector by the combined effect of government pricing and taxation measures.[48]

However, this unfavorable fiscal treatment has turned around over the past forty years, as it has in many other developing countries. In the 1950s and 1960s, successive Thai governments were concerned about the spread of communist influence in rural areas, and they started to invest in building up the peasantry as the "backbone of the nation."[49] The first National Social and Economic Development Plan set out a program of investment in rural infrastructure, research, extension, and credit that would "improve the social system of farmers so that they have a higher standard of living and better welfare, are unified, industrious and cooperate more with the government."[50] National commitment to investment in rural development was further encouraged by the brief period of open democratic government and political polarization in the first half of the 1970s. Politically assertive farmers' organizations, including the Peasants' Federation of Thailand, moved onto the national stage, and the communist successes in Indochina made the Thai state even more determined to win over rural hearts and minds. Since then, there have been important long-term shifts in the fiscal treatment of the countryside, laying the foundation for the emergence of a middle-income peasantry:

- As a result of changes implemented since the 1970s, government tax and trade policies no longer significantly reduce the crop prices received by farmers. As chart 3 shows, they now have a neutral or even positive effect. The rice premium peaked at about 60 percent in the early 1970s (i.e., prices paid to farmers were 60 percent lower than they would have been in an unregulated market), but it fell quickly in the years that followed, and by 1980 it made a negligible contribution to government revenue. The premium was abolished in 1986. Around this time the government introduced the first of its rice "mortgage" schemes under which farmers could receive income by pledging their rice to the government rather than having to sell it for low postharvest prices. If the market price rose above the pledging price, farmers could sell for the higher amount. These schemes expanded greatly, and became much more generous, under the Thaksin administration when the government-supported price was often set 20 or 30 percent higher than the prevailing market price.[51] By 2006, pledged rice accounted for about 25 percent of national rice production.[52] Beyond the benefits accruing directly to participants, these schemes had the effect of increasing the domestic rice price by giving farmers a fallback option if they were unhappy with the prices offered by millers or traders. Price support in the form of import restriction is also provided for some crops, such as sugar and soybeans, raising their prices about 25 percent above what they would be without government intervention.[53] A study undertaken by the World Trade Organization concluded that these price-support polices were specifically designed to "address the income gap between agriculture and industry."[54]
- Government spending on agriculture increased fifteenfold (in real terms) between 1960 and 2008 (chart 4). In the 1960s, government spending on agriculture represented about 4 percent of agricultural GDP, while in the 1990s it averaged 14 percent, falling back to 11 percent in the 2000s.[55] More than half

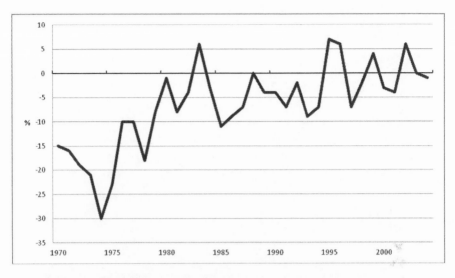

CHART 3. Impact of government policies in Thailand on agricultural prices, 1970–2006. (Based on appendix table 14 in Anderson and Martin, "Distortions to Agricultural Incentives.")

of the agricultural budget has been devoted to the expansion of irrigation infrastructure. During the 1970s and 1980s, the area of agricultural land with irrigation facilities increased by 250 percent with most investment taking place in the northeast and the north.[56] This has raised the productivity of wet-season agriculture and permitted a dramatic expansion in market-oriented dry-season cultivation. Agricultural research and extension, though rather lackluster by some standards, have been other areas of productivity-enhancing investment by the Thai state.[57] Government-funded research has improved the yield and quality of major crops such as rice, maize, cassava, sugar, and rubber, often laying the foundation for later research and development by private enterprise.[58] Investment in district-level agricultural cooperatives has improved marketing and provided farmers with access to subsidized inputs.

• In the 1960s and early 1970s, Thailand had a very weak rural credit system that was heavily dependent on informal moneylenders who often charged interest at between 25 and 100 percent per year.[59] Poorer farmers who had difficulty obtaining credit often presold unharvested "green rice" at a heavily discounted price. Indebtedness and land foreclosure were central issues raised by protesting farmers between 1973 and 1976. Responding to farmers' concerns, the government quadrupled the lending capacity of the state-run Bank for

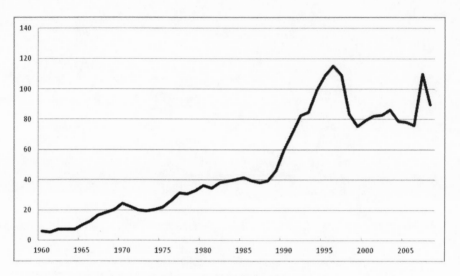

CHART 4. Spending on agriculture by the Thai government, 1960–2008, billions of baht, constant 2008 values. (Data from Alpha Research, *Thailand in Figures*; National Statistics Office, *Statistical Yearbook, Thailand*.)

Agriculture and Cooperatives (BAAC) in the second half of the 1970s, and private banks were required to lend a percentage of their deposits to farmers at below-market interest rates.[60] In the decades since, the real value of agricultural credit has increased dramatically, from about 15 billion baht in 1970 to more than 600 billion in 2007 (chart 5). The composition of credit has also changed. During the 1980s commercial institutions provided more than half of the agricultural credit (in 1991 it peaked at 72 percent), but in the wake of the Asian financial crisis, commercial lending slumped while government lending climbed sharply to reach 80 percent of agricultural credit in 2007. The Thaksin government provided a small-scale credit fund of 1 million baht for every village in Thailand in 2001, increasing the supply of rural credit by about 20 percent. The dramatic increase in rural credit since the 1970s has enabled farmers to invest much more in productivity-enhancing inputs. For example, in the 1960s, fertilizer application was estimated to average only 1.5 kilograms per hectare. By 2000 this had increased to about 78 kilograms per hectare.[61] Given the increase in formal sources of credit, borrowing from high-cost moneylenders now makes up less than 10 percent of agricultural credit.[62]

• There has been sustained public investment in rural infrastructure. During the 1980s and 1990s, rural road length increased nine times.[63] A 2003 survey in

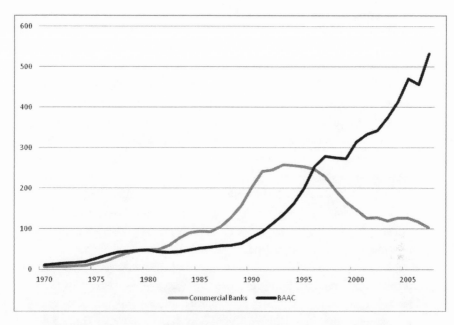

CHART 5. Agricultural credit in Thailand, 1970 to 2007, billions of baht, constant 2008 values. (Data from Bank of Thailand, "Private Bank Lending by Business Type"; Bank of Thailand, "Operations of the Bank for Agriculture and Agricultural Co-Operatives.")

the northeast, where rural road access is the worst in Thailand, found that "over a quarter of rural villages . . . were within 15 minutes of the nearest town or city by the most common mode of public transportation, and over 80 percent within 30 minutes."[64] Road construction has greatly facilitated the expansion of cash cropping and has been identified as an important contributor to Thailand's success in rural poverty reduction.[65] Other basic infrastructure also expanded rapidly in the 1980s and 1990s: rural electricity consumption increased seventeen times, and the number of rural telephone connections increased sixty-five times.[66] The UNDP reports that access to electricity, clean drinking water, and safe sanitation is now almost universal throughout rural areas of Thailand.[67]

• Government-funded health and education services in rural Thailand have also proliferated. In the mid-1970s there were only 169 hospitals in Thailand whereas by 2005 where were more than 900, covering almost every district within the country.[68] There are also more than 10,000 community health centers operating at subdistrict level.[69] In 1975 the Medical Welfare Scheme was introduced to provide free health care for those living beneath the poverty line. The scheme was expanded in the early 1980s and eventually covered around 30 percent of the population.[70] It was replaced by a universal coverage scheme introduced by the Thaksin government in 2001. The expansion in education since the 1970s is most marked in relation to secondary schooling, because Thailand had already achieved extensive primary school coverage by the 1950s. Between 1970 and 2007, there was a fivefold increase in the number of secondary schools throughout Thailand with an average of three in each district. Enrollments in lower secondary school increased by a factor of twelve while upper secondary enrollments increased by a factor of fifty-two (the total population less than doubled).[71] Secondary school attendance in rural areas has been supported by a well-funded loans scheme, scholarships, a school lunch program, and a bicycle-lending scheme for students living more than three kilometers from school.[72] Between 1980 and 2000, the average years of schooling of the rural population increased from 4.0 to 5.9 while rural literacy increased from 78 to 91 percent.[73] Educational improvements have had a significant impact on poverty: "The risk of poverty declined by 66 to 74 percent when the highest educated adult in the household had primary or secondary education, as compared to no education."[74]

- There has been considerable government investment in community development and poverty alleviation. The Accelerated Rural Development Program was established in 1966 with an initial focus on irrigation and highway construction, especially in the northeast, in order to prevent the spread of communism. It developed into a wide-ranging and well-resourced rural development program.[75] In 1975 the Subdistrict Development Program was established to distribute infrastructure budgets directly to local government units. According to one commentator at the time, this program "permanently and significantly altered government-village relations in Thailand."[76] This scheme was expanded in the 1980s and others followed, some of them locally coordinated by a nationwide network of community development offices established in 1977. Major schemes included the Rural Development Fund (1984), the Poverty Alleviation Project (1993), and the so-called Miyazawa Scheme (1999), funded by the Japanese government to help mitigate the impacts of the Asian financial crisis. Funding for the long-standing Accelerated Rural Development Program tripled during the 1990s.[77] The Thaksin government continued the trend with a series of local economic development and welfare schemes. Many of these have been retained by post-Thaksin governments, though often under new names.

- In 1999, the government embarked on an ambitious scheme of fiscal and administrative decentralization. This has greatly increased the responsibilities and resources of subdistrict administrative organizations and municipalities. There are almost eight thousand of these local government bodies in Thailand, each with an average of only ten or so villages. The proportion of central government revenue allocated to local government authorities has increased from 10 to about 25 percent.[78] Local government bodies have assumed a wide range of responsibilities, including local infrastructure, transport management, sanitation, some aspects of natural resource management, tourism promotion, cultural protection, local economic development, and some health and education functions. Decentralization has stimulated government employment in rural areas and greatly shortened the lines of funding between government agencies and rural villages. Local government authorities are governed by elected councils, so decentralization has intensified political competition for access to resource allocations.

- A final important policy development relates to land tenure. This is not a directly financial initiative, but tenure has a significant impact on farmers' ability to obtain credit for productivity-enhancing inputs and it also affects the confidence with which they make long-term investments in their land. According to political scientist Tomas Larsson, "[S]ince the early 1960s, the Thai state has formalized rural land rights on a massive scale with the land area under full formal title rising from [2.8 million hectares] in 1960 to [20.1 million] in 2000."[79] Concerned that rural conflict over land could provide an opportunity for communist agitation, the government started expanding its land registration bureaucracy in the 1950s. The land tenure effort accelerated in the mid-1970s following high-profile peasant protest about dispossession and landlordism. This effort was supported by a World Bank project that got under way in 1984. Despite concerns that formal tenure would facilitate market encroachment and land consolidation, data on land ownership suggest that tenure schemes have been successful in maintaining the predominance of smallholders in the rural land market.[80] The million or so farm households that occupy "public" lands in forest reserve areas have had much more limited access to formal tenure, but even they have enjoyed relatively secure status despite occasionally bellicose conservation rhetoric from the government.[81]

My intention in providing this summary is not to pay tribute to the Thai state's benevolence, although it is important to recognize Thailand's considerable achievements in rural development and poverty reduction, despite regular episodes of political instability. Rather, my intention is to suggest that the contemporary political energy of the peasantry does not come from fear about its dissolution but from the dilemmas of its preservation. Over the past half century, the Thai state has sought to address the political challenges of disparity in a rapidly growing economy by investing heavily in rural development. Government initiatives on price support, infrastructure, research, extension, credit, health, education, welfare, and land tenure have increased rural incomes and made livelihoods more secure. This spending has certainly not eliminated inequality, and investment in high-need agricultural areas such as the northeast still lags on a per capita basis.[82] Nevertheless, it has greatly enhanced the viability of the rural economy, especially when farming is combined with other sources of income and welfare. However, the overall impact of this state support for rural Thailand has been to help develop and maintain a middle-income peasantry rather than fundamentally transform it. Despite the amount of state investment, the rural economy remains relatively unproductive. Thailand's agricultural productivity improvements have been important in increasing rural incomes, but they have been much less impressive than those achieved by many of its regional neighbors. More important, as will become clear in the next chapter, the Thai state has been unsuccessful in developing the nonfarm sector in rural areas apart from some high-profile schemes producing handicrafts for niche markets. The expansion of secondary education in rural areas has been an important investment in human capital, but there are persistent doubts about its quality and its ability to adequately prepare rural people for higher-paid employment in the industrial economy.[83] The overall result is that the Thai state has helped to maintain a large rural population that, despite significant livelihood improvements, is insufficiently productive to fully meet the aspirations that economic growth has aroused.

THE NEW POLITICS OF RURAL PROTEST

In Thailand's modern era there has been a striking change in the political geography of rural protest. In the premodern rural economy, peasants aggrieved with the state sought to avoid it. The conspicuous consumption, military might, and religious glory of centers of state power depended on extracting rice and labor from peasant producers and monopolizing trade in desirable products from the forested hinterland. To govern was, in Thai terminology, to "eat the domain" (*kin muang*); from the paramount lords to lowly officials in muddy outposts, the accumulation of power was synonymous with controlling the labor, produce, and trade of the rural population. When the extractions of overlords threatened local subsistence norms, or when the fading potency of the center no longer justified its demands, a common response was flight. Land was abundant and population scarce, so oppressed peasants could shift to a more benign domain or they could melt into the hills where state power quickly receded as the forests closed in. In these hard-to-govern zones, seemingly haphazard cultivation bamboozled lowland tax collectors, and highly decentralized forms of political organization disrupted attempts at administrative incorporation. Occasional rebellions, which drew on the mystical potency of the periphery, challenged the extractive power of the state. Peasants who lived at the fringe of state power accumulated a rich store of spells, rituals, and cautionary tales to keep natural calamities, wild animals, and avaricious officials at bay. All this was recently described as the "art of not being governed" by James C. Scott, who writes that "it was very common for state subjects to run away. Living within the state meant, virtually by definition, taxes, conscription, corvée labor, and, for most, a condition of servitude; these conditions were at the core of the state's strategic and military advantages. When these burdens became overwhelming, subjects moved with alacrity to the periphery or to another state. . . . Much of the periphery of states became a zone of refuge or 'shatter zone,' where the human shards of state formation and rivalry accumulated willy nilly, creating regions of bewildering ethnic and linguistic complexity."[84]

In the modern rural economy, the geography of peasant protest is very different. Flight to the periphery has been replaced with assembly in the capital. Avoidance of the state has given way to encirclement of the principal sites of government administration. Rural invasion of the city first became a feature of Thai politics in the 1970s, as peasants joined students and workers in staging mass rallies in Bangkok. The tactic was refined during the civil society protests of the 1990s, culminating in the three-month "siege" of Government House staged by the Assembly of the Poor in 1997. In the countryside, protests in front of provincial offices have become a standard method for farmers to express their discontent about prices, land tenure, and failed development projects. The massive crowd of Thaksin Shinawatra's red-shirt supporters that descended on Bangkok in March 2010 provided the most recent demonstration that discontented peasants now focus their attention on the center of power, not its weakest margins. Their political desire is to attach themselves to the power of the state, not to avoid it.

In the modern economic context—characterized by a large smallholding population, the slow transfer of labor out of agriculture, relatively low agricultural productivity, and persistent inequality—the core political dynamic for the modern peasantry is not evading surplus extraction but maximizing state subsidies. State action and the persistence of the peasantry are now inseparable. It is no longer the intrusive presence of the state that is likely to prompt protest but, on the contrary, the state's disinterest, absence, or forced withdrawal as a result of austerity reforms imposed by international agencies. The expectation that the state will "deliver benefits directly to the popular classes" and actively intervene in unfavorable markets forms the basis for what the political scientist Kevin Hewison calls the "new social contract" that underpins modern political relationships.[85] In Thailand this populist social contract was most clearly evident during the Thaksin era, but he was capitalizing on a broad-based sentiment that had been evolving for several decades as the country moved into a middle-income position and as the state attempted to address growing disparities between urban and rural Thailand. This is a shift that is internationally commonplace as countries move out of poverty and face a new set of middle-income challenges. In this new political and economic context, dependent rural relationships with sources of power are potentially virtuous rather than necessarily exploitative or demeaning. The modern challenge for middle-income rural dwellers is to bind sources of power into relationships of productive exchange rather than to resist, subvert, or evade them.

2

Ban Tiam's Middle-Income Rural Economy

Ban Tiam is located in a narrow valley about one hour's drive from the city of Chiang Mai. The houses of the village are clustered around a long, straight road that runs south from the district center. It is the last village before the paved road fades into gravel and enters the densely forested Lanna National Park. To the west of the road, the Talat River winds its way through Ban Tiam's paddy fields. Even though the river is only a few meters across, it is the irrigation lifeblood of Ban Tiam, supporting cultivation throughout the year. The fertile river valley is about one kilometer wide, but it narrows dramatically just to the south of the village, pinching the paddy fields to a point. On either side of Ban Tiam, mountains rise precipitously. One is so high that if you climb to its summit you can hear the angels pounding their chili paste. On cold winter mornings it can be eight or nine o'clock before the sun rises above the mountain ridge, finally providing relief for grandparents and children huddled around improvised fires. The lower slopes of the mountains have been cleared for cultivation, but the higher reaches are heavily forested. A short journey along one of the tracks that winds into the mountains provides a magnificent view of the valley below: the meandering greenery of the river, a patchwork of cultivation on the paddy fields, roofs of the village just visible through thickets of trees, the glinting red and gold of the temple and its elaborate new drum tower, and swathes of fruit trees and teak plantations blending into the forested slopes (fig. 3).

The village itself is made up of about 130 houses, spread out on either side of the main north-south road. Scattered among the houses along the main road are several shops, a tiny petrol station where hand pumps decant fuel

FIGURE 3. Ban Tiam in the wet season, looking east. (Photo by the author.)

from large metal drums, and a couple of rustic restaurants selling noodle soup. Halfway along the road, a truly magnificent wooden gate marks the side road that leads down to the glittering temple. Follow this road a little farther and you arrive at a large wooden spirit house, built in the shade of the thousand-year-old "lucky tree" to honor Ban Tiam's supernatural lord. The temple and spirit house form the sacred center of the original village, but residential expansion means that they now lie toward its western edge (map 2). Most of the village's houses are made of timber, and many are raised up from the ground in typically northern Thai style. Newer concrete houses, including a couple of minimansions built by Ban Tiam's nouveau riche, are built on the ground, trapping the heat as their whitewash dazzles in the afternoon sun. Houses are located in compounds, which contain a miscellany of small gardens, fruit trees, scrawny chickens, sullen dogs, and abundant junk. Many of these compounds are big enough for a second house, often for the family of a married daughter. Household compounds are clearly demarcated and usually fenced, although there are numerous informal rights-of-way passing

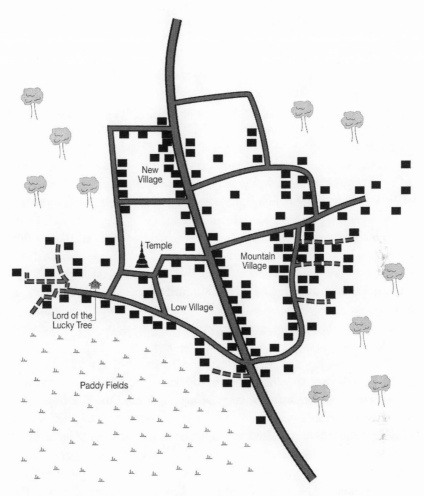

MAP 2. Ban Tiam, Thailand. (Map by Cartography Unit, College of Asia and the Pacific, Australian National University.)

through them so that pedestrians and motorbikes can avoid long detours along the public laneways. Many of the compounds feature large open sheds where garlic is hung to dry on long bamboo poles. Most have small shrines to the house plot's territorial spirit, and about twenty have slightly more elaborate shrines for the ancestral spirits of Ban Tiam's various lineages. Rice stores sit on sturdy poles, capped with iron in an attempt to keep rats at bay. A few households have carefully tended lawns, but these are an exceptional sign of domestic refinement.

The image is unmistakably rural, but Ban Tiam is certainly not isolated. Drive north out of the village and it takes only a few minutes to reach the district center with its market, hospital, banks, schools, shops, restaurants, and government offices. In a nice reversal of common northern Thai classification, this small center of civilization is locally referred to as Forest Village, because it was carved out of the forest only thirty years ago. Tigers used to roam there. Now there are government officials, potentially troublesome but much more amenable to domestication. Ban Tiam is one of six villages spread out around this district center, and, together with three other more remote villages, they form the municipality (*tesaban*) of Pad Siew. This is one of Thailand's least urban municipalities with a total population of about five thousand and a paltry tax base that contributes only 5 percent of municipal expenses. Nevertheless, Ban Tiam's incorporation into the municipality has been a boon. The decentralization of government finances in Thailand means that, despite its modest tax base, Pad Siew Municipality receives an increasing supply of central government funds for infrastructure, services, and an array of development projects. Ban Tiam has done well in capturing a share of municipal development, especially since one of its leading residents was elected mayor in 2002.

Most of the residents of Ban Tiam can be counted among Thailand's middle-income peasants. According to the "basic needs" survey undertaken by the Department of Community Development, the average household income in 2009 was 125,000 baht. This is 20 percent below the average rural income for northern Thailand but well above the northern Thai poverty mark of about 50,000 baht.[1] I estimate that about one in five households in Ban Tiam—mainly those of landless laborers or very small-scale farmers—could be classified as poor or near poor. A similar number comprises the commercial elite, with about 60 percent falling within the middle-income band. Within Pad Siew District, Ban Tiam's average income is comparable to those of most of its neighbors, but it is about 20 percent lower than those of the most agriculturally successful villages in the district and, on the other hand, more than double those of some of the more remote upland minority villages where the opportunities for cash cropping and off-farm employment are limited. There are plenty of other, less formal indicators of Ban Tiam's middle-income status. Most families live in solid and well-established houses, and new house construction is common (fig. 4). Modern consumer durables are ubiquitous. A survey conducted by the municipal administration in 2007 found that Ban Tiam's 130 households owned a total of 134 televisions,

129 refrigerators, 169 motorbikes, 134 mobile phones, 75 fixed phone lines, 81 tape or compact disc players, 26 cars or pickup trucks, and 29 computers. Local rice production is sufficient to cover subsistence requirements, there is a reliable electricity and domestic water supply, the main road is paved and the number of minor roads that are paved increases each year, all children have ready access to reasonable quality primary and secondary education, and the nearby district hospital provides a full range of basic health care.

The achievements and challenges of a middle-income economy are as evident in Ban Tiam as they are at a national level. There has been a considerable amount of income-enhancing diversification both within agriculture and outside of it. There is still a strong subsistence focus on rice, but there is also an active cash-crop sector that has flourished over the past thirty years. The nonfarm sector has also grown dramatically and now accounts for more than half of the income earned by Ban Tiam's households. This diversification, combined with substantial out-migration, underpins Ban Tiam's predominantly middle-income status. However, the performance in relation to improved productivity has been less impressive. There have been

FIGURE 4. Old and new housing, Ban Tiam, Thailand. (Photo by the author.)

some important land and labor productivity gains in relation to rice cultivation. This means that the previously persistent problem of food shortage
has been solved for most households. Nevertheless, the economic returns in
the rice sector are modest, and despite the substantial allocation of labor,
land, and water to its production, rice accounts for only a very modest portion of the village's overall income. Returns from cash cropping are potentially much better, and sometimes this potential is achieved. However, until
recently, cash cropping has relied heavily on a single crop, garlic, which has
experienced volatile fluctuations in both yield and price. Until the recent
arrival of contract farming, institutions that could encourage productivity-
enhancing investments in the volatile cash-cropping sector have been virtually nonexistent. There is little indication that agricultural profits have been
able to generate productivity-enhancing investment. External investment in
agroprocessing, tourism, or manufacturing is also minimal. Given these private sector limitations, it is unsurprising that the state plays a central role in
Ban Tiam's economy. State resources flow through many different channels
and support many different livelihood strategies.

This chapter provides an overview of Ban Tiam's demography and economy, as a foundation for the discussion of its political society in the chapters that follow. It examines the local manifestations of three of the general
themes explored in the first two chapters: rural diversification, productivity
constraints, and the importance of state support for the rural economy.

DEMOGRAPHIC TRANSFORMATIONS

About fifty years ago, Ban Tiam was a small hamlet of ten or twenty households clustered on a narrow strip of slightly elevated land between the temple and the paddy fields. This area is now referred to as the "low village."
Several of the "origin houses" of Ban Tiam's most important lineages are
located in this area. The first settlers probably came from downriver, following a long-established trade route upstream in search of timber, forest products, and new agricultural land. This was the period of Thailand's abundant
land frontier, when rural economic growth was achieved by opening up
new areas of productive land. Other early settlers were employees of logging
companies, which came to exploit the district's abundant teak reserves,
establishing several elephant camps in the vicinity. Several residents claim to
be descendants of migrant forest workers from northern Laos. As the population grew, new households were established along the edges of the paddy

fields and on the sloping land to the east of the temple. Gradually, houses were built farther up the eastern slope and a new hamlet, the "mountain village," took shape. About thirty years ago, a third hamlet, the "new village," was established when a small settlement of about six households from across the river shifted to Ban Tiam, tired of being cut off by floodwaters. This new hamlet, laid out on a nicely modern rectangular grid by the district administration, was a much more convenient location with a good road connection and ready access to the nearby school, government services, and electricity. Since then, Ban Tiam's population growth has been fueled by natural increase and the in-migration of farmers, traders, and laborers from the more densely populated areas on the Chiang Mai plain. The rate of growth slowed as two-child families became the norm in the 1980s and Thailand's AIDS epidemic caused a notable increase in mortality during the first half of the 1990s (the local health volunteer told me that twenty-three people in the village died between 1991 and 1994). But there is still modest expansion. In recent years some farmers have been selling parts of their paddy fields to provide housing plots for new arrivals: an official in the district administration has built an elaborate wooden house on a plot sold to him by the headman's wife, an irrigation engineer has built a new house only a stone's throw from the shrine of the village's protective spirit, and the German manager of an electronics firm in Chiang Mai has bought a prime piece of land on which to build a country retreat for his wife and parents-in-law.

It is difficult to provide a precise figure for Ban Tiam's population. A survey I carried out in 2003 showed that there were 386 people living in the village (in 126 households), but other surveys conducted by various state agencies suggest a higher population, including one estimate close to 500. This demographic uncertainty is directly related to the economic diversification of Thailand's rural economy. The spatially dispersed nature of contemporary rural livelihood means that household and village membership is not defined solely in terms of coresidence. Put simply, many people living outside the village are considered to be full household members. An indication of the significance of this demographic inclusiveness was provided by a supplementary survey I conducted in 2004. That survey sought information about "regular household members who were currently living elsewhere." Almost one-third of the village's households nominated someone in this position. Most of them were working or studying in surrounding districts or Chiang Mai. Some were even farther afield: several in Bangkok, 1 in Laos, and 1 in London. I counted 49 additional "residents" in this extralocal category, but there is nothing definitive about this figure because a survey term like *regular household members* is inevitably interpreted in many different ways. All in all, it is reasonable to say that the population of Ban Tiam is about 400. A census-style snapshot of the number of people resident in the village on any particular day would probably arrive at a total somewhat below 400, but if spatially dispersed household members are included the total rises by 10 or 20 percent.

The export of population, and the creation of extralocal livelihood networks, has been a central feature of Ban Tiam's economic development. Ban Tiam's location in a narrow valley means there is limited good agricultural land. This underlying resource constraint has forced many of those born in Ban Tiam to look elsewhere for viable livelihoods. This steady dispersion of Ban Tiam's population can be nicely illustrated by considering the descendants of great-great-grandmother Maew, one of Ban Tiam's important ancestral figures. I have been able to identify eighty-seven individuals who are descended from her, in more than twenty different households. Of these, only forty-four are still regularly living in Ban Tiam, or did so at the time of their death. I know of forty-three who are living outside the village, although there are probably considerably more because my genealogical information on these scattered descendants is much less complete.

One branch of this abundant lineage, the four daughters of one of Maew's grandsons, typifies the process of diversification and out-migration. The eldest daughter, Kluay (who we will meet again in the next chapter), was regularly resident in the village up until three years ago. She was an active farmer but relied heavily on land rental because most of her own land had been sold to pay for a succession of family medical bills and funerals. In 2005, partly in response to several expensive crop failures, she moved to southern Thailand to work as a full-time caregiver for the invalid mother of an affluent shopkeeper. Kluay's household in Ban Tiam is now maintained by her husband, who works as a carpenter, and her daughter, who recently commenced university education in Chiang Mai. Her son contracted AIDS and died while studying in Chiang Mai in the mid-1990s. Kluay's younger sister, Nok, left Ban Tiam in 1992 and worked in various jobs in Bangkok. She, too, contracted AIDS and died in 1996, leaving a daughter in the care of her sisters. Another daughter, Noi, also worked in Bangkok, where she met her husband, who works as an electrician on engineering projects in Thailand and Laos. Up until 2006, Noi maintained a household in the village, where her only daughter and orphaned niece lived under the supervision of her elderly mother. Now that her daughter and niece are attending university in Chiang Mai, Nòi spends almost all of her time with her husband. Another of Kluay's sisters, Mai, lived for a period with her husband in a neighboring province and has now moved to the Pad Siew District center where she operates a food stall in the district market. I expect that relatively few of the children of these four sisters will end up living in Ban Tiam once they have completed their secondary and, in most cases, tertiary education.

Ban Tiam's dispersed network of kin remains connected, though unevenly, with the local economy. Some of them move in and out of the village according to the stages of their life cycles and the vagaries of the broader economy. Many are still active members of households in Ban Tiam. Despite their regular absences, they remain "functionally and emotionally attached to their households."[2] Kluay, for example, has been able to fund the construction of a new house complete with elaborate furnishings, a computer, a refrigerator, and an automatic washing machine. She has purchased a motorbike for her daughter and is intending to fund the university education of both her daughter and her orphaned niece. Others are less closely connected with household economies in Ban Tiam—having established fully independent households elsewhere—but they continue to make contributions to household economies. They support day-to-day living expenses and often fund substantial outlays for medical treatment, motorbikes, and televisions. Others provide capital for the establishment of local businesses, such as a small restaurant or a shop. One young woman working in Bangkok urged her aging mother to give up farming and provided her with the funds to set up a noodle shop. Some are active moneylenders; others are generous donors to the village temple. The most successful part-time residents fund expensive house renovations for family members or even build their own minimansions in which they can enjoy occasional visits to their rural homes. On the occasion of important festivals, especially the Thai new-year celebrations in April, the village population swells with sons, daughters, cousins, brothers-in-law, heavy drinking uncles, and alluringly modern nieces. Domestic ritual events such as weddings and funerals create their own demographic bubbles. Life cycles in middle-income Ban Tiam are embedded in a wide web of extralocal connections.

AGRICULTURE

On its southwestern side, the residential area of Ban Tiam is bounded by an irrigation canal. Cross this, on any of the rickety wooden or bamboo bridges, and you arrive at the village's paddy fields. These run in a long north-south strip on either side of the river, filling the valley bottom in a cascade of unevenly shaped steps. The total area of Ban Tiam's irrigated paddy is about thirty hectares. Over the years, this expanded gradually as areas of swamp and secondary channels of the river were filled in by land-hungry farmers. The main channel itself narrowed as farmers drove wooden stakes into the riverbed and piled soil behind them to extend their fields. The river gets its revenge every few years when it breaks free of its newfound constrictions and turns the valley into a sea of muddy water and ruined rice, generating yet another compensation bill for the agricultural bureaucracy.

These fertile fields are irrigated by three locally managed irrigation systems. Each system has a small dam across the river. Two of the dams have been renovated and expanded with funds provided by agricultural development schemes as part of the Thai government's massive investment in irrigation infrastructure: the first was built with an Irrigation Department grant in 1997; the second is the product of an Accelerated Rural Development grant in 2003. Despite several representations, expansion of the third, which irrigates the largest area of land, has proven impossible: it is located well outside the village boundary, and a "person with connections" has illegally built a house next to it, meaning that the land necessary for the dam's renovation cannot be acquired. Each of the dams diverts a portion of the river's flow into a long canal, which runs along the upper side of the fields and channels water into them through a series of small gates and a network of minor channels. Water is retained in the fields by ridges of soil that are built up around the perimeter of each plot. Ban Tiam's irrigation systems are essential for providing the large water volumes required for rice cultivation. They also enable cultivation during the prolonged dry season. And there is an added bonus: the irrigation water provides an abundant harvest of small fish, tadpoles, and crabs which are enthusiastically grabbed, grilled, pounded, mixed with chili paste, and eaten with lumps of sticky rice.

Rice

During the wet season, which runs from April to October, Ban Tiam's paddy fields are covered with a lush green carpet of rice, which develops a yellow tinge as the seed heads ripen. Glutinous (sticky) rice is the primary staple in northern Thailand, consumed with almost every meal. It dominates wet-season cultivation in Ban Tiam, typically taking up 80 or 90 percent of the paddy fields. Rice seedlings are raised in bright green nursery plots. After about thirty days, they are pulled out, trimmed, and transplanted into flooded and plowed fields where they grow for about one hundred days before the rice is harvested (fig. 5). Transplanting, harvesting, and threshing are labor-intensive and nonmechanized processes. The potential for mechanization is limited because plot sizes are small and the terraced terrain is very uneven. The only exception is the adoption of small handheld tractors that can plow a typical rice plot in a matter of hours, compared to the days it used to take with a buffalo. Rice cultivation relies heavily on reciprocal exchange labor, although there is increasing use of wage labor as a result of competing demands on the available work force.

Compared to Thailand's unremarkable national average, paddy rice yields in Ban Tiam are usually very good, and there have been very significant improvements over the past twenty years, largely as a result of government investment in research, development, and extension. I surveyed rice production in 2003 and found the average yield to be close to 5 tonnes (1 tonne = 1,000 kilograms) per hectare, well above the national average (3.3 tonnes)

FIGURE 5. Preparing rice seedlings for transplanting, Ban Tiam, Thailand. (Photo by the author.)

reported in official statistics.[3] Like many of northern Thailand's intermontane valleys, Ban Tiam's has high-quality alluvial soil, well-constructed irrigation systems, and a good wet-season water supply. Labor-intensive transplanting techniques also provide higher yields than the "broadcast" sowing practiced in regions of more extensive rice cultivation. Recent increases in yield have resulted largely from the widespread adoption of improved rice varieties, especially one known as Sanpatong 1, which was developed at one of northern Thailand's agricultural research stations. Thailand has a low rate of cultivation of improved varieties—one of the reasons for its unimpressive national yield figures—but in Ban Tiam and other areas of northern Thailand there has been energetic promotion and widespread adoption. Generous fertilizer input means that Sanpatong 1 is more expensive to grow, but Ban Tiam's farmers are convinced that the greatly increased returns easily justify the additional outlay. Farmers occasionally express reservations about the taste of Sanpatong 1—and some continue to grow small plots of local varieties for home consumption or to feed to fighting cocks—but its advantages greatly outweigh culinary reservations.

Productivity gains brought about by improved irrigation infrastructure and high-yield varieties mean that, in very general terms, Ban Tiam is self-sufficient when it comes to rice. The rice subsistence requirement for the village as a whole is roughly 120 tonnes of unmilled rice.[4] Under good cultivation conditions the village produces about 140 tonnes of rice, most of it in irrigated paddy fields and a small amount in unirrigated upland fields. Of course, output can be substantially reduced by flooding—which is a regular occurrence—and disease and pest attack. But surpluses from good years can assist in tiding households over during bad years. Rice sufficiency is an impressive achievement for Ban Tiam's local economy. Numerous stories are told of rice shortages, hungry children, boiling twigs and bark to eat instead of rice, and long rice-purchasing treks to other villages (which were often reluctant to sell) in the years prior to the introduction of more modern rice-farming methods. These stark markers of absolute poverty are now, by and large, a thing of the past.

However, broad brush statements about rice sufficiency must be placed in perspective. There are three contextual issues to consider. First, local rice sufficiency is a result of the sustained export of population, a process made possible by an open land frontier up until the 1970s and, more recently, a rapidly expanding nonagricultural economy. If more people had remained in the village there simply would not be enough locally produced rice for local consumption needs. The viability of the middle-income peasant economy is heavily dependent on growth in the wider economy. Second, only about half of the village's households are engaged in rice cultivation. Ownership of Ban Tiam's paddy land is uneven, with only one-tenth of the village's households owning almost half of the paddy land. Inequalities in access to land are mitigated by the common practice of "borrowing" land from relatives who are not cultivating it and by land rental. Roughly half of the paddy land is cultivated by nonowners under rental or borrowing arrangements. Nevertheless, there is still a substantial proportion of the villagers without access to paddy fields on which they can cultivate rice. Some sharing of rice between closely related households takes place, but most non-rice-producing households obtain rice primarily by purchase, either within the village from rice-surplus households or from rice traders in the nearby district center. Some poor households receive rice as payment for agricultural labor. There is sometimes a tendency in commentary on Thai rural society to associate rice sufficiency with communitarian values, but for many households basic subsistence is met via market transactions and labor relationships. Third, it is important to remember that rice production has a quite limited role in Ban Tiam's overall economy. Rice is a low-value crop, and its real price has steadily declined since the 1960s.[5] Returns to labor are considerably lower than for most other crops commonly grown in the region.[6] Despite the very substantial investment of both land and labor, rice cultivation represents less than 10 percent of Ban Tiam's overall economic activity.[7] Increased rice yield has been important in addressing some dimensions of absolute poverty, and the cultivation of rice is certainly culturally important, but it has made very little contribution to Ban Tiam's middle-income status. For the past thirty or so years, the primary agricultural challenge has been market-oriented diversification.

Cash Crops

In Ban Tiam there is a strong demarcation between wet-season and dry-season cultivation. The rice harvest takes place around November. Once the rice is threshed, bagged, and carried back to the domestic rice stores, the rice stubble is burned and preparations begin for cash-crop production. Between November and April there is usually very little rain, so dry-season cultivation is almost completely dependent on the paddy fields' three irrigation systems. In most years there is sufficient water in the river, but if wet-season rainfall has been poor the water supply situation can become desperate. Water is rationed under a queuing system, with one farmer at a time diverting water, for a limited period, from the irrigation canal. If things get really dire, the municipality may provide a pump to draw the last remaining water out of the river and into the canal. In the 2003 dry season—after a particularly poor wet season—the head of one of the irrigation groups was forced to resign when his tardiness meant that the group missed out on the use of a municipal pump.

Ban Tiam is famous for its dry-season garlic production. For many years this was the mainstay of the cash-cropping sector, often supplemented by soybeans. However, in recent years price volatility, uneven yields, and growing indebtedness have brought about an important shift in cash cropping away from the garlic-soybean combination. Many new cash crops have been adopted: cabbages, eggplants, strawberries, gooseberries, sweet corn, peas, potatoes, zucchini, and tobacco. This is a typical transformation as Thai farmers have increasingly oriented their production to more diverse national and international consumer markets. Where possible, farmers grow a second dry-season crop before the start of the next rice cultivation season. Pigeon peas have proven to be a popular late-dry-season crop. They require a lot of labor, especially for harvesting, but they have a short cultivation period.

Ban Tiam's cash crops find their way onto the market in several different ways. Some cash crops are sold to traders within the village who then sell to larger-scale traders in Chiang Mai. Ban Tiam's local traders are usually successful farmers or shopkeepers who have been able to purchase a pickup truck and have ready access to the credit that is required to support a trading enterprise. Other cash crops, especially garlic, are sold to independent traders from Chiang Mai and surrounding districts. Many of these external traders have regular supply relationships with farmers in Ban Tiam, but there are enough of them to prevent any individual trader from exercising undue market power. A new marketing arrangement that has emerged in recent years is for crops to be sold to agribusinesses that have entered into contract-farming arrangements with local cultivators. The enthusiasm for contract farming is a result of the high level of risk, and resulting indebtedness, in the cash-cropping sector. Under current contract arrangements, the cost of most inputs is met by the contracting company, prices are agreed on in advance, and the company carries the cost in the case of crop failure. This is clearly an attractive arrangement for farmers in Ban Tiam as it addresses the primary challenge in the agricultural sector: increasing productivity by moving into higher value cash crops in a way that avoids the risk of indebtedness from price and yield fluctuation. The adoption of contract farming is discussed in detail in chapter 4.

Cash-crop cultivation plays an important role in Ban Tiam's middle-income economy. Among the paddy-farming households, about two-thirds indicated that cash crops were their most important source of cash income. Cash cropping also greatly increases opportunities for wage labor, much more so than rice cultivation, which frequently uses exchange labor. There are about twenty-five laboring households within the village whose primary source of income is agricultural wage labor, and a good number of the smaller farmers also obtain a portion of their income from working on the cash crops of other farmers, both within Ban Tiam and outside it. Overall, almost three-quarters of the households in the village cite agricultural wage labor as a primary or secondary source of noncrop income. Combining the contributions from independent farming and wage labor, I estimate that cash cropping accounts for about one-third of Ban Tiam's combined household income.

Upland Rice and Maize

So far I have concentrated on irrigated paddy fields, which represent the core of Ban Tiam's agricultural sector. Some cultivation of rice and cash crops also takes place on about twenty hectares of upland fields, which are scattered widely in the hills surrounding Ban Tiam. Cultivation of upland fields is less favorable for several reasons. Their soil is usually less fertile than the rich alluvium that makes up the paddy fields. In the past, regular fallow and rotation of fields helped to maintain fertility, but forestry regulations now prevent this. Upland fields also lack irrigation and are only cultivated in the wet season. One well-off farmer has installed an upland sprinkler system, but this is an exceptional investment. Weed and insect infestation is a persistent challenge, and it is compounded by excessive cultivation with insufficient fallow. Adding to the disadvantage of upland farming is the fact that many upland fields are remote and inaccessible. This increases travel time to and from the fields and also significantly increases transport costs for harvested crops. Given these various challenges, many households in Ban Tiam have abandoned upland cultivation altogether. In 2003, about one-third of the village cultivated upland fields. For a little over half of these households, low-productivity upland fields were their only agricultural option, while the rest combined paddy and upland cultivation. Interestingly, all of the households entirely dependent on upland fields are located in Ban Tiam's newer hamlets, suggesting that they are the families of more recent migrants who arrived too late to secure a share of the limited paddy fields. These households have a tenuous foothold in the least productive sector of Ban Tiam's economy.

Rice has been a popular upland crop, but it is much less dominant than rice grown on irrigated paddy. In 2003, about 40 percent of the upland fields were devoted to rice production, achieving an average yield of 2.3 tonnes per hectare, about half of the yield achieved on paddy. Upland yields are quite good by national standards, partly a result of improved upland varieties distributed by a government extension station operating within the district. Nevertheless, when surveyed, 70 percent of the upland rice farmers rated their rice yields as bad.[8] Some upland farmers, especially those who also have high-yield paddy fields, are coming to the conclusion that upland rice culti-vation is simply not worth the effort. In 2003, a greater percentage of upland cultivation (45 percent) was devoted to maize than to rice. Some farmers have started planting peanuts, and other nitrogen-fixing crops, in an attempt to restore upland soil fertility. Tobacco is also increasingly being grown on upland fields under contract-farming arrangements. The marginal character of upland agriculture is demonstrated by the fact that among the farmers that rely entirely on upland cultivation, only one reported that cash crops were her primary source of cash income. And even this farmer complained that in the previous year her crop of pumpkins had been almost completely eaten by rats, leaving her an agricultural income of only one thousand baht. All of the other farmers that own only upland fields said they were primarily depen-dant on wage labor, mostly within the cash-crop agricultural sector.[9]

The Nonagricultural Economy

According to Thailand's national agriculture survey, the number of farming households that derived all of their income from agriculture declined sharply from 46 percent in 1993 to only 21 percent in 2003.[10] The national "basic needs survey" reported that in 2008 rural people derived 59 percent of their income from off-farm employment and enterprise.[11] In Ban Tiam the basic needs survey results suggest that the proportion of off-farm income is 73 percent, considerably higher than the national average. There are problems with this sort of data collection—and I suspect that the basic needs survey understates the contribution of cash crops and agricultural wage labor—but these data show that Ban Tiam is certainly part of the sustained shift in Thai-land's rural economy away from agricultural pursuits. However, these rural households are not making a straightforward transformation from agrarian to nonagrarian lifestyles, or following the path of proletarianization predicted by some peasant studies scholars. Thailand's rural residents, like rural people in many parts of the world, are developing economically diversified and spatially dispersed livelihood strategies in which agricultural and nonagricultural pursuits are intertwined. As a result of this livelihood complexity, rural households are increasingly multifunctional and multisited, combining an economically and spatially stretched portfolio of livelihood activities.

In Ban Tiam only about one in ten households derive all their income from agricultural activities (farming and/or agricultural wage labor). As table 4 shows, the vast majority derive at least some of their income from nonfarm employment or enterprise. For more than one in three households this is their most important source of income. This group includes both households that are not involved in independent farming at all and about one in four farming households that earn most of their income off-farm. Some of the households that rely heavily on nonfarm income make up the more affluent socioeconomic strata in the village, and they are involved in relatively lucrative nonagricultural pursuits such as public administration, shopkeeping, moneylending, wage-labor recruitment, rice milling, handicrafts, food processing, and construction. Others are much worse off and survive by combining nonagricultural employment with intermittent agricultural labor. Many households also receive regular and intermittent income from family members who live and work outside the village, but estimating the magnitude of these remittances is very difficult. Data from previous studies suggest that remittances may comprise up to one-third of the income of receiving households.[12]

Government Employment

Government employment is an important component of Ban Tiam's economy. A survey I undertook in 2006 found that 41 percent of Ban Tiam's households derived some income from work in the government sector. This was the second most important source of employment, exceeded only by agricultural wage labor. Given that wages and salaries are generally higher in the government sector, and employment is much less seasonal, it is probably the most important source of employment in financial terms. Pad Siew Municipality is a substantial employer. It has grown considerably in size and importance since its establishment in 1999. It now has an annual budget of over 30 million baht, and it employs about fifty full-time staff. Positions held by Ban Tiam residents within the municipality include senior administration,

TABLE 4. Incidence of nonagricultural employment and enterprise in Ban Tiam, Thailand (percentages).

	Government	Community Projects	Construction	Business Owner	Business Employee	Employment Elsewhere in Thailand or Overseas	Agricultural Wage Labor
Primary source of noncrop income	27	7	5	18	5	2	30
Secondary source of noncrop income	14	27	27	9	7	20	43

SOURCE: Field survey by the author, August 2006.

NOTE: Figures are the percentage of fifty-six surveyed households. Household members were asked to nominate their primary and secondary sources of income from employment or enterprise. Agricultural wage labor is included for comparison. For the primary source, some households didn't nominate any employment or enterprise. For the secondary source, households could nominate more than one option.

clerical work, driving, market fee collection, and cleaning. Some residents also hold positions within the district administration: two work in the community development department, another runs a shop selling local handicrafts, and some of the younger women have clerical positions. Government-run services are also sources of professional and less skilled employment. Ban Tiam has a primary school teacher, two cooks at the district high school, one masseuse at the hospital, and one police officer. Forest management is also important. There are no less than four government offices involved in managing the forest areas surrounding Ban Tiam: a national park protection office located to the south of the village; the local office of the Royal Forest Department located in the nearby district center; and two watershed protection offices, both about ten kilometers away. Several villagers have salaried positions in these offices, and a good number of the village's poorer residents are employed in various environmental projects aimed at national park management and watershed rehabilitation. Unskilled laboring employment is available in two large agricultural development stations located about five kilometers from Ban Tiam. A medium-scale hydroelectric scheme located on the river a few kilometers downstream from Ban Tiam employs villagers in several positions ranging from housekeeper to engineer.

Construction

Construction activity is undertaken by private contractors, but it is heavily underwritten by government finance. There is some nongovernment construction, such as house building and temple improvements, but a good proportion of this private or communal construction is generated by the salaries of government officials or the patronage of politicians. Over the past decade Ban Tiam has witnessed an array of government-funded construction projects, significantly boosted by the municipality's annual allocation of 800,000 baht for infrastructure within Ban Tiam. Infrastructure development has long been a central component of the Thai government's strategy for rural development. In recent years, construction projects in Ban Tiam have included the widening of the road from the district center to the village, the paving of village roads, a handicraft center, a large concrete pavilion for village rituals, two new water supply systems, two bridges, expansion of the storm-water drainage system, two new irrigation weirs, a community rice mill, and a village meeting hall. A large and very thick concrete slab on vacant land in the center of the village is the product of some quick end-of-year spending of an unused municipal budget allocation. A similar array of projects is evident in the surrounding villages. In the local imagination, the proliferation of government-funded construction projects is a clear marker of Ban Tiam's emerging modernity, prosperity, and development.

The most direct beneficiaries of these construction projects are the two local contractors who are resident in the village. One is a highly successful businessman who has won a steady supply of construction work from the municipality, no doubt linked to the fact that his father-in-law is the mayor. Another contractor focuses on the design and construction of private residences in Ban Tiam and neighboring villages. There is also another wealthy contractor in the district who has close links with Ban Tiam, having acquired significant landholdings there. Each of these contractors employs Ban Tiam residents to work on various construction projects. Construction work usually pays considerably more than casual wage labor in the agricultural sector, especially for those undertaking skilled activities such as carpentry or bricklaying. However, on some projects local employment opportunities are reduced by the contractors' use of teams of low-wage construction workers from Burma. Overall, construction laboring provides a supplementary source of income for almost 30 percent of households within the village.

Community Projects

Community development projects comprise another sector of economic activity in the village. Government agencies support an array of livelihood, environmental, and welfare projects that provide various forms of employment and income. The important role of the state in these community activities is underlined by the fact that many villagers found it hard to distinguish between "working for the community" and "working for the government" when I surveyed them about wage labor. Once the rather artificial distinction was explained, 7 percent of those surveyed said that community projects were their most important source of cash income and 27 percent said they were a supplementary source. This income derives both from direct employment and from various "allowances" and "dividends" paid to those involved in the management of the projects. These projects are discussed in detail in chapter 5.

Private Sector

Apart from the state-dependent construction businesses, the private commercial sector in Ban Tiam is small scale and informal. There are seven shops, two small restaurants, two tiny petrol stations, several crop traders, and several stall holders in the nearby district market. About 8 percent of the village lives mainly off shopkeeping. The shops sell an array of basic consumer durables and some locally produced fresh vegetables. Much of their custom is from Ban Tiam, but some of the shops have an active trade with residents of an upland village that is located in the national park about ten kilometers to the east. Shops and restaurants in the nearby district center also employ a number of Ban Tiam residents. The manufacturing and food-processing sector within the village is very small scale. Two households operate small rice mills, one produces fried bananas, another steams bamboo shoots for sale in the district market, and several men are involved in furniture manufacture and other forms of woodworking. These small-scale processing enterprises make a substantial financial contribution to only about 3 percent of households. Local capital accumulation in the private sector is virtually nonexistent, and employment opportunities are limited. In fact, the largest "private-sector" employer in the local area is an elaborate meditation temple, which is supported by a wide network of affluent disciples based in both Chiang Mai and Bangkok. Despite the proximity of Chiang Mai, and the district's environmental and cultural charms, the tourism sector is moribund with only a couple of ramshackle tourist "resorts."

Official survey data for Pad Siew Municipality, of which Ban Tiam is a part, confirms this rather dismal private-sector picture. The industrial survey undertaken by the National Statistics Office in 2007 recorded a total of 159 establishments, of which 121 (76 percent) were shops or restaurants.[13] Only 11 were classified as manufacturing enterprises. These were not identified, but my strong impression is that all of them are household-based microenterprises or small rice mills. The small scale of the private sector in the municipality is also revealed by the fact that 149 of the enterprises employed fewer than five workers, 152 were run by individual proprietors, only 1 was a "branch" with a head office outside the district, and, not surprisingly, none was the recipient of any foreign investment. Some older data from the early 1970s provide an interesting comparison.[14] The overall size of the sector was smaller, with only 53 establishments in the area that now comprises the municipality. Clearly there has been considerable growth in the number of enterprises (300 percent), substantially greater than population growth over the same period (about 80 percent).[15] However, the enterprise structure in the 1970s was broadly similar to what it is now: shops and restaurants predominated (65 percent) followed by rice mills (13 percent), dressmaking services (10 percent), and an alcohol distillery. There is, however, an important difference.

In the early 1970s there was a single substantial enterprise in the form of a tobacco-processing factory, which was established by a businessman from Chiang Mai, who later became the provincial assemblyman for Pad Siew District. This employed thirty-nine people, almost one-quarter of private-sector employment at the time within the municipality. In a neighboring subdistrict there was also a tin mine and various processing facilities, which employed more than two hundred people. These two enterprises represented more substantial private sector activity than anything currently operating in the district. The closure of both the tobacco factory (in about 1976 after its owner was bankrupted by excessive gambling) and the tin mine (in the early 1990s) amounts to very significant local deindustrialization. Over the same period the local timber industry also disappeared.

The attempts by the Thai government to promote rural industrialization and transform the economic structure of the peasantry have had very limited success. One review of government policy concludes that "while the promotion of rural small-scale industrial enterprises in Thailand has long been an aspect of state policy, it has been relatively ineffectual and its impact has been minimal."[16] Rural enterprise schemes have tended to be tokenistic, poorly implemented, and often focused on the production of low-value handicrafts that have provided only supplementary employment for a very limited number of people in rural communities. The Thaksin government's local economic development schemes, such as the famous One Tambol [Subdistrict] One Product (OTOP) program, have continued this trend. In Ban Tiam, the most notable OTOP-supported project is a small backyard enterprise producing sweets made from bananas. There is a very lightly patronized OTOP shop in the district center, which sells exotic and expensive handicraft goods. Similarly, the Small-Medium-Large (SML) scheme, which provided grants of up to 300,000 baht to villages throughout Thailand, has made some contribution to job creation and local infrastructure, but there are indications that its main contribution has been to strengthen the already robust construction sector.[17] In Ban Tiam, the SML scheme funded the construction of a community rice mill, which operated primarily by taking business away from the privately owned mills already operating in the village. Overall the situation in Ban Tiam resonates with the conclusions drawn by the Japanese economist Yoko Ueda in her analysis of northeastern Thailand in the early 1990s: "[E]conomic backwardness in provincial economies in Thailand can be best summarized in the following three points: small-scale business, weak manufacturing, and few exportable manufactured products."[18]

Diversity, Productivity, and
Inequality in a Middle-Income Economy

In describing the contemporary challenges faced by Ban Tiam's economy, I find it useful to consider political scientist Richard Doner's analysis of Thailand's uneven development. Doner makes an important distinction between economic "diversification" and "upgrading."[19] Thailand has been successful in diversifying its economic activity, moving from an economy largely dependent on agriculture to one dominated by manufacturing and services. Even within the agricultural sector, there has been impressive diversification with a much broader mix of cultivation and export than there was in the rice-dominated 1960s. However, the national record in terms of upgrading—"moving into higher value-added products, at higher levels of efficiency, with local inputs"—has been much poorer.[20] By and large, Thailand's economic growth has relied on higher levels of inputs (more agricultural land, foreign investment, and domestic labor) rather than on their more efficient use. Even the dramatic growth in manufacturing has been heavily reliant on relatively low technology and labor-intensive goods, with domestic firms tending to focus on assembly rather than design, production, and innovation. Doner argues that without substantial productivity increases via upgrading, Thailand runs the risk of becoming stuck in its middle-income position, especially as competition from lower-wage economies undermines the advantage of Thailand's labor-intensive exports.

How does Ban Tiam perform in terms of diversification and upgrading? Ban Tiam clearly has a diverse economy, both within and outside the agricultural sector. This diversification is evident in the development of an active, and innovative, cash-crop sector and in the large proportion of income earned from off-farm employment and enterprise. This diversification has been facilitated by the Thai state's long-term policy shift from taxing the rural economy to subsidizing it. In Ban Tiam, the state has supported the adoption of high-yield rice, invested in irrigation infrastructure, dramatically expanded rural credit provision, and funded an array of local development projects. Road construction has opened up access to regional, national, and international markets. This public investment has increased the productivity of agricultural labor in Ban Tiam, as it has done throughout Thailand.[21] A dense local network of government offices and ongoing state investment in infrastructure also provide a wide range of off-farm employment. The private sector's role in diversification has been very modest by comparison, although recent investment in contract farming is providing a greater range of crop choice. There is no doubt that, as in rural areas throughout the world, Ban Tiam's economic diversification, especially the increase in nonfarm income, has played a crucially important role in reducing poverty and lifting the village into a middle-income position.

However, Ban Tiam's performance in relation to upgrading has been much less impressive. Diversification has certainly increased the range of economic activity, and the nonagricultural sector has grown in both absolute and relative terms, but many of the basic structures of economic activity remain unchanged. Overall, the local economy is still strongly oriented to lower-value forms of production. The state has become a very important source of income, but state expenditure has done little to produce more productive forms of economic activity. State intervention has preserved rather than transformed this rural economy. Rural diversification from subsistence farming to cash cropping and from on-farm to off-farm plays an important role in poverty alleviation, but international experience strongly suggests that sustained and broad-based livelihood improvements require the development of the more lucrative manufacturing and service sectors of local economies. Without this, national disparities between rural and urban areas persist, or even widen, and local versions of these disparities are produced as social groups achieve differential access to the limited sectors of the economy where higher levels of income are possible. This uneven development is evident within Ban Tiam itself.

For the most economically marginal households within Ban Tiam, economic diversification has provided a basic safety net, but it has made only a modest contribution to productivity enhancement and livelihood improvement. This is most evident among the landless poor (comprising about 20 percent of the village) and the least successful farming households, especially those that only have access to less productive upland fields. The diversification that has taken place in many of these marginal households has been motivated principally by the force of economic circumstances—the geographer Jonathan Rigg calls it "distress diversification"—rather than by opportunity-seeking entrepreneurialism.[22] Some of the landless have lost their agricultural land as a result of foreclosure on debts or forced sale to meet pressing household expenses. Others are landless because of an unfavorable inheritance or because they moved into the village after all the good agricultural land was claimed. Some small farming households have had little choice but to increase their off-farm activities as a result of crop failure, low prices, and indebtedness. State restrictions on cultivation have also limited agricultural options for some of the poorer non-paddy-owning farmers. Of course, even distress diversification can enhance overall productivity if labor shifts from agriculture into more productive sectors. Out-migration to urban areas is one way in which this has been achieved; however, some poorer households are unable to do this due to a shortage of funds for relocation, a lack of social networks, and lower educational achievement. Within the local economy, productivity gains from distress diversification have been modest as it has commonly resulted in people moving from independent farming into low-skill and irregular employment, much of it within the agricultural sector itself. As one recent analysis of rural economic development argues, "[R]eliance on agricultural labor markets alone will not reduce poverty to a significant extent."[23] Agricultural wages in Ban Tiam are around the minimum provincial rate of 140 baht per day, and work is intermittent. Laboring opportunities in the agricultural sector are restricted by the use of exchange labor by capital-short farming households. As a result, agricultural wage laborers complain of chronic underemployment. The construction sector is another source of employment, although payment for unskilled work is also low, partly as a result of the ample supply of immigrant laborers from Burma. In addition, construction work is often short term, irregular, and highly dependent on the flow of government development grants.

A quite different form of economic diversification is evident among the most economically successful households in the village. The village elite consist of an upper-middle-income and rich group of successful farmers, traders, shopkeepers, moneylenders, construction contractors, and government administrators. Profits from garlic production played a part in launching some of them into business—and farming remains an important source of income for some elite families—but the main source of contemporary capital accumulation is state financial support. This is most evident in the construction sector, which, as in many other parts of Thailand, is an important site of economic and political power. The most successful members of the local elite have been able to create profitable links between political office and their construction businesses. Most notable is the village's richest member, Witoon Siwila, whose business interests expanded as he rose from headman to district head and then to provincial assemblyman. He got rich on road-building contracts during the 1980s when there was rapid development of the road network within the district as part of the nationwide boom in rural roads. His finances were enhanced by acting as a local vote canvasser for national politicians, and he later became an active local campaigner for Thaksin's Thai Rak Thai party. In 2002, Witoon successfully backed one of his colleagues in the construction business, Somsak, who was elected mayor of the newly established Pad Siew Municipality. In turn, Mayor Somsak passed his construction business to his son-in-law. Construction contractors, and the government officials who deal with them, are widely rumored to maximize their financial benefits by means of price collusion in the preparation of tenders, overcharging, cutting corners on construction specifications, and substituting raw materials of lower quality than those specified in the contracts. Income from these lucrative linkages has also enabled elite families to expand their shopkeeping, crop-trading, moneylending, rice-milling, and tractor-plowing enterprises and, in some cases, to acquire tracts of agricultural land that generate rental income. In a couple of cases, marriages with government officials have provided a reliable salaried income and consolidated bureaucratic connections.

Ban Tiam's elite residents are very much like the "local powers" that the anthropologist Andrew Turton described in northern Thailand in the 1980s:

> At the "village level" we find . . . a small minority . . . of households which possess a degree of wealth, control of resources, prestige, and power which sets them apart from the majority. . . . Many of [their strategies of accumulation] involve varying degrees of direct and indirect state patronage. Among these are privileged access to low-interest credit and limited inputs provided on credit; access to state-owned land . . . ; access to contracts to supply quotas; access to limited official budgets for development projects . . . and guaranteed prices . . . ; and access to the benefits of infrastructural development.[24]

The enduring relevance of this description highlights an important point about this economically dominant group in Ban Tiam: there is nothing particularly new about it. Economic power still lies in establishing productive connections between state resources and local enterprise rather than in pursuing more independent forms of capital accumulation. What has changed is that the growth and diversification of the economy and the proliferation of state administration mean that the ability of these local leaders to command loyal entourages has been diminished.

About 60 percent of the village lies between these two socioeconomic poles, forming the core of Ban Tiam's middle-income peasantry. This group is made up principally of smallholding farmers who combine agricultural pursuits with various forms of off-farm enterprise and employment. They, too, have benefited from state investment in the rural economy, though rather less ostentatiously than their elite neighbors. They have achieved some important productivity gains, particularly in relation to rice production, largely as a result of government investment in research and extension. The government's expansion of agricultural credit and investment in irrigation infrastructure and roads have also been essential for the expansion of cash cropping. Commercial agriculture in Ban Tiam has raised the incomes of farming households and increased the demand for wage labor. Nevertheless, there are important productivity constraints. Rice is a low-value crop and contributes very little to increasing income. Garlic is much more lucrative, but yields have stagnated and garlic prices have been very unstable. Problems with garlic have prompted a new phase of diversification via contract farming. This has facilitated some productivity-enhancing adoption of high-input and high-value vegetable crops, but the most popular contract crop has turned out to be low-risk and low-value tobacco.

Given these productivity constraints, the ability of the agricultural sector to contribute to ongoing livelihood improvement is limited, and Ban Tiam's farming households have become highly diversified. For 30 percent of farming households, off-farm employment or enterprise is their most important source of cash income, and for another 35 percent it is a supplementary source of income. The government plays an important part in this off-farm sector, both by providing direct employment and by funding the active construction sector. Some farmers grumble about the lack of independence involved in wage labor—and some successful farmers proudly declare that they have no time for it—but it is well recognized that income from wages can help mitigate the risks involved in cultivation, for "if you work for wages you are sure of getting the money, but with farming the money only comes once in a while." These farming households are strongly represented in Ban Tiam's various committees and political offices (such as headman and assistant headman) and, as such, are well placed to benefit from the government-funded development projects implemented within the village. However, as with their poorer landless neighbors, much of this off-farm economic activity is in relatively nonproductive sectors of the economy and is heavily dependent on government finance. Despite its growth, the agricultural sector has been insufficiently productive to generate capital investment in alternative forms of economic activity, and government efforts to promote private sector activity have had a limited impact.

3

Drawing Power into Private Realms

On the morning of Monday, 14 April 2008, Aunt Kluay prepared an elaborate feast. It was the second day of the new-year celebration and Kluay wanted to honor the spirits that had overseen her newfound prosperity. Early in the morning she made the short journey to the district market and spent a thousand baht buying two pig's heads, the accompanying sets of trotters, and some choice portions of intestine and flesh. Back at her mother's house, which lay just next to her own, Kluay carefully arranged the heads and trotters in large metal bowls. Working with her daughter and niece, she prepared fifteen bowls of curry, blood-soaked *larb*, and fried pork.[1] The bowls were divided onto three platters. On each of these she added a small container of sticky rice, a bowl of vegetable soup, a bowl of sweet coconut jelly, two small bottles of orange juice, and a cup of water. Shortly before ten o'clock in the morning, Kluay and her daughter carried one of the pig's heads and two of the platters upstairs to the main bedroom of her mother's house. They were joined there by Grandmother Thip and Grandmother Duang, maternal relatives of Kluay's deceased father. Grandmother Thip was the custodian of the protective spirit that resided on a small wooden shelf located in the northeast corner of the bedroom. Sitting before the shelf, Thip raised one of the platters of food above her head and, with a few words of offering, presented it to the spirit. Kluay then placed the platter on the spirit's wooden shelf. The second platter, along with the pig's head, was left on the floor. This platter of food was offered to another protective spirit that normally resided in a small wooden shrine just outside the house. This spirit was invited inside to join the feast and share in the honor of the pig's head. The three women said some brief prayers and urged the spirits to eat.

Kluay then turned her attention to a much more public demonstration of her relationship with the spirit world. Just outside her family compound, many of the men of the village had assembled to present the new-year offering to the village's guardian spirit, the Lord of the Lucky Tree. Giant woks of pork curry were bubbling away over outdoor fires. A small group of women carefully folded large leaves to make rustic platters on which the food would be presented to the lord and his assistants. Inside the lord's shrine, which had been swept and washed for the occasion, a member of the village committee was collecting donations to help defray the costs. Suddenly, Kluay and her husband marched into the midst of the preparations, bearing the second pig's head, a bottle of whisky, and the third platter of food. Their presence was all the more notable because both were wearing bright yellow shirts, the auspicious color of both Monday and Thailand's king. They climbed the steps of the shrine and knelt before the long wooden shelf where the lord resides. The lord's custodian then held the pig's head and whisky above his head and presented them to the guardian spirit. He placed these offerings, along with the platter of food, on the wooden shelf. Kluay and her husband then returned to their home, while preparations for the village's communal offering continued.

Aunt Kluay embodies some of the main socioeconomic changes that have occurred in Ban Tiam over the past decade. When I first met her in late 2002 she was one of the most active farmers in the village with almost two hectares of garlic fields. Most of the land that she farmed with her husband was rented because she had sold land, and her house, to cover the medical and funeral expenses of her sister and her son, who had both died of AIDS. Along with her husband and daughter she was living in a temporary bamboo hut on a spare plot of land next to her mother's house. She was determined to recover her former status by means of heavy investment in cash cropping. However, disappointing crop yields and a couple of outright failures left her further in debt. Kluay started talking about giving up agriculture altogether, and for a while she sold food in the district market. As another sideline, she occasionally did odd jobs at the nearby meditation temple, where she was a disciple of a locally famous Buddhist nun. It was at the temple that she met a wealthy shopkeeper from southern Thailand who offered Kluay long-term employment as a caregiver for her elderly mother. Kluay took up the offer and left Ban Tiam in early 2005, earning over ten thousand baht per month plus numerous allowances. Her husband stayed in the village and worked full time as a carpenter. By 2007, Kluay was able to fund the construction and lavish furnishing of a new house, which replaced the bamboo hut. When she first left the village, and each time she departed after a return visit, Kluay made modest offerings to the spirits; she told them where she was going and asked for their guidance and protection. She had prospered under the supervision of these spirits, and it was now time to acknowledge their role and draw them more closely into the successful trajectory of her life.

The spirit world is a useful place to commence a detailed exploration of Ban Tiam's political society. Attitudes toward spirits reflect quite fundamental orientations toward power. These orientations are not fundamental in the sense that they derive from some unchanging cultural foundation. On the contrary, as this chapter will show, there is a significant degree of pragmatism and adaptability in dealings with the spirit world. Rather, orientations toward the supernatural power of spirits are fundamental because they relate to very basic concerns about safety, morality, health, and prosperity. Exploring the ritual relationships between the social and supernatural domains provides useful insights into the way in which dispersed and malleable nodes of power are drawn into the day-to-day worlds of livelihood, aspiration, and ambition. Aunt Kluay was an excellent networker, and she was determined to create an appropriate place for her spiritual guardians in the increasingly prosperous network of connections that she was building around her.

Pu Nya Spirits

The spirit (*phi*) that resides in the main bedroom of the house of Kluay's mother is a *pu nya* spirit.[2] This is not a straightforward term to translate. In standard central Thai, *pu ya* refers to one's paternal grandparents, but in northern Thai the similar term, *pu nya*, can refer to various categories of senior relatives. In Ban Tiam, the term is often used to refer to a broad category of older relatives, both living and dead. Given that *pu nya* is a kinship term that refers to older, and often deceased, relatives, some observers have taken the view that *pu nya* spirits are spirits of the ancestors. This view gains some support in Ban Tiam, where the *pu nya* spirits are sometimes explicitly referred to as ancestral spirits (*phi banphaburut*) and the deference granted to them is described as being similar to that granted to senior members of a lineage. But it must be said that this ancestral identification is vague, and the *pu nya* spirits are not associated, either through naming or through narrative, with any particular ancestor. In fact, it may be more in keeping with local belief to see the *pu nya* spirits as "spirits that belonged to the ancestors" rather than spirits *of* the ancestors.[3] This interpretation leads us to an even more general meaning of the term *pu nya*. The villagers of Ban Tiam most commonly use the term to refer to what is best described as an authoritative past. For example, the typical answer provided when villagers are asked why a ritual is undertaken is that it came to them from the *pu nya*. This use of the term is not meant to refer to people in any specific kin relationship— nor to older (or deceased) people more generally—but to a vaguely defined past era that is selectively drawn on to justify contemporary practice. So, whatever the specific relationship between *pu nya* spirits and actual ancestors, the important thing is that the spirits have been inherited from the time of the ancestors and their moral force and potency derives from this ancestral period. This is the moral authority that Aunt Kluay was tapping into when she performed her offering.

The potency of *pu nya* spirits is intimately embedded in Ban Tiam's residential landscape. As in other areas of northern Thailand, the *pu nya* spirits in Ban Tiam are resident in a limited number of "origin" houses (*huen kao*). Kluay's mother lives in one such house. The presence of a *pu nya* spirit in these origin houses is marked by a small, nondescript, wooden shelf (*hing*) located in the main bedroom. These shelves are small, private, and very unremarkable spirit "shrines." Ban Tiam has seventeen such origin houses, many of them clustered around the original site of settlement within the lower part of the village. Most people living in the village have an affiliation with one or another of these local origin houses, while about a quarter of the residents are linked to origin houses in other villages and districts. The origin houses are usually home to the most senior woman within the group that is affiliated with the spirit. This senior woman is responsible for making offerings to the spirit, although a closely related kinswoman can act on her behalf if circumstances require (fig. 6). For reasons that I will explain below, Kluay's mother is not responsible for the spirit that resides in her house. That responsibility lies with Grandmother Thip, who is Kluay's deceased father's maternal cousin. The spirit group has about twenty local members.

Pu nya spirits are very intimate manifestations of the diverse and dispersed network of power in which Ban Tiam's residents seek to favorably situate themselves. Connections within this spiritual sphere of political society must be cultivated with regular inducements, especially offerings of food. Like people, spirits get hungry, and in order to maintain good relations with *pu nya* spirits it is important to feed them. Persistent neglect or outright abandonment may lead to the *pu nya* spirit taking on a malevolent and disruptive form. Fortunately, *pu nya* spirit appetites only need to be satisfied a few times

FIGURE 6. Making an offering to a *pu nya* spirit, Ban Tiam, Thailand. (Photo by the author.)

each year. The most important occasion for offering is the ninth northern Thai month, which commences in late May or early June. Ideally all members of the spirit group should assemble at the origin house for the feast, but attendance is very uneven and dominated by women. Many members of the group only send a small offering of food. The usual ninth-month offering is a chicken, although some participants not resident at the origin house may only contribute an egg. Food and drink offerings are accompanied by a few flowers, candles, and sticks of incense. In many origin houses a pig's head is offered every six years. Once the food is presented to the spirit a small candle is lit to signal that the spirit is eating. Once the candle has completely burned down and gone out, the spirit has eaten its fill and the members of the spirit group can then feast on the "leftovers." Those who have contributed food but not attended often come to collect their donated portion, perhaps just an egg with the donor's name written on it. Apart from the ninth-month feast, offerings are made during the new-year festival (in April) and on other, less regular occasions: when members of the spirit group are getting married, when members of the group are traveling away from the village, and when a household member or lineage relative dies.

Cultivating good relations with the *pu nya* spirits is important because they have considerable retributive and protective power. Spirits are temperamental masters, and they can be angered and disturbed in any number of mundane ways: by strangers entering into the main bedroom, by a persistently crying baby, by a child playing near the spirit shelf, or by other disturbances to the regular domestic routine such as a village festival, which attracts rowdy visitors to the house. Movement of the spirit shrine to a new house can also upset the spirit. The most serious form of offense is inappropriate sexual behavior by women within the spirit group. Older people in Bam Tiam report that the spirits used to play an important role in regulating the sexual behavior of young women. Illness (especially fevers) and misfortune were often interpreted as arising from the spirit's anger at extramarital sexual behavior, ranging from sexual intercourse to much more minor infractions such as an inappropriate or even accidental touch. When unexplained sickness occurred, the *pu nya* spirit was called on to guide divination sessions that could determine which girl in the group was responsible for the offense. Naturally, these sessions would cause great stress to young women who could easily be blamed for causing misfortune within the spirit group. Offerings to the spirit were required to redress the offense. For more serious cases a pig's head or even a sacrificial buffalo was the only thing that could placate the angry spirit. In extreme cases, failure to make these offerings or making them incorrectly could lead to the death of someone in the spirit group.

Currently, there is a lot more emphasis on the *pu nya* spirit's protective power than on its retributive power largely because it is widely acknowledged that women's increased mobility for study, work, and marriage has reduced the regulatory influence of the spirits over sexual behavior. In Ban Tiam the *pu nya* spirits are now most commonly spoken of in terms of their role in securing the peace and safety of their descendants and in providing protection when these descendants travel away from the village. The standard request made to the *pu nya* spirits is that they will enable the members of the lineage to *yu yen pen suk*, a term that can be literally translated as "living coolly and happily" but embraces a range of meanings related to security, health, and prosperity. It is an expression broadly associated with good government and righteous rule and nicely illustrates some of the symbolic continuities between different domains of political society. This invocation of benevolent power was clearly expressed when Grandmother Ying made her yearly offering in early June 2004. The occasion was quieter than she had hoped, with only two of her eight daughters present, despite the fact that she had informed them all. She prepared the food for the offerings and took them to the bedroom. She lit some candles as she spoke to the spirit: "On this day in the ninth month we have these things for you to eat. Please make us live and eat well and give us good luck and good health. Today we are presenting chicken and other offerings. Please protect us. Please, grandparents, come and eat. After that make us live and eat well and protect your children and grandchildren."

Through standard invocations like this, reciprocal relationships are established with supernatural powers. Food and respectful words are offered in return for protection. The power of the cosmos is condensed into the figure of the *pu nya* spirit and drawn into an intimate familial domain. The intimacy of this particular form of power is underlined by the spirit's presence in the main bedroom, an exceptionally private place saturated with domesticity and sexual intimacy.

MATRILINEAL DESCENT AND LOCALITY

Kluay's elaborate new-year offering was designed to honor a somewhat capricious *pu nya* spirit and bind its protective power into the newly prosperous trajectory of her family's life. Her actions are a good illustration of the pragmatism and adaptability of rural political society. For some years, the *pu nya* spirit that received Kluay's offering had been rather isolated from the domestic world of the family compound. The house where it lived had been all but abandoned. In the mid-1990s, not long after her husband's death, Kluay's mother moved out of the house's main bedroom and took up residence in a small partitioned room located downstairs. The main residential area upstairs was never used; in fact the house's main entrance was often blocked by boards and bricks to stop chickens from roosting on the steep flight of stairs leading to the door. The only occasions when the upstairs area was opened was when members of the spirit group assembled to make their offerings there. When Kluay and her husband were forced to sell their own house, which was located in another part of the village, they didn't move into her mother's virtually empty house but built their own rough bamboo hut next door to it. Relatives joked that neither Kluay nor her mother wanted to live under the watchful eye of the spirit. There had been a spate of deaths in the family— Kluay's father, her sister, and her son—and there was a real possibility that the spirit was angry. The dubious career of Kluay's sister in Bangkok, which ended in her death from AIDS, was a particular cause for concern. For a short period, the spirit had been moved to the house of Kluay's father's aunt, who had become the most senior woman in the spirit group, but she claimed that the spirit had possessed her and expressed its displeasure at the relocation. The uncooperative spirit was quickly moved back to its rather lonely home.

The somewhat forlorn circumstances of this spirit, and the innovative significance of Kluay's honoring of it, can be understood by reference to the principle of matrilineal descent. The moral authority of the *pu nya* spirits derives from the past, but the relationship with the past is constructed quite specifically in terms of connections that run through women. For most people in Ban Tiam, and in other parts of northern Thailand, connections to the *pu nya* spirits are reckoned matrilineally—people inherit the spirits of their mothers, not their fathers. A girl takes on the spirit of her mother, and she is obliged to pass that affiliation on to her own children, especially her daughters. A boy also inherits his mother's spirit, but he does not pass it on to his children. The descent ideology is expressed in regular references to those sharing the same spirit as forming a lineage (*trakul*). There is also talk of bloodlines (*say luat*, literally, "strings of blood"), which connect people both to the past and, in the present, to their origin houses. The senior woman who is the spirit's custodian is referred to as the "origin of the lineage." The matrilineal principle means that women are much more intimately involved with *pu nya* spirits and much less likely to abandon them.

However, matrilineal principles don't always match neatly with the vagaries of marriage, residence, and inheritance. These vagaries posed a particular problem for Aunt Kluay and her mother. In current memory, the founder of the lineage that "owns" the spirit resident in the house of Kluay's mother was Great-great-grandmother Maew (chart 6). When she died, responsibility for the spirit passed to her daughter, Grandmother Mon, who also inherited the house. However, Mon had three sons, and on her death, custodianship of the spirit passed to her younger sister, Grandmother La, who lived in a house about one hundred meters away. It was La who was possessed by the spirit when it was temporarily moved to her house. Despite this disconcerting experience, La continued to act as custodian of the spirit until her death in 2004. The position then passed to her younger sister, Duang, who held it for only a short period. Duang told me that she gave up the position because she had no children and was worried that there would be no one to look after the spirit when she died. Kluay, in a not so subtle attempt to undermine

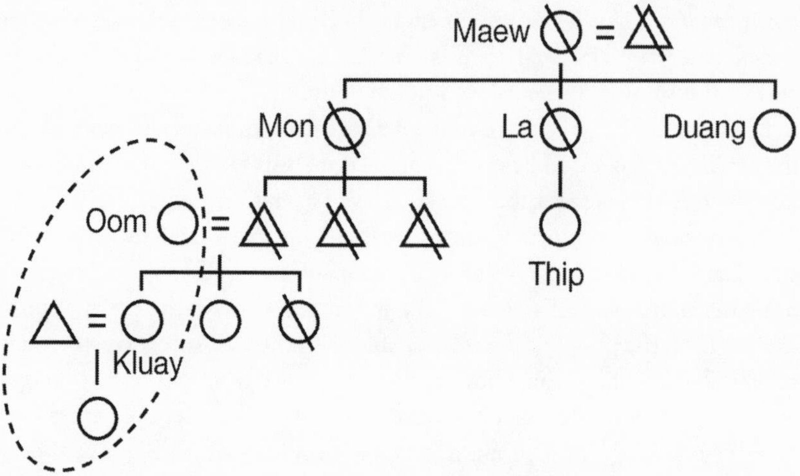

CHART 6. Kluay's family and close relatives. The dotted line surrounds the current residents of the household compound. (Diagram by Cartography Unit, College of Asia and the Pacific, Australian National University.)

matrilineal authority, told me that Duang had offended the spirit by dropping the offering tray when she was presenting it with food. Whatever the reason, the responsibility for the spirit now lies with La's daughter, Grandmother Thip, who lives in a house on the other side of Ban Tiam.

Where does Kluay's mother, Grandmother Oom, the current owner of the origin house, fit into this picture? Oom was an in-marrying woman from a neighboring village (Ban Khua) and came to live with her husband and his mother, Mon. Following matrilineal principles, Oom did not worship the spirit in her husband's house but maintained her ritual connection with her mother's spirit in her natal village. She once told me emphatically that she could not make offerings to the spirit in her current house of residence because she is a daughter-in-law (*saphay*) who married into the household, not an actual descendant. Matrilineal ideology holds that a mother-in-law and daughter-in-law living together like this is hazardous, as their different spirits are unlikely to get on. But in this case the situation was unavoidable as Mon, the mother-in-law, had only three sons so the household could only be maintained by bringing in a wife. As a result, since the death of her mother-in-law and husband, Oom has had to live with the disconcerting situation whereby the house, which she inherited from her husband, is in one important ritual sense controlled by people living elsewhere given that custodianship of the spirit had passed outside of the origin house to Grandmother La, her mother-in-law's sister, and most recently to La's daughter, Thip. Kluay has inherited this anomaly. Her *pu nya* spirit is, in fact, the spirit in her mother's natal home in Ban Khua. According to matrilineal principles she has no role or responsibilities in relation to the spirit that lives in her mother's marital home—the house were Kluay herself grew up.

However, things turned out to be not quite so clear-cut. Attachments to power are malleable, and they can be reconfigured. In April 2005, I received a message from my research assistant that Kluay's mother was claiming that I had offended the spirit in her house, where I stayed during my research visits. Oom claimed that I had disturbed the spirit by entering the room and taking photographs when an offering was made in March 2004. In its annoyance, the spirit had caused her second daughter (who was living in Bangkok with her husband) to fall in the bathroom and break her nose, which required surgery. In order to remedy the situation it was necessary for me to make an offering of a pig's head. I was puzzled about this development. According to the matrilineal principle to which Oom subscribes, her daughters came under the authority of the spirit in her natal village, Ban Khua. I have had no dealings at all with that spirit. My assistant asked Oom to explain why the spirit in her house was exercising its retributive authority over a person who was not a member of its matrilineal group. Oom's answer was very important. She said that her daughters had regularly eaten in the house and lived their lives there. In other words they had grown up there. For this reason, she explained, they belonged to the spirit in the house more than they belonged to Oom's own spirit in Ban Khua. Oom was asserting that localized domesticity is relevant, and perhaps even more relevant than the matrilineal linkage, in orienting people toward sources of spiritual power.

In June 2005, on my next visit to Ban Tiam, I made the necessary arrangements for the offering and purchased a pig's head and some pork at the district market. Interestingly, Oom took an active part in preparing the offerings. These were similar, though less elaborate, to the offerings prepared by Kluay described at the beginning of this chapter. Even though she insisted that she could not actually present the offerings to the spirit, Oom participated in the ceremony: carrying the offerings into the bedroom, placing the tray of food on the spirit shelf, and lighting the candle that marked the spirit's feast. She also took the largest share of what was left over after the spirit had eaten its fill (although she didn't actually join in the small communal feast that followed the offering). Oom was making small, but significant, steps to align herself with the spirit of her late husband's matrilineage. The matrilineal principle had left her spiritually marginalized in her house of residence, especially after her husband's death, and she was now realigning herself with one source of local power. I suspect that her actions may have been partly motivated by the fact that at the end of my previous two visits I had paid my "rental" money to Kluay—rather than to Oom herself—naively assuming that Kluay would pass the money on to her mother. Oom was angry about this because it was her house that I actually slept in, and I have little doubt that she was mobilizing the house's supernatural resources in order to assert some domestic and financial authority over me. With Kluay away working in southern Thailand, the way was clear for her mother to reclaim a dominant position in the household compound.

The importance of residence, rather than matrilineal descent, in forging connections with spirits is also evident in Kluay's behavior. When I surveyed Kluay about *pu nya* spirit practice in 2004 she reported that she had two *pu nya* spirits: her mother's spirit in Ban Khua and her father's spirit in Ban Tiam. In 2005, when she was leaving to return to work in southern Thailand (having briefly returned home to cast her vote in the national election), she made modest offerings to the *pu nya* spirit in her house (her father's spirit) and to various other protective spirits in the vicinity. Having done this, she told me that all her ancestors, and her ancestor's friends (*phuan pu nya*), now knew where she was going and would protect her on her travels. She made no such offerings to her mother's spirit in Ban Khua. By 2008, when she made the large offering described at the beginning of this chapter, there was no reference at all to her mother's spirit. Kluay had several motives for this shift toward the spirit of her father's lineage. She told me on several occasions that she was much closer to her father than her mother. Relations with her mother became particularly tense after her marriage, because her mother never accepted her husband and, in fact, refused to perform the usual wrist-tying ritual at their wedding. So she had strong emotional reasons to seek to ally herself with the spiritual power of her father's lineage. There were also more pragmatic factors. After investigating the possibility of purchasing a new block of land on which to build their planned new house, Kluay and her husband had ultimately decided to build it within her family compound. This required prolonged negotiations with her mother about subdivision of the household compound and also inflamed simmering tensions about inheritance between Kluay and one of her sisters. Cultivating her relationship with the *pu nya* spirits was one way in which Kluay was asserting her legitimate rights within the household compound, perhaps even challenging the similar claims that her mother was making. When Kluay made her elaborate offerings in April 2008, her mother played no role in the ceremony.

THE PROTECTIVE AHAK SPIRIT

So far I have dealt with only one of the platters of food offerings prepared by Aunt Kluay: the platter that she presented to her father's *pu nya* spirit. The second platter, which was also taken up to the bedroom in her mother's house, was provided for a second, but closely related, protective spirit known as the *ahak*. This spirit resides in a rather ramshackle wooden shrine located in the household compound a few meters to the east of the house (fig. 7). This three-walled, houselike shrine is built on small stilts, which raise it about half a meter off the ground. There is a small set of rickety steps that facilitate the spirit's access. The floor of the shrine is often littered with fallen leaves, among which there are remnants of incense, candles, flowers, and

FIGURE 7. *Ahak* shrine next to Kluay's mother's house, Ban Tiam, Thailand. (Photo by the author.)

puffed rice. Leftover food offerings are quickly taken care of by cats and chickens. At the back of the shrine there is a rough wooden shelf where the offerings to the spirit are provided. Similar external shrines are found at almost all of the houses in the village where *pu nya* spirits reside.

The *ahak* is an important element in the supernatural sphere of Ban Tiam's political society, and it is worth considering in some detail given the insight it can provide into local orientations toward external power. *Ahak* is a word that is widely used in northern Thailand, and elsewhere in the region, to refer to various types of protective spirits. As some Ban Tiam villagers point out, the word is similar to the central Thai word *arakkha*, which means "care" and "protection."[4] The presence of the *ahak* appears to be a rather common aspect of *pu nya* spirit practice in northern Thailand. In their survey of the relevant literature, the anthropologists Paul Cohen and Gehan Wijeye-wardene state that some *pu nya* spirit groups "have two shrines, one internal and another in the northeast or southeast corner of the house compound."[5] They refer to these external shrines as "the slightest elaboration of the [*pu nya* spirit] cult," making the important point that with these external shrines "the practice begins to look more like the rituals associated with locality shrines." Wijeyewardene reports that these external spirit houses are "often said to be the abode of the 'protecting spirit.'"[6] Cohen's data, from Chiang Mai Province, indicate that over half of the spirit groups he studied "had two shrines, one in the main bedroom . . . and one in the compound called the *hau phi aahag* [*ahak*] ('shrine of the guardian spirit')."[7] Similar observations about the *ahak* are made by a number of other writers who have worked in different provinces of northern Thailand.[8]

Before exploring the distinctions Ban Tiam villagers make between the *pu nya* spirit and the *ahak*, it should be noted that in the minds of many vil-lagers these two powerful entities are merged, with people regularly referring to them as the "same ancestral spirit." Significantly, almost all survey respon-dents stated that their *pu nya* spirit and *ahak* are located at the same origin house. The only respondents who nominated a different location for their *ahak* were those for whom there was no *ahak* shrine present at the local ori-gin house. Most of these nominated an *ahak* at a house in a nearby village, to which they are matrilineally related. Ban Tiam residents also point out that the *pu nya* spirit and *ahak* are worshipped at the same time, and, as one woman stated, "the steps for making offerings are the same and the same food is provided to both each year." Another emphasized that "when women get married it is necessary to tell both the *pu nya* and the *ahak*."

However, within this strong sense of common identity there is simultaneously a strong sense of distinction. Most simply, the distinction is expressed spatially—the *pu nya* spirit lives (and takes care of) the upstairs while the *ahak* lives (and takes care of) the downstairs. This is not just a matter of elevation. What is being said is that the *pu nya* spirit lives within the house while the *ahak* resides outside it. There is some ambiguity in the symbolism of this spatial configuration. The *ahak's* common location to the auspicious east of the house signals ritual superiority, but its placement well below the shelf of the *pu nya* spirit signals inferiority, although, at the same time, its proximity to the earth suggests an alternative locus of power. The spatial statement (with its inherent ambiguities) is fundamentally a statement about gender. It is commonly said that the *ahak* is oriented toward men. Kluay's husband told me that the external spirit is the *pu* (grandfather) while the spirit in the bedroom is the *nya* (grandmother) and that together they make up the *pu nya* spirit. Another man said that the duties of the *ahak* "relate to men, and men have the responsibility to serve it." Some villagers assert that men follow the *ahak* while women follow the *pu nya* spirit. One elderly woman stated that "women go upstairs, men live downstairs, so we make the place for offerings for the *ahak* downstairs so it can protect the men and can follow them to protect them wherever they go." Another elderly woman, who is the custodian of an origin house, stated that "the *ahak* has a more widespread power, to protect men who go out to work." And a man who is widely recognized for his detailed knowledge of spirits stated, "The *ahak* is an ancestral spirit. It lives downstairs and is responsible for protecting the peace for the people in the house like a bodyguard and creating security for the members of the lineage. The *ahak* works harder than the *pu nya* spirit. It is responsible for a much wider area. Some people believe that it is stronger. When young people go a long way away they take some charcoal and mark their foreheads with black and ask the *ahak* for protection, just like a soldier going off to battle."

Given the clear masculine symbolism of the *ahak*, it is not surprising that their spiritual custodians are usually men. When offerings are made to the *pu nya* spirit within the house, parallel offerings are often made by a male custodian at the *ahak's* external shrine. As a result of the close relationship between the *ahak* and *pu nya* spirits, this male role contributes to some dilution of matrilineal ideology. In Ban Tiam it is now commonly claimed that responsibility for the *ahak* should be passed from father to son. Some villagers indicate that this patrilineal principle exists alongside the matrilineal principle that applies to the *pu nya* spirits: sons inherit the *ahak* from the father while daughters inherit the *pu nya* from the mother.

It is likely that the emphasis on the masculine symbolism of the *ahak* and the system of patrilineal inheritance have been strengthened by the relatively recent adoption of surnames. These surnames have contributed to some attenuation of the potency of matrilineal linkages with the ancestral past.[9] Surnames were introduced in Thailand in a 1913 decree that also required married women to take the surname of their husbands and children to take the surname of their fathers. While it has been suggested that surnames have had a minimal impact on rural Thai sociality, in Ban Tiam it is clear that the presence of surnames creates flexibility, and some confusion, about the concept of lineage.[10] On the one hand, lineages are defined matrilineally by reference to their origin houses and, as noted earlier, the female custodian of the *pu nya* spirit resident in these houses is referred to as the "origin of the lineage." However, when Ban Tiam residents are asked to name the main lineages in the village their answers invariably refer to surname groups. It is clear that in the day-to-day social life of the village, groups of patrilineally related kin are much more explicitly marked (given their surnames) than groups of matrilineally related kin, and in discussions of lineage there is constant slippage into patrilineal terms. Sometimes even the predominantly matrilineally constituted spirit groups are referred to in terms of a surname, where that surname is the patrilineally inherited surname of the husband of the custodian of the group.

Surnames provide for alternative connections with the power of the past. Surname groups are the patrilineally related descendants of the original surname-founding male ancestors. Discussions of genealogy often make their way, eventually, to these origin males, who arrived, often as traders or timber workers, and married local women, thus bringing their surnames to the area. This is a reference to nonparochial, mobile, and masculine agency, quite different from the highly localized embedding of matrilineal *pu nya* spirits in the bedrooms of origin houses. Grandmother Sai provides a good illustration of this alternative orientation toward supernatural power. She is the custodian of an origin house, which she inherited from her mother and mother's mother. She speaks proudly of her lineage but in doing so recounts a story about the origin of her surname (her knowledge of her mother's family is very sketchy). She claims that her "surname-founding" ancestor came from an aristocratic family in Chiang Mai. However as a result of a family dispute he was forced to leave Chiang Mai and come and live in a nearby village.

He married locally, passing his surname to his descendants, who are now numerous, and politically influential, in Ban Tiam and surrounding villages. Despite the long period that has passed and the considerable genealogical distance involved, this connection to Chiang Mai aristocracy is remembered and, in Sai's eyes, given added weight and ritual authority by the fact that her son (who died two years ago) was a spirit medium for one of Chiang Mai's main protective spirits. She still carefully maintains an elaborate shrine behind her house where her son used to hold spirit medium sessions for his clients from Chiang Mai. So, for Grandmother Sai—the custodian of the spirit of a matrilineage—it is the patrilineal connection to Chiang Mai aristocracy that gives her lineage status and has contributed to its present-day prosperity and political influence.

The relationship between the *pu nya* spirit and the *ahak* is a good illustration of the way in which different types of power are intermingled. In local perception, there is a very close relationship between these two entities, but, at the same time, they reflect quite different orientations. In simple terms the *ahak* spirits represent a masculine and territorial form of power, which is contrasted with the female-focused and lineage-derived potency of the *pu nya* spirits. The power of both descent and locality is bought together in a single spirit complex.

The Hierarchy of Spirit Administration

Two of Kluay's platters of food have now been discussed: one was for her *pu nya* spirit and the other for the *ahak*, who was invited inside the house to join in the communal feast. The third was for the protective spirit of the village itself. In making this offering Kluay was ritually enacting the political connections between her domestic spirits and the aristocratic lords of the land.

The landscape of power in Ban Tiam is populated by an enormous number of territorial spirits. Most of them are "lords of the place" (*chao thi*)— minor territorial spirits that protect specific local areas. Most houses have small *chao thi* shrines where regular offerings are made to secure domestic prosperity and security. The irrigation weirs have their own minor lords, and small feasts are held for them as part of the annual calendar of irrigation maintenance. They are asked to ensure a good water supply and abundant harvests. Nearby there are guardians of the rice fields who must be appropriately informed when rice is being planted. They are promised a chicken at harvest time if they protect the crop diligently. Next to the natural springs that bubble out at the foot of mountains there are small shrines, draped with decaying garlands of flowers and littered with sticks of incense. The springs are said to be linked to a massive cave system located far to the north where one of the region's most famous supernatural lords resides. High in the mountains above the village there are forest spirits, which are visited a few times each year and urged to guard against floods and drought and to punish evildoers who enter the forest to cut down trees. Even the village temple, despite its spiritual potency, has its own protective spirit who receives a share of the offerings that are brought along each time the congregation assembles. The landscape is littered with sites of exchange where human enterprises intersect with supernatural power.

Within Ban Tiam's crowded panoply of spirits, the most impressive is the Lord of the Lucky Tree (*jao nai ton chock*). This spirit was the recipient of Aunt Kluay's third platter of food. His shrine is located about twenty meters from Aunt Kluay's house on a patch of public land behind the village temple (fig. 8). It stands next to the ancient "lucky tree," so named because its sap is believed to form the shape of lottery-winning numbers when the bark is scratched. The shrine is a sturdy wooden pavilion, standing on posts a meter or so above the ground. Inside, it is large enough for the lord's custodian, and other devotees, to assemble when offerings are made to him. Fragments of local legend recall the foundational role of masculine agency in establishing relations with this source of protective power. The lord's first shrine, which was considerably smaller than it is now, is said to have been built by a group of three men who were Ban Tiam's original settlers. After building Ban Tiam's first Buddhist temple—really just a very small hut in which Buddha images were worshipped—these village pioneers entered into a deal with one of the powerful spirits resident in the locality. They gave the spirit his honorable title, built him a rustic palace, and agreed to feast him regularly in order "to protect the village from outside spirits so the villagers could live together in tranquility." Two of the men were former monks, charged with spiritual power, and they were well placed to deal with the potentially hazardous forces that resided in the natural environment. These first settlers also built another shrine for a forest spirit that lived to the auspicious east of the village. With the expansion of Ban Tiam, this has now become the protective spirit for the residential area now known as "hill village." He is known as the Lord of the Northern Palace. Later these two local lords were joined by a third, the Lord of the Cool Forest, a reference to the small but dense patch of forest that surrounds his shrine. This lord watches over the "new village,"

FIGURE 8. The shrine of the Lord of the Lucky Tree, Ban Tiam, Thailand.
(Photo by the author.)

which was established when the hamlet across the river was relocated to
Ban Tiam.

These three village spirits are territorial rather than ancestral or descent
spirits. People are affiliated to the protective power of these spirits as a result
of residence in a particular area. The territorial domain of these spirits is
often expressed as paralleling the modern administrative structure: increasingly inclusive areas are ruled by increasingly powerful officials. It is no accident that each of the three locally recognized hamlets in Ban Tiam has its own
spirit, with the spirit of the original hamlet—the Lord of the Lucky Tree—
sometimes described as the "chairman" who presides over the other two
assistant spirits, just as the village headman has two deputies. In fact, this territorial hierarchy extends well beyond the village: first to the "district spirit,"
located a few kilometers to the north at the site of a natural spring, and then
to the protective spirits of Chiang Mai itself. In northern Thailand, there is
a common folk and academic perception that village spirits and higher level

guardian spirits "are part of the same network" despite the significant differences in their level of power.[11] This is underlined by the high level of symbolic continuity in ritual practices associated with spirits at the village, district, and provincial levels.

The presence of these protective spirits is a clear sign of the ability of villagers to draw seemingly remote forms of power and authority into local domains and to replicate the trappings of chiefly authority. Despite their modest administrative reach, village spirits are referred to as "lords" or "princes" (chao) and occasionally given other aristocratic titles. Their rustic shrines are sometimes referred to as "prince's houses" (khum), "palaces" (ho), or even "offices" (thi thamngan or opfit). They are staffed by servants (saena) and surrounded by tethering posts (lak chang lak ma) to which the lord can tie his elephants and horses. When offerings are made to the more important spirits, these tethering posts (some of which are not visible) receive special reverential attention. This lordly power is clearly masculine. The custodians of these spirits are usually men, and, at the main new-year offering for the Lord of the Lucky Tree in Ban Tiam, men predominate among those assembled for the ritual. When these guardian spirits possess their mediums, they express a masculine persona. The mediums, who are often women, dress up as princes and engage in stereotypically male behavior—drinking alcohol, smoking, and speaking assertively in deep voices. The guardian spirits are also associated with military power. According to one story, the people in Ban Tiam first recognized the power of the Lord of the Lucky Tree when invading Burmese troops decided to rest near the tree where he resided. The spirit caused the soldiers to fall into a deep slumber, making their capture easy. Some villagers also link these village spirits with "city pillars" (lak muang), which appear in larger settlements throughout Thailand and which some consider to have phallic connotations.[12] These lak muang are closely associated with chiefly power. In Ban Tiam a number of villagers take the view that the lucky tree is, in fact, the lak muang of the village. In brief, supernatural power's aristocratic splendor is re-created within the village itself.

How do these village-level spirits relate to the pu nya spirits? My view is that the ahak represent an important point of connection between territorial and ancestral spirits. A very useful insight into this was provided by a young monk from a neighboring village who is particularly well versed in local culture. When I asked him about the ahak I had encountered in Ban Tiam he told me that ahak are spirits that live in the forest, particularly in large trees, and their presence is often marked by small shrines. The ahak, he said, represent sacred things in natural areas, and they guard against inappropriate behavior. What is interesting is that he described the *ahak* as precisely those forest spirits (resident in large trees) that are domesticated to become the village protective spirits in Ban Tiam. Associations between village spirits and large trees are a common feature in neighboring villages, and, in fact, throughout the region the relationship between tree spirits and guardian spirits is well established.[13] When I asked the monk why *ahak* shrines in Ban Tiam were located within the village (rather than in the forest) and at individual origin houses, he replied that these were the "branch offices" of the major *ahak* (although it was not clear where the "head office" actually was).

A woman who is the custodian of an origin house in a village a few kilometers from Ban Tiam made observations that had similar implications about the connection between different types of spiritual power. She told how she originally split her *pu nya* spirit from her home in a neighboring district. The spirit is represented, as it usually is, by a wooden shelf in her bedroom. As in Ban Tiam, she also has an external shrine, which houses a spirit she refers to not as *ahak* but as "lord *pu* lord *nya*" (*jaw pu jaw nya*). This terminology is also sometimes used in Ban Tiam and seems to indicate an elevation in status of the *pu nya* spirits toward that of the territorial "lords." She said that she erected this external shrine some years ago—on the advice of a spirit medium when she fell ill—to accommodate the village protective spirit from her natal village. Significantly, she also referred to this village-level spirit as the origin of her lineage. She said that the external shrine at her origin house was the "branch" of the village protective spirit (seemingly referring to the village spirit in both her natal village and her current village). In other words she was well on the way to fusing the domestic power of her ancestral *pu nya* spirit with the much more wide-ranging and "administrative" power of her village's guardian spirit.

There are a number of other elements that point to attempts to ritually connect the domestic *ahak* spirits with the wider-ranging power of the territorial spirits. To begin with, the design of the *ahak* shrines and the larger spirit houses is similar. In Ban Tiam the domestic *ahak* shrines are considerably smaller than the major village spirit shrine—though comparable to the shrines of the two "assistant" village spirits—but their general form is similar. At least one of the domestic *ahak* shrines has an elephant-tethering post (*lak chang*) standing next to it, clearly marking the aristocratic pretensions of its resident. In the nearby village of Ban Peung, the spirit house for one domestic *ahak* (to which a number of Ban Tiam residents are linked) is an impressive structure, comparable to that of any of the village protective spirits I have seen in the local area.

In additional to architectural pretensions, some of the domestic *ahak* also take on identities that are the same as those of protective spirits that have local and regional influence. Most generally, this is evident in the use of the word *ahak* itself, but there are also cases in which domestic spirits and territorial spirits share more specific names. The general term *ahak* is used throughout the region to refer to protective spirits of widely varying scope and power, underlining the hierarchical continuity among lineage, village, and regional spirits. In a village near Ban Tiam, the major guardian spirit is actually referred to as the *ahak*. In another nearby village, the village protective spirit is referred to as Lord Khamdaeng. This is also the name of a spirit that is said to possess a woman who is the head of one of the main *pu nya* spirit groups in this village (a number of Ban Tiam villagers are members of this group). In fact, Khamdaeng is a famous legendary figure in Chiang Mai and is reportedly worshipped in many areas of the province, with his headquarters in a major cave system in the northern part of the province.[14] According to one account, Khamdaeng was referred to as the *ahak luang* (great protector) of Chiang Mai.[15] In neighboring Chiang Rai, Andrew Turton found that Khamdaeng was present both as a "village cluster locality spirit" and as one of the lineage spirits.[16] He writes that Khamdaeng's cult occupied an "intermediary position" between the *pu nya* cults and the state-level cults centered on the city pillar (*lak muang*). Similarly, the domestic *ahak* in Ban Peung mentioned in the previous paragraph is referred to by a number of aristocratic names, with clear links to the guardian figures of Chiang Mai. And in Ban Tiam itself, one elderly woman who is custodian of a *pu nya* origin house claims to be a medium for her *ahak*, who she refers to as Lord Somphet, another figure from the panoply of Chiang Mai spirits.[17] Until early 2005 her *ahak* had no shrine, a fact that she lamented. Initially she marked the presence of this aristocratic spirit by placing a child's pink umbrella in the midst of a pile of wood. Later she persuaded her son to construct a rather elaborate shrine—built of corrugated roofing material and decorated with colorful garlands—so the spirit could be appropriately worshipped during the new-year celebrations.

These observations about the connections among *pu nya* spirits, *ahak*, and guardian lords can help us interpret the actions of Aunt Kluay when she made her offering to the Lord of the Lucky Tree. There was a lot that was unorthodox about her action. Her offering took place in the middle of a communal ritual. It was an event for which labor and resources were pooled to produce a combined offering that represented the symbolic unity of the village. Kluay used a communal occasion to highlight her family's specific connection with the village's protective lord, publicly linking her newfound prosperity to the village's supernatural authority. As a woman, Kluay was also entering into a distinctly masculine domain. The Lord of the Lucky Tree has a male custodian, and the communal offerings for him are predominantly prepared and presented by men. Of course, Kluay involved her husband—in fact he led the miniprocession from their house to the lord's shrine—but among those present nobody doubted that she was the driving force behind this initiative. Kluay also had no hesitation in entering into the slightly raised "inner sanctum" of the lord's shrine. It was very unusual for a woman to do this. However, despite the bold innovation that her actions entailed, Kluay was not breaking completely new ground. In fact, she was elaborating on the symbolic connections that already existed between the intimate, domestic, and feminine domain of the *pu nya* spirits and the public, administrative, and masculine world of the guardian lords. As the daughter of an in-marrying woman, she faced challenges in establishing credible relations with the *pu nya* spirits resident in her mother's house, so it made good sense for her to combine *pu nya* relationships with the more genealogically neutral territorial power of the Lord of the Lucky Tree. Given the links that exist between these different domains of spiritual power, represented most clearly by the *ahak*, Kluay had plenty of cultural resources at her disposal in making her rather ostentatious claim.

Flexibility and Articulation

I would only be a little surprised if, in fifty years or so, the villagers in Ban Tiam and other parts of Thailand make offerings to Lord Thaksin. The spiritual domain of rural political society is an ideal forum for situating local lives within the potent flow of history. The supernatural authority of ancestors and princes can be used to strengthen local efforts to create prosperous and secure livelihoods.

In Ban Tiam spirits are drawn into familiar networks of power by providing them with food, gifts, and housing. Their supernatural potency is congealed in origin houses scattered throughout the village and in an array of rustic shrines and palaces. The protective power of spirits contributes to a sense of security, coolness, and good health. They help to maintain domestic harmony and bring about prosperity. Their retributive power—sometimes made real in the form of accident, sickness, possession, and even death—underlines the importance of maintaining good relations with them. Although there are some risks in recognizing the authority of these spirits, there are also substantial benefits. The ultimate source of the spiritual potency that is tapped by the residents of Ban Tiam varies, but the power of the past looms large. The *pu nya* spirits reflect the authority of ancestors. This authority is given a strongly feminine coloring, with maternal connections to the *pu nya* past given the highest priority. The territorial lords draw on a more complex mix of potency: the forces of nature, the domesticating skills of the original male settlers, military might, and administrative organization. The *ahak* represent a fascinating point of articulation between the two, simultaneously looking inward to the domestic realm and outward to the cosmopolitan power of the guardian lords.

There are elements of hierarchy and inequality in this network of supernatural power, but this domain of Ban Tiam's political society is open and loosely structured and based on an ethic of exchange rather than domination. Some *pu nya* spirits have authority over relatively large groups, and some custodians attempt to elevate the status of their spirits with elaborate rituals and ambitious titles, but the creation of hierarchy is mitigated by the ability of households, or sublineages, to "divide" the spirit that resides in the origin house and establish their own independent sites of spiritual affiliation. When one woman was told that her lineage's spirit did not approve of her daughter's job in a Chiang Mai karaoke bar, she simply established a new spirit shelf in her own house. The *pu nya* spirits are also ritually articulated with the pseudo-administrative power of the guardian spirits—via the *ahak*—but they are not subordinate to the lords' authority. I have never heard of the male custodians of the *ahak* or the territorial lords making any effort to intrude into the ritual sphere of the *pu nya* spirits. The predominant view is that the lords, the *ahak*, and the *pu nya* are complementary, with a broadly gender-based division of responsibilities that provides for an inclusive domain of power and protection. Some villagers assert that the *ahak* spirits and the village guardian spirits are superior to the *pu nya*, but this superiority is expressed in terms of their greater territorial jurisdiction, and sometimes in terms of their relationship with the powerful forces of the forest, rather than in terms of control over subordinate *pu nya* spirits.[18] In sociological terms, the *ahak* and the village lords may have greater "power to" (capability or potency) but not "power over" (domination). Even the most impressive guardian spirit, the Lord of the Lucky Tree, lives within a network of otherworldly nobles who can offer their own idiosyncratic rewards and punishments without reference to any overarching schema of authority.

These reflections on the spirit world can assist us in conceptualizing the relationship between rural communities and higher levels of power such as the state. As noted earlier, it is commonly observed that northern Thai spirits are part of an extralocal hierarchy, with networks that extend to Chiang Mai and even to Bangkok itself.[19] However, while the symbolic continuity between different types of spirit belief is commonly recognized, several anthropologists have argued that there is a disconnect between "higher-" and "lower-level" spirits. This approach is a product of the academic interest in class conflict and the resistant autonomy of community culture. This is clearly evident in Shigeharu Tanabe's work on the Tai in southern China, who share many cultural attributes with the northern Thai. Reflecting the interest in ideological domination in the 1980s, Tanabe argued that state-level "guardian cults" are part of an "ideological apparatus employed by a ruling class as an alternative to the exercise of violence."[20] They help to legitimate the exploitation of the peasantry by the dominant ruling class. By contrast, Tanabe argued, village and domestic spirits are part of the resistant identity of subaltern groups. They represent the autonomy of the village and its collective antagonism toward outsiders. A similar position is adopted by the Thai anthropologist Anan Ganjanapan when he argues that Chiang Mai's chiefly spirit rituals were oriented toward the establishment of state legitimacy while similar rituals performed in local communities were primarily concerned with satisfying the emotional needs of villages.[21] This separation between levels is also conveyed by Andrew Turton when he describes the city pillar ritual previously held in the district where he worked as representing "remote" and "alien" princely power. In contrast to the more intimate offerings made to the *pu nya* spirits, villagers were "unwilling" or, at best, "ambivalent" participants in the city pillar ritual.[22] In other words, spirit practices can be understood in terms of the classic tension between state domination and local resistance.

Of course, it would be absurd to deny the ideological importance of public spirit rituals undertaken by the region's premodern chiefs. Nor is it unreasonable to argue that the contemporary symbolic parallels between spirit hierarchies and administrative hierarchies add some ideological legitimacy to modern bureaucratic incorporation. And there is no doubt that *pu nya* and *ahak* rituals are usually rather private events, often with quite domestic and personal objectives. But the radical separation of function proposed by these observers of rural society ends up characterizing local attachments to non-local supernatural power as a form of false consciousness that ideologically conceals underlying conflicts of interest and facilitates exploitation. I propose an alternative perspective that can help us to understand some of the basic cultural orientations underpinning Ban Tiam's political society. In Ban Tiam the *ahak* shrines present at *pu nya* origin houses are an attempt to draw external power into more intimate and localized spheres. The *ahak* are an important point of connection between the domestic power of the *pu nya* spirits and the chiefly power of the supernatural lords. They link very private concerns about morality, health, and prosperity to the highly public pretensions of chiefship and territorial rule. This emphasis on the localization and domestication of external power is made quite explicit when, on the occasion of major offerings to the *pu nya* spirits, the offering tray for the *ahak* is often taken not to the outdoor shrine but to the bedroom where the *pu nya* shelf is located. The *ahak* must enter the bedroom in order to join the feast. In other words, a primary concern of village practice is to enter into familiar relations of exchange with representatives of external power. It is well recognized that the potency of the *pu nya* spirits is limited and that forces with a broader jurisdictional range must be drawn on. In this sphere of Ban Tiam's political society, the aim is to draw external lords and masters into the intimacy of domestic life.

4

Contracts, Private Capital, and the State

My first research trip to Ban Tiam was in December 2002. I was planning to spend a couple of months looking at how the village managed water allocation for the dry-season cultivation of cash crops. However, when I arrived in the village in late December, it was clear that water allocation was not going to be an issue. I drove along one of the rough tracks that ran from the main road down to the paddy fields and stopped to talk with a group of farmers who were standing in the middle of a vast swathe of very sad looking garlic. After brief introductions, they told me that heavy rain over the past few days had caused the river to break its banks several times, inundating the low-lying areas of cultivation. The rain was very unusual: Chiang Mai's average rainfall for December is 16 millimeters, but in 2002 about 116 fell.[1] This freak weather was a disaster for the garlic, which, the farmers told me, liked cool and dry conditions. The excessive moisture in the waterlogged fields provided perfect conditions for disease and threatened to rot the garlic bulbs. The problems were compounded because the floodwaters had left behind a thick layer of sand and silt, smothering many of the garlic seedlings. Even in the fields above the clearly visible flood line, the farmers were worried that the unseasonal rain—combined with unusually warm weather—would ruin the crop. The protective spirits that watch over the fields had not been doing their job well.

The unseasonal rain meant that my original plans to investigate dry-season water allocation were dashed, but I was lucky to witness an important turning point in Ban Tiam's agricultural history. The (not so) dry season of 2002 marked the end of garlic's domination in Ban Tiam's cash-cropping sector. Disillusionment with garlic had been building for some time as garlic growers were increasingly troubled by low yields and unreliable prices. The bad weather of late 2002 compounded their anxiety and frustration. By the end of the 2002 season, most farmers had decided to abandon garlic production and explore other options. The most attractive option on offer was contract farming. Several companies had become active in the district, seeking out farmers who were willing to grow crops to supply the agroprocessing plants that had been established around Chiang Mai. It was a big change—abandoning independent production and entering into contracts to grow crops according to predefined schedules and techniques—but in uncertain times many of Ban Tiam's farmers were willing to give it a go.

The emergence of contract farming has introduced an important new dimension into Ban Tiam's evolving political society. Until the arrival of corporate agricultural players like Leo, Union Foods, Far East, and CM Enterprise in 2003, the private sector played a very limited role in the local network of connections that sustained the village's middle-income livelihoods. However, through contracts, Ban Tiam's farmers have been able to draw the economic power of agroindustrial capital into the village, using the capital of contracting companies to make up for some of the main deficiencies in the local economy. These farmers have actively participated in what is often clumsily described as the "penetration" of capital into the countryside. Of course, their agency and enthusiasm in this process are not unqualified, far from it. Farmers in Ban Tiam draw on an array of values to evaluate and critique their new forms of agricultural practice and the role of corporate capital in agricultural transformation. Dealings with the private sector also create new tensions in the much more established relationship with the state. It is inevitable that new economic arrangements will be uneven in their effects and that some aspects of them will prompt discomfort, resentment, and even outright anger. These acts of "resistance" are important, but they must be understood in terms of a broader experimental orientation toward the emergence of new economic relationships in a middle-income economy.

AGRICULTURAL CHALLENGES

As in many other parts of rural Thailand, dry-season cash crops are an important part of Ban Tiam's economy. During the dry season of 2002, two crops predominated in Ban Tiam's paddy fields: garlic (56 percent of the area) and soybeans (33 percent). Both of these crops were independently grown: the farmers purchased all the inputs, managed the cultivation schedule, and sold the produce to private traders. Between them, these two crops highlight some of the main opportunities and constraints that have emerged in Ban Tiam's agricultural sector.

Garlic has been cultivated in Ban Tiam for many years, but in the past production was considerably lower. Farmers recall that thirty or so years ago less than one plot in three was planted with garlic (fig. 9). This was because the work was more labor intensive (plowing with buffalo rather than using handheld tractors) and many of the dry-season fields were devoted to raising cattle. Since then the extent of garlic production has steadily increased, as part of a general trend that made Chiang Mai province the country's biggest garlic producer and Thailand the ninth-largest garlic producer in the world.[2] Many farmers recall that around twenty years ago garlic became the basis for Ban Tiam's prosperity. Revenue from garlic funded houses, pickup trucks, and children's university education. Very healthy prices in the mid-1990s generated unprecedented profits. One well-off farmer colorfully described the large garlic-drying sheds behind her house as a "source of gold." Garlic itself has become a symbol of good fortune; generous bunches, with intricately

FIGURE 9. Planting garlic, Ban Tiam, Thailand. (Photo by the author.)

plaited stems and swollen bulbs, are commonly presented as temple offerings or housewarming gifts. The popularity of garlic is unsurprising: by one recent estimate, garlic is the second most lucrative of the crops commonly grown in Chiang Mai, generating net returns (in 2003) of over 100,000 baht per hectare and returns to labor of around 400 baht per day, well above the provincial minimum wage of 140 baht per day.[3] Garlic has been an important component of higher-productivity diversification in the agricultural systems of northern Thailand.

However, there are several interlinked vulnerabilities in this production system, which, for the farmers of Ban Tiam, came to a head in the 2002–3 growing season. To begin with, garlic is a very expensive crop to grow; in fact it is one of the most expensive crops commonly grown in northern Thailand. The largest cost component for farmers in Ban Tiam is the seed stock, which must be purchased each year. Farmers consistently state that using their own garlic production as a source of seed stock results in very low yields so they buy new bulbs every year from other provinces or even from across the border in Burma. Purchase of bulbs for planting typically makes up between one-third and one-half of the investment cost. Other costly inputs include generous applications of fertilizer, herbicide, and pesticide. Garlic is also labor intensive, requiring about three times as much labor as rice. While much of this is provided by the household itself, or recruited via exchange labor, increasing use is made of paid laborers. Overall, the investment cost for garlic is close to 100,000 baht per hectare.[4] This high cost means that the cultivation of garlic is heavily dependent on access to credit. In Ban Tiam the two major lenders are the government-run Bank for Agriculture and Cooperatives and the district's Agricultural Cooperative. Most farmers have been able to access credit from these sources because they have formal title to their paddy fields, which can be used to secure loans. Higher-cost loans are sometimes obtained from informal moneylenders, especially once farmers have reached their credit limits with formal lenders. When the village credit fund of 1 million baht was established under the Thaksin administration, a portion of the funds available for loans was pooled and used to buy seed stock for member households. Suppliers of seed and fertilizer also sometimes provide credit to their regular customers.

The large expansion in rural credit provision in the 1980s and 1990s played an important role in enhancing the productivity of Ban Tiam's agricultural economy by facilitating investment in garlic. However, there have been significant risks associated with this transformation. Since at least the 1980s the price of garlic has followed a roller-coaster path (chart 7). The

overall trend in prices has been slightly upward, partly as a result of government restrictions on imports, but the fluctuation has been dramatic. The
price has peaked several times, resulting in windfall profits, but each peak has
been followed a few years later by an equally striking trough in which prices
sometimes fail to cover costs. The reasons for this fluctuation are not well
understood. Demand for garlic is stable because there are no obvious sub-
stitutes, so price fluctuations are probably caused by supply factors. A possible cause is variation in supply brought about by farmers entering into and
leaving the garlic market in response to price changes. In Ban Tiam there
was also speculation that large garlic traders were involved in price manipulation, possibly in collaboration with government agencies. Anxieties about
the garlic price became particularly intense in the early 2000s, in the lead-
up to the agricultural trade agreement between Thailand and China, which
would abolish import duties on many agricultural products, including Thailand's 30 percent tariff on garlic.[5] It was widely rumored that following the
implementation of the agreement, duty-free Chinese garlic would flood into
the Thai market where it could be sold at a price lower than local production costs. Doubts about garlic cultivation in Thailand were compounded
when the government announced an adjustment scheme that would make
cash payments to farmers who gave up garlic cultivation.

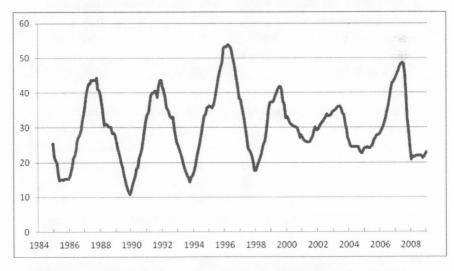

CHART 7. Garlic prices in Thailand, 1984 to 2009, baht per kilogram of dried
garlic, constant 2009 values. (Data from Office of Agricultural Economics, "Rakha
Sinkha Kaset" [Agricultural Commodity Prices], accessed 10 June 2009.)

Apart from the investment cost and price fluctuations, the third important vulnerability in Ban Tiam's garlic production system was its lackluster
productivity. In garlic-producing areas of Thailand as a whole, productivity
gains have been modest, especially compared to those of other major garlic-
producing countries in Asia.[6] There was some increase in productivity in the
1970s, probably a result of greater investment in crop inputs following the
rapid expansion of agricultural credit, but since then garlic yields have stagnated. There is little evidence of state investment in extension, education,
processing, or marketing in the garlic sector. In Ban Tiam itself garlic yields
are said to have been declining for several years. The most popular explana-
tion for this decline is reduced soil fertility as a result of an unrelenting cultivation schedule. In the 2002–3 season, anxieties about yield came to a head,
compounded by the unseasonal rainfall and flooding, combined with disease
and insect infestation. The harvest was very disappointing, and almost all
the farmers I consulted indicated that they had lost money on their crop, for
"the heads were small, the leaves were short, and the crop developed slowly."
When asked to subjectively rate their garlic yields, farmers indicated that
70 percent of plots had provided "bad" or "very bad" returns. Only one plot
out of thirty surveyed was described as returning a "very good" yield, and
only two others were rated "good."

Garlic's risky combination of high input costs, substantial fluctuation in
output prices, and stagnant or declining yields has produced a major problem
of agricultural debt. Of course, garlic production is not the only source of
indebtedness in Ban Tiam, but it has been a very significant contributing
factor, especially as some farmers have attempted, unsuccessfully, to cultivate
their way out of debt by borrowing even more heavily to produce a bumper
garlic crop. It is not uncommon for garlic cultivators in Ban Tiam to report
debts of between 50,000 and 100,000 baht, with some notable cases reporting debts over 200,000. Ban Tiam's headman, who had compiled some data
on the issue for an official poverty alleviation scheme, told me that there was
a total of around 10 million baht of debt within the village, an average of about
77,000 per household. In an economy where the average household income
is 125,000 baht per year, these debts represent very substantial financial challenges, and they are an important source of anxiety, and some resentment.
The desire to reduce exposure to agricultural debt has been one of the primary drivers of the adoption of contract farming in Ban Tiam.

Before considering this change, it is useful to briefly consider the second
most popular crop grown in the 2002–3 dry season as it represents one

possible response to the vulnerabilities of garlic cultivation. Whereas garlic represents the high-return and high-risk end of the agricultural spectrum, soybeans are a poor farmer's crop, and they have an important insurance and social security role in a middle-income rural economy. Chiang Mai is now the largest producer of soybeans in Thailand.[7] Compared to garlic, soybeans are a very low value crop, with estimated returns of only 12,000 baht per hectare, and returns to labor of only 150 baht per day.[8] This is not much more than the returns generated by rice. Nevertheless soybeans remain popular for three main reasons. First, as a legume they are nitrogen fixing and, as such, they have soil-restoring properties. In Ban Tiam, farmers often comment that other crops grow well after soybeans have been cultivated and that lower applications of fertilizer are required. Second, soybeans require minimal investment (about one-quarter of the cash input of garlic) and they are easy to cultivate. When asked why they are growing soybeans, most farmers respond that they don't have the capital to invest in garlic cultivation. Finally, even though soybeans generate much less income than garlic, and real prices have declined slowly since the late 1980s, soybean prices have been relatively stable with very little year-to-year fluctuation. Soybean prices are also 30 to 40 percent higher than they would be without government price support in the form of import restrictions.[9]

New Crops

Cultivating soybeans is a low-risk and low-return alternative to the economic roller-coaster of garlic cultivation. However, since 2003 many farmers in Ban Tiam have explored more radical alternatives. In late 2003 I surveyed farmers and asked them what crop they planned to grow in the coming dry season. Almost 40 percent said that they would grow sweet corn, and 15 percent nominated tobacco. Both of these crops would be grown under contract for agribusinesses based in Chiang Mai. After the disastrous harvest in March 2003, it was no surprise that only 9 percent planned to persevere with garlic. One of the reasons for the popularity of sweet corn was that the two farmers who had grown it in 2002 achieved good yields and had been paid a reasonable price by a food-processing company. A persuasive and well-connected local broker (who was also the assistant village headman) assisted in promoting the new crop, with contracts offering an attractive three baht per kilogram. Another advantage was that sweet corn is an easy crop to grow, requiring minimal labor input or supervision. Tobacco was also attracting some local interest. In part, this was due to the fact that a number of the older farmers had grown tobacco up until the mid-1970s when there was a tobacco-drying factory in the district owned by a local businessman and politician. Oriental, a company from one of the region's major tobacco-processing areas, was now seeking tobacco growers to fill orders for export to Europe. Oriental's local extension efforts were managed by a skilled and personable extension agent who had established a seedling nursery in a village about ten kilometers from Ban Tiam. He had a local production quota of twenty-two hectares and was keen to fill it. Smaller numbers of farmers said that they would grow cabbages, peas, maize, potatoes, and eggplants under a variety of contract and independent arrangements.

These intentions were borne out when actual planting decisions were made in the 2003 dry season. There was a strong move to sweet corn, and it accounted for 47 percent of the cultivated area. The second most popular crop was tobacco (24 percent). Garlic rated a distant third (13 percent) followed by potatoes (8 percent), soybeans (5 percent), and a few plots of cabbages, beans, and coriander. The newfound popularity of sweet corn was underlined when fourteen farmers grew it as a second dry-season crop.

However, the experiment in sweet corn gave mixed results. Twelve farmers considered the yield to be "bad" or "very bad," nine considered it "average," and only six thought it was "good" or "very good." Apart from the yield, farmers complained about the low price paid by the company as a result of the low grade of the corn. The story for tobacco was rather different. Only one farmer considered the yield to be "bad," nine considered it "average," and four considered it "good." This did not amount to a strong endorsement, but the returns were sufficiently attractive to consolidate interest in tobacco as a contract crop. Surprisingly, the picture for garlic was also rather positive. Only one farmer considered the yield "bad," eight considered it "average," and two considered it "good."

The dry seasons of 2004 and 2005 showed signs of both reversion and innovation. After the solid experiment in 2003, the contract farming of sweet corn was abandoned. The new favorite was tobacco, which covered a little more than 40 percent of the cultivated area in both years. Ban Tiam had become Oriental's most important production site in the district, filling about 60 percent of the company's local quota, despite some grumbling about lower than expected prices and rising input costs. The next two most popular crops in Ban Tiam were the old favorites: garlic (about 30 percent in both years) and soybeans (about 20 percent). Reversion to garlic was encouraged by improved yields in 2003 and also by early indications that the price impact of the trade agreement with China would be short-lived. As the optimistic village headman commented to me, "No crop has a good price like garlic." Soybeans remained a valued standby for farmers wanting a low-cost, low-input, soil-restoring crop. There was also ongoing experimentation with other crops, in particular cabbages, chilies, potatoes, tomatoes, Japanese melons, peanuts, and eggplants. The area devoted to the contract farming of eggplants was small, but it was a high-labor-input and high-value contract crop that was attracting the interest of some of the village's most influential farmers. One farmer made a remarkable profit of forty thousand baht from only one-quarter of a hectare. Another farmer made thirty thousand from an even smaller plot of tomatoes grown for a Chiang Mai cannery. These good news stories were bound to attract imitators who had sufficient labor to cultivate demanding crops for which quality standards are often very high.

In the following years, contract farming continued to be a feature of Ban Tiam's agricultural landscape. Tobacco maintained its popularity. It is easy to grow, yields are consistent, the contracting company is reliable, and it generates a steady cash flow because leaves are harvested several times during the growing season. It is a solid performer but certainly not spectacular. Average returns from tobacco in Ban Tiam have been around thirty thousand baht per hectare, less than a third of what garlic can generate in a reasonably good year. In this respect the popularity of tobacco cultivation in Ban Tiam reflects the tendency of the rural economy to be strong on diversification but less so on productivity upgrading. Nevertheless, high-value contract crops like eggplants, zucchinis, beans, and tomatoes have some strong supporters in Ban Tiam. Beans are popular as a short-duration crop that can be grown at the end of the dry season prior to the wet-season cultivation of rice. In fact, in the wet season of 2009 a number of farmers carried on growing beans rather than planting rice. This was an important departure from the usual practice of maintaining a clear distinction between dry-season cash-crop production and wet-season subsistence production. Beans return about twenty-five thousand baht per hectare after only sixty days. Garlic is still cultivated, but it is very unlikely that it will ever be as dominant as it was prior to the advent of contract farming.

THE LIVELIHOOD LOGIC OF CONTRACT FARMING

Throughout the world, food-processing and retailing firms are increasingly securing low-cost, low-risk, and highly flexible sources of supply by entering into production agreements with independent smallholders. In Thailand, contract crop production has expanded dramatically since the 1970s, becoming an important feature of diversification within the agricultural sector. Crops grown under contract in Thailand include asparagus, beans, capsicum, corn, cassava, cut flowers, eggplants, jasmine rice, ginger, maize, pineapples, potatoes, soybeans, sugarcane, tobacco, and tomatoes. Baby corn grown by Thai farmers is sold in supermarkets throughout the world. Tomatoes grown in the north and northeast end up as sauce in canned fish shipped out of southern Thailand. Potatoes grown under contract in Chiang Mai supply Thailand's rapidly expanding potato chip market. In 2002 there were estimated to be almost eighty vegetable-processing firms located in northern Thailand, many of them around Chiang Mai.

The international expansion of contract farming has attracted very mixed reviews. For its critics, contract farming is an important contributor to the ongoing destruction of the peasantry whereby independent smallholders become "what Lenin called propertied proletarians" as capitalist control is extended into the agricultural labor process.[10] A common argument is that this process of subordination and exploitation is disguised by the seemingly free and reciprocal contract agreement. As Roger Clapp argues in a study of agribusiness expansion in Latin America, "[T]he widely promoted view of the contract as a bargain freely made by two equal parties is a form of mystification which is central to the effectiveness of the company's domination."[11] An important aspect of this domination is that the debt relationships that are often embedded in contract arrangements can lock farmers into the production of cash crops, compromising subsistence security and exposing livelihoods to volatile global commodity markets.[12] Critics acknowledge that there can be financial benefits from contract farming, and that proletarianization is not necessarily universal, but they argue that benefits are unevenly spread as it is usually the more affluent farmers who can afford to allocate resources to nonsubsistence crops and these farmers often have better organizational capacity to negotiate with companies. At the same time resource rights of vulnerable household and community members can be undermined as land and labor are commoditized and drawn into new spheres of commercial production. Tanya Korovkin provides a good illustration of this process of differentiation in her account of contract fruit production in Chile: "[T]he fruit boom increased the gap between the rich and poor peasants. It transformed the former into peasant capitalists and reduced the latter to the status of seasonal wage laborers . . . without a stable source of income."[13] All in all, the aim of much of this critical literature is to shift the discussion of contract farming away from the idea of a voluntary agreement between independent actors and toward the contextual structures of capitalist penetration, dependency, exploitation, and differentiation.

While not denying some of contract farming's negative impacts, other commentators adopt a much more benign, and even favorable, view. This alternative perspective is more inclined to place contract farming within a more locally specific framework of household adaptation and peasant persistence, promoting the idea of dynamic partnerships between firms and rural households. As households respond to demographic pressures, market uncertainty, and environmental change, contract farming represents a livelihood option that can provide access to markets, increase incomes, and generate agricultural employment for laboring households. It does not necessarily favor affluent farmers, nor is it necessarily repressive: "Contract farming holds far less possibility for coercion than traditional agricultural relations between smallholders and the rural elite."[14] Contract farming can also make up for institutional deficiencies in the agricultural sector, providing farmers with more accessible forms of credit and insurance against the risk of crop failure, though often at relatively high cost. Agricultural corporations and their local brokers can also be sources of technical advice and innovation in production techniques. While accounts of rural proletarianization may suggest labor force deskilling, in fact the technical demands of corporations and increasingly specific consumer preferences can increase the complexity and sophistication of the agricultural labor process. In brief this alternative view sees contract farming as potentially contributing to the diversified resilience of rural smallholders: "Contract farming offers many benefits for growers, including access to new markets, technical assistance, specialized inputs, and financial resources. Contracts can also reduce crop price variation, helping farmers bear the risk of non-traditional crop production. To the extent that firms contract with smallholders, contract farming has the potential to raise incomes of the poor and promote rural development."[15]

Although there are widely divergent views on contract farming, there is some agreement that both the reasons for its adoption and its socioeconomic impacts are locationally specific. Conclusions drawn in an area of heavy reliance on agriculture, marked rural differentiation, and authoritarian political structures will be quite different from those drawn from areas where the economy is more diverse, independent smallholders predominate, and there are opportunities for various forms of political participation. This may sound like a very obvious point, but it is crucial for understanding what is going on in places like Ban Tiam where contract farming has been adopted in response to specific vulnerabilities in the local economy. In Ban Tiam, contract farming is an adaptive and, for the time being, experimental response to the hazards of garlic cultivation and, more fundamentally, to the relative absence of private investment in local enterprise. In specific terms, the primary attractiveness of contract farming for Ban Tiam's dry-season cultivators lies in the fact that they do not have to pay the crop's input costs. Under the terms of the various contracts, the contracting companies provide the farmers with seedlings (or seed) and agrochemicals. The cost of these inputs is deducted from the selling price of the crop. If the crop fails, the "debt" is written off and the loss is borne by the company. One farmer summed up the widely acknowledged benefits of this arrangement: "We are growing for the companies because at least they are willing to invest the capital. We don't have to hurt ourselves with debt. We don't have to get stressed or tired. Investing labor is not as stressful as investing money." Of course, crop failure is still regarded as something of a disaster, but farmers regularly state that their only loss is the time they have invested in the crop and that their debt situation is not worsened. Given that they have grown a subsistence rice crop in the wet season, they still have a very basic level of subsistence security and most have other sources of income from wage labor, government employment, and local enterprise.

In essence, the companies in Ban Tiam are offering a form of crop insurance, an institutional arrangement completely lacking for the independent cultivation of garlic. This company-provided insurance supports the diversification of the agricultural economy and encourages the adoption of new crops that may enhance productivity. In an economy in which debt arising out of crop failure is a fundamental concern, this confidence-enhancing insurance is crucially important. Of course there is some premium paid for this insurance because the input costs deducted by the companies are somewhat higher than their cost on the open market. This generates some resentment, but most farmers consider the insurance to be well worth the cost because of their overwhelming desire to avoid further indebtedness. Another aspect of the insurance arrangement is that the companies offer the prospect of price stability. Contracts with farmers typically set out a schedule of prices to be paid for the crop at the time of harvest. Some contracts will guarantee to match the market price if it is higher than the contract price at the time of purchase. There is plenty of room for companies to adjust prices on the basis of quality, but these socially embedded and usually face-to-face negotiations are generally regarded as less threatening than the anonymous and unpredictable volatility of the open market.

The fact that contracting companies pay for agricultural inputs also means that contract farming is one of the few ways in which external capital is drawn into the local production process. As discussed in chapter 2, there is a marked lack of private capital investment in the local economy. Local agricultural activity has generated very little capital investment beyond land acquisition (by the most successful farmers) and modest investment in mechanization (such as handheld tractors). Much of the profit from the good years of garlic production was invested in private consumption, especially education, house building, and the purchase of pickup trucks and motorbikes. External investment in local enterprise has also been minimal since the decline of resource extraction and processing enterprises: logging, sawmilling, tin mining, and tobacco processing. In this economic context, contract farming represents a rare source of external capital that can enhance the productivity of Ban Tiam's well-irrigated land and its underemployed agricultural labor. Put simply, the private capital made available through contract farming increases the productivity of land and agricultural labor. Without this injection of capital, many farmers seeking to avoid the debt risks of garlic cultivation would either have to resort to low-value soybean cultivation or attempt to secure low-paid wage labor in more agriculturally successful villages.

For these various reasons, contract farming in Ban Tiam is widely welcomed as providing a new range of low-risk agricultural alternatives and as filling an important livelihood gap opened up by the decline in garlic cultivation. This support is far from unqualified, as we will see, but it is based on a pragmatic assessment of the agricultural options currently available. One farmer neatly summed up the prevailing feeling.

The companies have been coming for a long time, but people were not interested because people just wanted to grow garlic. People only really became interested in the past few years. The first person to grow peas for a company was the headman. The first year he grew [2.5 hectares] and made about two hundred thousand baht. The second year he could not rent so much land so grew a lot less. This year I tried out one tiny plot and I made six thousand baht from just that little bit. And if the crop fails there is no cost and no problem. New Asia Food has a quota of about [80 hectares] for the whole district. So why not grow for them? If you grow your own crops you have to go and borrow from the cooperative, and if the crop fails you are in debt and the interest just mounts up and up and up. And you get more and more into debt. But there is no problem with the company. All you lose if it fails is your labor.

But is this a sustainable relationship? Some observers of contract farming urge caution. They argue that farmer-friendly arrangements initially put in place by companies commonly undergo a process of "contract normalization," which gradually reveals the true face of agricultural exploitation. Companies may only be absorbing losses in the case of crop failure and offering attractive prices as promotional strategies to draw cultivators into their corporate sphere of operation. As farmers commit more and more of their land and labor resources to contract production, they may find themselves locked into asymmetric contract provisions under which debts are enforced and low crop prices are unilaterally set. As an international overview of contract farming notes, "The typical outcome is for the firm to begin to squeeze the growers just at the time that farmers have become more dependent on the scheme."[16]

This is an important caveat on the experience of the farmers in Ban Tiam, especially with contract farming still at an early stage, but it would be a mistake to overstate the risks of these new connections. Relationships with companies are certainly unequal, but as with other power relationships cultivated by the residents of Ban Tiam, they do not necessarily result in domination or socially unacceptable levels of exploitation. There are underlying economic factors that mitigate the asymmetries between company and farmer. To begin with, crop trading and processing are competitive and dynamic sectors in middle-income Thailand. A vibrant national and international agrocommodity trade means that companies are keen to secure contracts with farmers who own land in suitable agroecological zones. There is considerable competition between buyers—both contracting firms and independent traders—to secure output from farmers. Firms regularly face problems of farmers diverting inputs to noncontracted crops and selling contracted crops on the open market when prices are higher than the level specified in contracts. This competition is one of the reasons that companies in Ban Tiam cover input costs. As one farmer noted, "The company does not want us to invest our own money because they are afraid we will sell to other companies. There are several of them that would want to buy." Companies that attempted to enforce debts in the case of crop failure or consistently offered low prices would find farmers quickly switching to their competitors. The universal abandonment of sweet corn after the 2003 harvest, and potatoes after the disappointing 2004 harvest, demonstrates the ability of farmers to select the best contract option on offer. Intercompany competition, and the room for maneuver that it gives farmers, is an internationally common problem for contractors, but it appears to be particularly marked in Thailand's very diverse agricultural sector.

The diversity of the local economy itself also places limits on the power of contracting companies. Ban Tiam's households have adopted many different livelihood strategies, and companies recognize that contract farming is not the sole, or even most important, source of local income. Put simply, farmers have to be convinced that contract crops are a better option than other livelihood alternatives on offer. Critics of contract farming sometimes lament the fact that contract payments cannot fully support smallholders, forcing them to pursue other income sources.[17] However for the farmers in Ban Tiam a multistranded livelihood portfolio is, in fact, an entirely desirable way to avoid becoming locked into unfavorable relationships with contracting firms. Ban Tiam's farmers generally maintain a clear separation between cultivation of a subsistence crop in the wet season and contract crops in the dry season, providing them with a very basic level of subsistence security regardless of market fluctuations or corporate manipulation. For some farmers, garlic remains an option. Beginning in 2004 there was something of a revival in garlic cultivation, demonstrating that the move to contracting has not been a one-way street. Soybeans remain a low-cost and low-risk fallback. Remember, too, that off-farm employment is the primary or secondary source of cash income for many of Ban Tiam's farming households. Farmers are often cautious about getting heavily involved in labor-intensive contract crops, despite their attractive returns, as they would restrict the ability of family members to work off-farm. This pattern of intrahousehold livelihood diversification has been found among contract farmers in other parts of Thailand. As one survey of contract-farming households in nine provinces in central and southern Thailand notes, "Nearly all the farmers . . . have diversified their production. Their income comes from both on-farm and off-farm activities. . . . Normally, farmers produce both cash crops for sale, and subsistence crops like paddy, vegetables and fruit trees for their own consumption. Diversification is favoured as a way to reduce the risks inherent in monoculture production. . . . Diversification therefore helps reduce barriers to exit . . . and also reduces their risks."[18]

KEEPING GOOD COMPANY

As individual economic agents, the companies are certainly much more powerful than the farmers of Ban Tiam. Accounts of corporate proletarianization rightly point out that seemingly reciprocal agricultural contracts gloss over substantial disparities in economic resources and sociopolitical influence. But relationships of power are not simply determined by structural position. In the everyday exercise of power within rural political society, contracting companies have to operate in an environment where there is considerable competition for the land and labor of farmers. In this climate of economic diversity and choice, companies cannot simply impose their will. Inevitably they are drawn into locally valued systems of sociality and exchange.

This process of engagement and domestication commences when the companies first introduce themselves to Ban Tiam's farmers by organizing a public meeting, either in the hall next to the village temple or at the agricultural cooperative in the district center. The formats of the meetings vary, but the overall content is generally similar: an overview of the crops that the company is interested in, discussions of likely yields, pricing policies, production techniques, and possible problems. There are often vigorous question and answer sessions where the company representatives try to deal with farmer skepticism about the promised rewards. Promotional meetings are often accompanied by other gestures of goodwill, which signal a willingness on the part of the company representatives to become engaged in local systems of exchange. A free lunch may be provided at the meeting or the company representative may supply calendars, agricultural inputs, or even T-shirts for the village soccer team. Clever company representatives will also make a point of attending local ritual events, such as temple festivals and funerals, and making informal social visits to opinion leaders, such as the village headman or leaders of the irrigation groups.

The mutual engagement of companies in local systems of sociality is evident in two aspects of contract farming: the nature of the contracts themselves and the use of local brokers. Initially most of the companies use formal written contracts. These contracts take the form of a legalistic agreement between the "seller" (the farmer) and the "buyer" (the company). The farmer agrees to plant a specified crop on a specified area and to sell it to the company. Contracts may include provisions about the timing of the planting and harvesting and the timing and rates of application of agrochemicals. The company agrees to purchase the crop (often with certain quality provisions specified) at an agreed price with payment made within a defined period. The contracts also specify the inputs that will be provided by the company and the cost of the inputs that will be deducted from the contract payment for the produce. Some contracts are made directly with individual farmers while others are made with a local broker who then subcontracts individual farmers. These written contracts provide a formal institutional underpinning for the relationship between company and farmer. However, once relations between the companies and farmers became well established, formal written contracts often give way to informal verbal agreements. When I asked about this, farmers indicated to me that contracts soon become unnecessary as they and the company now "understood each other" or had achieved a degree of "solidarity." They also said that the detailed specification of techniques was unnecessary as they were now completely familiar with the production process. Contracting quickly becomes immersed in the everyday language of cooperation and mutual understanding.

This embedding of contract arrangements in local systems of sociality is facilitated by the use of brokers. Brokers play an important role in recruiting farmers, coordinating production schedules, distributing inputs, providing training, and facilitating communication between farmers and the company. They are an important component of the company's indirect management of the agricultural process, and they assist in making the company more socially legible. Some companies use local farmers to act as brokers. Often these are village leaders (headmen or assistant headmen), and they are usually active and skilled farmers who have been early innovators and adopters of new crops. Local brokers may also be recruited on the basis of kin relations. Uan, for example, became Ban Tiam's main tobacco broker mainly due to the fact that his father-in-law is also a company broker in the village where the company's local nursery had been established. Typically local brokers will get a small percentage of the total sale price as a reward for their services. This additional income, perhaps as much as five or ten thousand baht per year, is likely to attract gossip and some resentment, but there is also grudging acknowledgment that being a broker involves a considerable amount of work, expense, and stress that warrants some reward. As an alternative to—or in addition to—these local brokers some companies also base company employees in the district, where they can manage company assets and maintain close relations with farmers. Almost inevitably these employees are drawn into local social networks, not infrequently forming sexual liaisons with women in the district. In one much-discussed case a company broker had established a second family in the local area, a particularly strategic liaison given that his "minor wife" held an official position in the district's agricultural administration.

This corporate embedding in local systems of sociality means that companies are subject to the critical commentary that emerges from local value systems. Most farmers have a clear idea about what constitutes appropriate corporate behavior. The ideal mode of company behavior runs something like this: companies will provide clear instructions for the production of the crops; company extension agents and brokers will visit regularly and provide guidance on all the stages of production; agricultural inputs will be provided promptly, even on the weekend; company representatives will be accessible and respectful and "talk well" with farmers; agricultural produce will be collected as close to the field as possible; financial records will be clear and transparent; payments will be prompt; and companies will not be overly strict about quality regulations. Of course no company, or individual representative, can live up to all these provisions on all occasions, and it is inevitable that company behavior is subject to local critique, and sometimes outright anger.

Local critiques of company behavior focus on several issues. Probably the most common source of discontent is late payment for produce. Income from cash cropping is important for many farmers to meet day-to-day living expenses—electricity and telephone bills, fuel, education and health expenses, ritual obligations, and a wide range of consumer items. Notwithstanding companies' provision of agricultural inputs there are also costs associated with cultivation, in particular the employment of supplementary labor for intensive periods of work, such as harvesting. Carrying considerable debts, most farmers have very limited cash reserves, and prompt payment for crops is important in maintaining cash flow. Delayed payments are a common feature of exchange within the local economy, but companies are not yet sufficiently socially embedded—or their sometimes ponderous procedures sufficiently understood—to be given the benefit of the doubt. Anxieties about payment are compounded by stories from other villages about companies that have collected the produce and then "disappeared," never returning to make payment.

In 2004, a number of farmers who had grown peas for a Chiang Mai–based cannery were increasingly anxious about their nonreceipt of payment. When one of the company's extension officers came to the village he was harangued about the delay. Particular concern was expressed about the nonappearance of the company's local broker (who lived in a neighboring subdistrict): "We haven't seen his face for a long time, it's like he's scared of meeting a tiger in the fields." The extension officer told the farmers that the issue of payment was not his responsibility and that they should talk to someone in the company's finance department. His bureaucratic response underlined the social distance between company and farmer and the illegibility of its administrative procedures. Another group of farmers in Ban Tiam also experienced persistent problems in relation to payment for eggplants. In this case the extension officer was somewhat more diplomatic, sympathizing with the farmers and complaining that he had not been paid his salary in three months. But the company's credibility declined further when only some farmers were paid (those who were owed the smallest amounts) and later when partial payments were made in bulk to growers' groups without any indication of how the payment should be distributed to individual farmers—an inevitable recipe for local conflict.

Quality standards enforced by companies are another source of discontent, complaint, and occasional dispute. These standards give companies considerable leeway in the observance of the price guarantees set out in the (formal or informal) contracts. Quality downgrades can result in very large reductions in the payment made to the farmer. Claims about quality can be made in relation to chemical residue, damage by disease or insects, and produce being undersized or over-sized—zucchinis, for example, have to be between four and six inches long. Quality standards, particularly those relating to chemical residue, which strictly schedule the application of agrochemicals and often require a prolonged period of nonapplication prior to harvest, can undermine farmers' sense of being able to adaptively manage the production of the crops. Chemical application schedules may be surreptitiously ignored, but farmers run the real risk of rejection of the crop if residues are detected. Residue detection is a highly technical issue on which farmers have little ability to respond. Some companies have developed a reputation for being unreasonably strict in relation to these standards, and in one particularly egregious case the agent rejected all the crops of one farmer because one portion of one of his crops was deemed to be below standard. In another case, a farmer exploded with rage when his eggplant harvest was downgraded, resulting in a large reduction in income. What particularly annoyed the farmer was that the extension officer had inspected the crop shortly before harvest and had made no adverse comment about its quality. "Why did you let me harvest it?" the farmer protested. "I have wasted my time, and I have wasted money hiring people to help me harvest." With that he struck out, aiming a punch at the agent's face. The agent managed to evade the punch, but, according to local gossip, he would have to be very careful in his future dealings in the village. By contrast, one of the reasons for the popularity of tobacco is that quality standards are liberal and the company even knowingly turns a blind eye to the common practice of harvesting the leaves very early in the morning when their moisture content is highest. Farmers do this to increase the weight and, as a result, the price of their crop (fig. 10).

A number of other operational issues can also attract farmers' ire. The location where the companies come to collect the crop is one common source of complaint. Few companies are willing to collect the produce direct from the farmers' fields. Not only would this be overly time consuming, but company representatives also claim that the rough tracks down to the paddy fields are not suited to their trucks and pickups. Farmers accept these practical reasons, although the refusal of some company agents to bring their vehicles into the fields is sometimes interpreted as a reluctance to share in the inconveniences that Ban Tiam's farmers face every day. Some farmers also interpret it as unwillingness on the part of company agents to mix with

FIGURE 10. Weighing tobacco, Ban Tiam, Thailand. (Photo by the author.)

the hoi polloi in the hot, dusty, and unmistakably rural context of the paddy fields. Complaints are likely to become explicit when companies insist that farmers transport their produce to central collection points in villages closer to the district center. Many farmers are reluctant to incur this additional inconvenience and cost, especially when they have to pay inflated transport costs to the few farmers in the village who own pickup trucks (some of whom are also company brokers). Again, the Oriental tobacco company displayed admirable sensitivity to local concerns when it changed its collection point from the agricultural cooperative (about six kilometers from Ban Tiam) to a large concrete pavilion that had been erected at the center of the village for the conduct of village rituals.

There is another, much less frequently expressed line of critique of contract farming. This is not so much directed at the companies as at the arrangement more generally and even at the farmers who enter into contracts. Some residents of Ban Tiam, including the locally influential Mayor Somsak (a shopkeeper and former construction contractor), argue that the village has become overly reliant on contracts and has lost its sense of agricultural independence and entrepreneurship. While these critics acknowledge the difficulties of garlic production, some of them argue that the farmers need to make more effort to help themselves. On the occasion of a local festival, one of the farmers was harangued by his son, a schoolteacher who had returned home for the occasion. "Ban Tiam has become too lazy" he claimed. "Why should farmers wait for companies to bring the market to them? They have to go out and find a market for themselves." In some cases this critique is accompanied by claims about the undesirable environmental impact of some of the contract crops. A former village headman, and highly influential figure in some quarters, was vocal in his opposition to sweet corn cultivation. He claimed that it depleted the soil of nutrients completely and used too much water. No doubt his motivation was partly political (the sweet corn broker was a newly appointed assistant headman who represented the new generation of leadership in the village), but it expressed the potential for local environmental uncertainties to become implicated in local assessments of agricultural transformation.

THE GARLIC ADJUSTMENT SCHEME

In formal terms, contract farming involves bilateral relationships between farmers and private firms; however, the state often plays a role in encouraging these new partnerships. Since the 1980s, state agencies in Thailand have actively promoted contract farming in an effort to increase rural incomes and support the profitability of domestic capital in the agroindustrial sphere. In Ban Tiam, and many other parts of northern Thailand, government action played an important role in encouraging the shift from garlic to the production of alternative crops under contract. In mid-2003 the Ministry of Agriculture launched a garlic adjustment scheme under which farmers who switched to alternative crops would be paid a subsidy of nine thousand baht per hectare. This adjustment subsidy was motivated by concerns that garlic prices would fall dramatically as a result of the agricultural trade agreement with China. Official documents circulated in garlic-growing districts stated bluntly that the import price of Chinese garlic would be lower than garlic production costs in Thailand and that farmers needed to move out of garlic production. The ministry set an ambitious target of a 40 percent national reduction in garlic cultivation. The scheme specifically encouraged farmers to adopt contract farming. Officials insisted that those who wished to receive the subsidy had to provide a copy of a contract for the cultivation of alternative crops. Paperwork distributed to farmers included a model contract in which the farmer, the company, and the relevant state agency would agree to jointly develop plans for the production of contract crops. The government agreed to make the subsidy payments to the farmers, and the company agreed to pay, within twenty days of collection, either the stipulated price for the crop or the prevailing market price, whichever was higher. The farmer had to take full responsibility for cultivation, harvesting, and sourcing inputs. Farmers also had to undertake not to return to garlic cultivation. As it had done several times in the past, the Thai government was hoping that private capital could help drive an agricultural reform agenda.

Ban Tiam farmers responded to the garlic replacement scheme favorably. Although the compensation payments were modest, representing only about 10 percent of returns from garlic in a good year, many farmers were already seriously considering moving out of garlic as a result of declining yields. A cash payment held out the prospect of at least some level of guaranteed return, and there was also the attractive prospect of overclaiming. Coming on top of a range of local economic development programs, the garlic substitution scheme was seen by some as further evidence of the Thaksin government's support for rural livelihoods. Soon after it was announced, almost all of Ban Tiam's farmers had signed up to participate, registering their intentions to grow alternative crops. Only a handful of farmers who grew garlic in 2002 did not register.

Despite the initial enthusiasm, problems soon started to emerge. There was confusion about how the scheme would actually operate. There were several vigorous discussions and arguments among farmers in Ban Tiam who put forward varying interpretations of the government's proposal. Some argued, correctly, that the payment was only intended for those farmers who grew alternative crops on plots where they had actually grown garlic in the 2002–3 season. Others insisted that garlic farmers would be compensated for their entire cropping area whether or not they actually shifted away from garlic production. And others seemed to think, or hope, that all agricultural land would be eligible for garlic compensation. One particularly vigorous argument broke out among a group of women who were harvesting peas. They ended up trading insults given their different interpretations of the scheme's rules. The argument may have escalated further if one of the younger women had not interrupted it by loudly declaring, "Let's change the subject. Let's talk about something more enjoyable. Let's talk about the size of Promin's cock."

In many respects the confusion about the scheme was self-serving and provided some justification for attempts to manipulate the scheme and submit excessive claims. In the latter half of 2003 there were persistent rumors, and more direct charges, that a good number of farmers who had registered had exaggerated the area of their former garlic fields in order to increase their crop-substitution payment. At least one farmer registered land on which he had no intention of shifting out of garlic production. And several farmers registered land on which they had long-established orchards, much to the chagrin of district agriculture officials. The most blatant case of manipulation of the scheme involved the village's largest landowner (and member of the provincial assembly), who claimed the subsidy for his entire landholding (eight hectares) even though he rented all of the land out to other farmers who themselves had claimed the subsidy for their rented land. The overall impact of these manipulations was very substantial. Whereas almost forty hectares of converted garlic fields were registered for subsidy, my survey data from the 2002 dry season suggested that there had been only about fourteen hectares of garlic actually cultivated![19] In other words, with this highly inflated claim, farmers were hoping to receive a generous twenty-seven thousand baht per hectare windfall for the land on which they were actually replacing garlic with other crops.

Local attitudes toward this sort of behavior were informed by a common view that petty corruption is acceptable provided that excessive benefit is not gained at the expense of others within the village. Manipulation of the garlic adjustment scheme was generally regarded as morally acceptable because the state is well resourced and has a responsibility to support the livelihoods of rural people, especially those who were bearing the brunt of the economic adjustment brought about by the free-trade agreement with China. There was also a strong feeling that local officials were likely to be deriving some benefit from the scheme's implementation so farmers certainly had a right to capture their share. However, the ambitious claim of the village's largest landowner strained the credibility of this moral reasoning. There were some who regarded his potential cash windfall as consistent with his high social and economic status—"the benefit of someone with property" was how one farmer described it. But others were more openly critical, questioning the justice of an arrangement whereby someone who did not even farm his own land—"just sitting back and collecting rent"—could also obtain unearned income of almost eighty thousand baht. The unfairness of his behavior was not so much a matter of his taking advantage of the state as of the state and the rich collaborating in delivering a benefit far in excess of that available to less well-connected farmers. And there was also the risk that his blatant manipulation threatened the credibility of the entire village's adjustment claims.

Ultimately what undermined public confidence in the scheme most dramatically was the long delay in the receipt of the garlic substitution payments. As in dealings with contracting companies, delayed payments from the state undermine confidence in the relationships villagers have established with state officials. Both company agents and state officials can appear remote, and their procedures illegible, when the flow of transaction is disrupted. In the case of the garlic substitution scheme this crisis of confidence was compounded by administrative complexity and confusion. When the scheme was announced farmers were asked to register either at the district agriculture office or, if they were members, the agriculture cooperative. This added another layer of confusion to a scheme that was already poorly understood. Several farmers responded by registering some land with the district office and some with the cooperative. Others registered the same land in both places. But when some compensation funds were finally forthcoming in July 2004 only those who had registered with the district office received their payments. At a village meeting the rather embarrassed director of the cooperative, who had several close relatives in Ban Tiam, explained that there had been a breakdown in communication with the district office and that in the preparation of a consolidated list for submission to the provincial office for processing almost all of those who had registered at the cooperative had been left out. Despite the administrative muck-up, she also took the opportunity to go on the offensive about farmers who had registered their well-established fruit orchards for garlic compensation, suggesting that fraudulent claims had contributed to administrative delays. After the meeting, Ban Tiam's volunteer agricultural leader, who had coordinated the submission of the paperwork for the scheme, became a target of vigorous criticism. Some alleged that he had been inefficient in advising farmers about how to correctly submit their claims. Others went further, claiming that those who had received payments were his friends and relatives, who had received preferential treatment. There was talk of forcing him out of his position because he had only taken care of his own "faction" (*phuak phong*). All in all, the scheme had succeeded in straining relations with agricultural officials and in adding further fuel to the persistent local climate of gossip, charge, and complaint about the intravillage distribution of government funds.

Another reason for discontent related to the garlic market itself. In 2004, prices did drop substantially (chart 7). The provincial assemblyman commented that "reducing the garlic price was the same as killing the farmers" (remember that he had claimed compensation for the eight hectares of garlic fields that he rented out!). However, garlic prices recovered in the years that followed. This improvement in the market was a reflection of the success of the government's scheme in reducing domestic production and of lower than expected garlic imports from China. The price recovery prompted some farmers to speculate that "people with influence" within the government had encouraged farmers to withdraw from garlic production in order to increase their own profits. There was local gossip that people connected with the Ministry of Agriculture had bought up large quantities of garlic when the price was low and sold when the price was high. Some farmers, who were still growing garlic, were reluctant to provide the district agricultural office with information about the extent of their cultivation. They were concerned that the office would pass information about garlic production onto garlic traders who would use the information in "making plans" to minimize the price they offered to local producers. These suspicious were encouraged by media reports that the trade agreement with China served the interests of large traders who now dominated the garlic market and could easily manipulate domestic prices by releasing or withholding stock.[20]

The recovery in garlic prices after 2004 opened up another line of opposition to the garlic reduction scheme. Despite their undertakings that they would permanently cease garlic cultivation on the nominated plots, many farmers responded to the rising market by returning to garlic, especially after a dramatic price spike in 2006, which saw dry garlic reach an unprecedented fifty baht per kilogram.[21] Some farmers who had scruples about returning to garlic after having accepted the substitution payment rented their land to other garlic cultivators. Soil nutrients had been restored by the cultivation of alternative crops in the preceding few years, and the garlic yields were surprisingly good. In the 2007 dry season, the garlic revival continued; however, by April 2008, when the garlic had been harvested and dried, prices had plummeted to seventeen baht per kilogram, barely above the cost of production. Farmers throughout northern Thailand's garlic-growing districts faced substantial losses. In early April a "garlic mob" of three hundred farmers blocked the entrance to the Chiang Mai provincial hall demanding that the government intervene in the market and guarantee a price of twenty-five baht per kilogram. They also demanded that the government suspend farmers' debt repayments, stop the smuggling of Chinese garlic, reduce official imports, and open a debate about the negative impact of free trade agreements. They threatened to close major roads around Chiang Mai if their demands were not met.[22] Some farmers from Pad Siew District joined the protests, but farmers from Ban Tiam did not. Nevertheless, Ban Tiam's garlic cultivators were strongly of the view that the government should support the price. As one of them commented, "The government has plenty of money; they should just buy garlic and bury it in a hole if necessary or they could grind it up and use it to make fertilizer."

The government's response to farmers' concerns was limited. Officials expressed frustration that many farmers had returned to garlic cultivation despite previously undertaking to switch to other crops. They argued that the drop in price had been caused by an increase in domestic cultivation rather than any sudden increase in imports from China. Nationally, there had been a 15 percent increase in the area cultivated over the previous year, a sharp departure from the reductions in domestic production that had contributed to high prices in 2006 and 2007.[23] Officials argued that farmers who had previously received payments to switch out of garlic production could not expect further assistance, and they rejected calls for the government to step in and buy garlic at above-market rates. Instead they encouraged farmers to store garlic until the price improved. Provincial officials also attempted to facilitate direct transactions between farmers and large-scale garlic buyers. The Customs Department was urged to increase its vigilance and crack down on garlic smuggling along the Mekong River from China. Farmers themselves were asked to be the "eyes and ears" in the campaign against garlic smuggling.[24]

The government's handling of the garlic market, and its enthusiastic promotion of contract farming, brought an important point of tension in Ban Tiam's contemporary political society to a head. On the one hand, the growing importance of private capital in Ban Tiam's agricultural economy was welcomed by farmers as providing a low-risk source of diversification, productivity improvement, and on-farm employment. This enthusiasm is understandable given the very low level of private sector investment in the district's economy. However, at the same time there is a clear expectation that the Thai state will continue to provide a livelihood safety net if corporate relations and market fluctuations threaten their income. Despite the good relations they have cultivated, company agents have certainly not supplanted state officials as the legitimate guarantors of livelihood security. Farmers want to be free to pursue the most attractive option on offer—whether it be contract farming or the independent production of garlic—but they also expect the state to back them up if their chosen option fails to deliver. The private sector in Ban Tiam is simply not extensive or resilient enough for farmers to give up their expectation that the state should be the ultimate guarantor of economic security. Contemporary political society is not informed by an ideology of autonomous responsibility but by a social contract premised on state support for rural livelihoods. On this score the government was vulnerable to critique. Within Ban Tiam there was a view that there was a larger agenda behind the garlic substitution scheme: it was an attempt by the state to expand the agricultural extension role of companies and to reduce its own obligation to provide agricultural subsidies and support services. As one Ban Tiam farmer commented, "The government wants us to shift to planting crops for companies, and they want the company extension staff to help carry the burden that the government has to take responsibility for." These critical sentiments were reinforced by the very low profile of the government extension workers, many of whom were regarded as office-bound processors of paperwork that were rarely seen in the field actually providing advice or assistance to farmers. Government mix-ups and delays in garlic adjustment payments and the perceived role of state agencies in garlic price manipulation compounded the discontent. As I will discuss in chapter 7, critical sentiment was also fueled by an emerging view that the Thaksin government had done less than it could to address agricultural challenges in the rural economy.

RESISTANCE AND EXPERIMENTATION

The reaction of Ban Tiam's farmers to contract farming and the garlic adjustment scheme can tell us a great deal about political culture in Thailand's middle-income rural economy. These reactions illustrate a shift from the old-style rural politics of protest and resistance to contemporary political society's emphasis on experimental engagement.

Since publication of James C. Scott's classic *Weapons of the Weak*, it has been internationally commonplace to discuss responses to the transformation of peasant economies within the framework of resistance. Scott documents the reaction of farmers in a Malaysian village (which he calls Sedaka) to the double cropping of rice and the introduction of mechanized harvesting. According to Scott, these very typical green revolution changes resulted in the economic and ritual marginalization of poor peasants: they had less access to rental land, suffered a sharp reduction in laboring income, and received less charity and ritual munificence from the rich. How did the poor react to these changes? They certainly didn't attempt to overthrow the new socioeconomic order—their response was nostalgic rather than revolutionary. Farmers adversely affected by the changes in Sedaka drew on a preexisting moral order to stage a symbolic and practical "rearguard action" against the rich.[25] They accused the rich of exploitation, stinginess, arrogance, callousness, and failing to meet the moral expectations and obligations associated with their social position. At times this symbolic struggle was translated into more direct action such as the collective withdrawal of labor, sabotage, and theft.[26] The ideological reference point for this repertoire of resistance was a selectively remembered precapitalist moral order in which the rich and poor were linked "in a symbiosis of dependency and exploitation."[27]

Similar strategies of everyday resistance are evident in the response of Ban Tiam's farmers to the fluctuating fortunes of garlic cultivation and the rise of contract farming. The farmers in Ban Tiam are like those in many other parts of the world who have expressed their dissatisfaction about various aspects of contract farming and its impact on their autonomy and livelihood security. They complain bitterly about late payment for their contract crops and the seemingly unreasonable quality standards that companies enforce, they harvest their crops in ways that maximize their weight, they sometimes neglect to follow the strict production schedules insisted on by the companies, they circulate cautionary tales about companies that have failed to appear when crops are harvested, and they gossip about the private lives of company representatives. They also resist the intrusion of commercial agriculture into the subsistence sector, maintaining a distinction between the cultivation of rice in the wet season and cash crops in the dry season. The state is also a target of ideological and practical weaponry: administrative guidelines are misinterpreted, fraudulent claims for state subsidies are submitted, late payments are condemned, information collection and surveillance by state officials is resented, local agents of the state are accused of favoritism, and the withdrawal of the state from the agricultural sector generates political discontent. Sharp fluctuations in the price of garlic generate protests at the state's lack of market intervention.

So Scott's "weapons of the weak" are undoubtedly present in Ban Tiam. But some caution is warranted in interpreting the meaning and assessing the cultural significance of the "resistant" actions of Ban Tiam's farmers, especially given the very different context of a middle-income rural economy. There is a risk of oversimplifying the intentions underpinning these various acts and statements and framing them within the reassuringly familiar narrative of a local community resisting the incursion of the capitalist market and the modern state. This simplifying tendency is what the anthropologist Sherry B. Ortner refers to as the "problem of ethnographic refusal" in many resistance studies.[28] She argues that political complexity and cultural richness can be lost when resistance studies provide ethnographically "thin" accounts that are organized in terms of a simple relationship between dominant and subordinate groups. It is important to remember that the classic studies of rural resistance were concerned with disruptive moments of transition, as new economic and political forces emerged that undermined preexisting social protections and imposed new systems of exploitation. Although some observers may be inclined to interpret the emergence of contract farming in these terms, I find it more helpful to consider reactions to contract farming in the middle-income context of rising rural incomes, economic diversification, and widespread expectations of state subsidy for rural livelihoods.

In Ban Tiam's middle-income economy, characterized by a high level of commercial engagement and livelihood diversification, the ideological point of reference in the evaluation of new farming systems is experimentation rather than nostalgia. Unlike the poor rice cultivators and laborers of 1970s Sedaka—who were at the cutting edge of a profound rural transformation— middle-income peasants can afford to engage in trial and error. Discussions of commercial agriculture in Ban Tiam are permeated by the language of experimentation. Farmers often comment that they are experimenting (*thot*

long) on a new crop or technique or that they are trying it out (*long du*). In a
very typical discussion, a woman planting eggplants under contract told me
that she had no idea what the return from the crop would be; she was just
trying it out, largely because she had insufficient capital to grow garlic on all
her land. Another farmer described his contract-farming venture as "a rat
nibbling at the grass," suggesting that this was a relatively small and explor-
atory venture. Sometimes the verb *to play* (*len*) is used to suggest that this
"experimental" activity is, in a sense, separate from mainstream farming. One
farmer commented that he had been "playing with organic farming" (*len insi*)
in response to company expectations of a chemical-free crop. This experimental orientation is explicitly comparative. Walking through the paddy fields,
farmers regularly and spontaneously comment on the state of the various
crops they pass, speculating about the inputs and techniques that may have
caused various outcomes: "The garlic on that plot is beautiful because they
used 1:14:12 [fertilizer]"; "She has a good tobacco crop because she planted
soybeans last year"; "The company only paid them two baht for those cabbages, but I would want ten before I would be interested." On trips outside
the village, similar comparative comments are made: "The garlic in this village is good because they have only been growing it for a few years"; "They
make a good profit on eggplants because they are very diligent and produce
good quality"; "This village grew a lot of sweet corn, but the company never
came to collect it."

As other studies of agricultural transformation have noted, a great deal of
experimentation takes place at the margin.[29] My survey data show that each
year there is a modest percentage of Ban Tiam's land allocated to several secondary crops. This experimental area covered about 20 percent of the paddy
fields in the 2005 dry season, reflecting growing interest in the new crops on
offer after the initial flush of enthusiasm for tobacco. In the overall context of
the agricultural economy, these plots may not appear to be overly important,
but they may well be the testing ground for what turns out to be the next big
thing. A small number of farmers—"early adopters" to use the agricultural-
extension jargon—play an important role in this process. Aunt Jiab, an influential and well-respected farmer, is a good example. Over the course of four
years she grew broccoli, peas, potatoes, beans, zucchinis, eggplants, gooseberries, and tomatoes under a number of different contract arrangements.
Some of these were abject failures. The broccoli was eaten by grubs, the potatoes required too much labor and ultimately rotted in the ground, and the
company rejected most of the gooseberries because the fragile sheaths that

surround the fruit were damaged by unseasonal rain. But some, like peas, eggplants, and zucchinis, generated good returns and were quickly taken up by other farmers. By 2006, Jiab's husband was the local broker for eggplant production with about six other farmers helping him to fill his quota.

In suggesting that farmers' ideological orientation toward contemporary economic transformation is experimental rather than nostalgic I am not suggesting that the past is irrelevant. Clearly, the evaluation of new economic and administrative relationships in a middle-income economy involves some reference to long-standing (and often idealized) sentiments of village solidarity, ritual cooperation, and benevolent patronage. There is a real attempt to draw new economic actors into these "traditional" webs of meaning. Yet in relation to commercial agriculture, the past and traditional modes of behavior do not occupy a privileged ideological position; there is no particular moral value placed on preexisting arrangements. In an experimental orientation, traditional values are combined with other points of reference. Ban Tiam's farmers' contemporary ideological frameworks draw on the importance of expert knowledge from external sources, the role of government funds in contributing to local development, the desirability of administration that is transparent (*prongsay*) and fair (*yutitham*), and the importance of fairly sharing the windfall benefits of corruption. In complaining about overly strict enforcement of companies' quality standards, Ban Tiam's farmers are drawing to some extent on a premarket ideology of mutual support and reciprocity, but they are also experimentally deploying a new language of equitable and transparent market access. In submitting fraudulent claims for garlic compensation, farmers are not seeking to disrupt or subvert the state's intervention in local agriculture in favor of more communal or traditional forms of resource management. The ideological goal is to draw the state into more lucrative forms of livelihood support. The petty (and not so petty) corruption of the villagers is not a rejection of the ways of the state but an experimental imitation of the ways in which state officials themselves administer rural development schemes.

Ban Tiam's agricultural experiments are complex and uncertain, and it is inevitable that there will be problems and some cases of outright failure. Not surprisingly, farmers respond to these failures with frustration, anger, gossip, and condemnation. But it would be a mistake to separate these particular responses as resistance and divorce them from the broader experimental context in which they are embedded. An experimental orientation is relatively open-minded about the risk of failure, the possibility of success, and the potential benefits of collaboration. It seeks to explore alternatives rather than defend a particular position. This is well illustrated by the anthropologist Holly High in her account of farmers' response to collectivization and mechanized irrigation in southern Laos. High does not shy away from the negative impacts of these state-imposed schemes.[30] She vividly documents the climate of fear in which the Lao state operates, but she describes villagers' involvement in these schemes in terms of an "experimental consensus . . . where policy is consented to, but as a basis of ongoing renegotiations and manoeuvrings." These consensus arrangements, she writes, are not "a final agreement, not an end-game, but an opening scene, a basis upon which ongoing renegotiation is commenced. By consenting to engage with state projects such as irrigation and collectivization, farmers gain a toe-hold from which they can manoeuvre to a more advantageous position."[31]

In middle-income Ban Tiam, the overall results of the recent phase of agricultural experimentation have, on the whole, been positive. Farmers readily acknowledge that contract farming has provided a range of relatively low-risk agricultural alternatives that can provide some protection from the volatility of the garlic market. There is some selective nostalgia for the good old garlic days of high yields and prices, but there is recognition that a more diversified agricultural economy entails less risk and that some degree of crop rotation has a beneficial impact on soil fertility. What is most appreciated is that contract farming does not expose farmers to the high risk of indebtedness associated with the independent farming of garlic. Ban Tiam's farmers are by no means unusual in coming to these conclusions. Local studies of contract farming, both in Thailand and internationally, have often found that contracting households experience higher incomes and productivity and that these benefits are by no means confined to the wealthiest strata. This may change as broader trends in the Thai and international economy alter the terms of exchange between farmer and company. In the future, for example, farmers may have to pay some, or all, of the input costs in the case of crop failure, but, as High reminds us, an "experimental consensus" does not involve a one-off agreement. It is an ongoing process of culturally informed engagement and evaluation.

5

The Political Economy of Projects

One morning in early June 2006, a group of three men set out from Ban Tiam along a forest trail to the east of the village. One of them was representing the village's water supply committee. The other two were members of a newly formed watershed protection committee. The trail followed the course of a mountain stream that provided the village's domestic water supply, and the men stopped occasionally to inspect the plastic pipes that conveyed water to the village. After an hour or so, they arrived at a small dilapidated shrine that lay in a narrow forest clearing. The shrine was home to the spirit that protected the stream and the forest around it. They had come to make the ninth-month offering to the spirit. This was an annual event, but it was usually done quietly by just one of the men. This year, however, the watershed protection committee wanted to make the event "look important" with more people involved and more elaborate offerings. The committee had also decided to renovate the shrine itself. The men were disappointed that more members of the two committees had not come along. They had even hoped that Mayor Somsak, who was a member of the water supply committee, might attend. There was muttering that he no longer took an interest in village affairs. Their disappointment was compounded by the absence of their main government contact in the watershed protection office, who was on leave for the day. Even Ban Tiam's headman was unavailable because he was attending a meeting about compost production. Luckily my research assistant, who the headman had asked to photograph and record the event, was able to join the men for their ritual trek into the mountains.

Despite the small size of the entourage, the spirit would have been well pleased with the offerings. A pig's head held pride of place. One of the men presented it to the spirit, placing it on a large banana leaf laid at the base of a tree just behind the shrine. He spoke to the spirit, emphasizing that the offering was from all the villagers, "together with the watershed protection committee." This year, he said, a pig's head was being offered in place of the usual chicken. He asked the spirit to protect the soil and stream "so that the water will flow all year and never dry up." His quiet words of offering were interrupted by the noise of the other two taking apart the dilapidated shrine. They removed the corrugated iron roof, quickly replaced a couple of rotten posts, reinforced joints with new nails, wove a new floor out of strips of bamboo, and placed the rusted iron roof back on top. Once the shrine was reassembled, offerings of rice, pork curry, and whiskey were placed inside, accompanied by further requests that the spirit punish people who committed illegal acts in the forest. As they waited for the spirit to eat its fill, one of the men explained that the expenses for the occasion had been taken out of the village's domestic water supply budget. This was fair, they felt, because the spirit protected the water for the entire village. But they had balked at replacing the shrine's old roof, preferring to wait until the watershed protection committee was in a position to fund a more complete renovation.

This small act of government came at an important time for Ban Tiam's watershed protection committee. Under the enthusiastic leadership of the headman, the committee was in the process of applying for a fifty-thousand-baht grant from the watershed protection office for a local forest protection project. There had been extensive discussions with local forestry officials, projects in other villages had been inspected, and an application had been carefully drafted and submitted to the regional watershed office in Chiang Mai. Given the strength of their interpersonal connections with the local forestry officials, members of the committee were confident of success. One of the officials was a regular visitor to the village, often dining with the headman and participating in communal rituals. Nevertheless, they still thought it advisable to underline their communal solidarity and commitment to environmental customs, especially since they had heard that the officer in charge of the local watershed administration had a strong interest in local resource-management traditions. As one of the men making the offering said, their forest protection project "had to be the real thing," and the video and photographic evidence of the ritual would prove very useful in demonstrating that their project proposal was embedded in customary practice.

The renovation of the watershed spirit's shrine is just one of many similar moments of intersection between state power and local programs for conservation, livelihood support, and development. In rural Thailand, these intersections often take a distinctive form: the project (*khrongkan*). Local development projects, funded both by the state and by private donors, are an important component of Ban Tiam's political society. In fact, they have become one of the central preoccupations of political discussion within the village. I have counted almost forty projects that have been implemented in Ban Tiam since the late 1990s. Some projects, especially infrastructure projects, are implemented directly by government agencies or through contracts with local construction companies. However, in this chapter I am interested in more clearly community-based projects that are initiated by residents of the village and managed by local committees for local benefit. Unlike broad-based state subsidy schemes—like the garlic adjustment program—which attempt, often unsuccessfully, to implement impersonal resource transfers based on standard eligibility criteria, community projects are based on an explicit logic of local and personal relationships. Projects draw on political-society idioms of context-specific and bounded exchange and collaboration rather than the civil society notion that all citizens have a right to the benefits of development. Local development projects provide an institutional context in which state power can be condensed, domesticated, and productively mingled with local livelihoods and the moral appeal of community. Given the weakness of the private sector in the economy, projects have become an important vehicle for entrepreneurialism and the development of new styles of leadership.

FOUR PROJECTS

From among the many projects that I have observed in Ban Tiam, I have chosen four to use as a basis for this discussion. Taken together, these four projects capture the diversity of local community development initiatives, and they also encapsulate many of the core political society dynamics involved in project implementation.

Banana Project

The banana project was established in 2000 by Mrs. Bun with funding from the municipal administration. Its overall objectives were to generate employment, strengthen the community, and provide small loans to project members. The project's primary activity was to make sweets out of boiled banana. These were carefully wrapped in banana leaf and placed into tiny decorative baskets woven out of thin bamboo strips. They were sold in shops in the district town and to specialist retailers in Chiang Mai and Bangkok; some were distributed under the nationwide One Tambol [Subdistrict] One Product banner. Mrs. Bun told me about orders from Japan, Taiwan, and Switzerland and also about a visit from an Australian government trade representative. When I visited the project in 2004, it was based in a room at the back of Mrs. Bun's house where several paid workers produced the banana sweets. By then it had been renamed the Ban Tiam Development Group and claimed to have fifty-three members within the village. Mrs. Bun told me that she had more orders than she could fill, primarily because the project had insufficient cash to pay for the time-consuming processing and wrapping of the sweets. Others in the village commented that they were reluctant to work for the banana project because they were not convinced that they would be paid. Undeterred, Mrs. Bun spoke of her plans to create a "village knowledge center," which would generate local jobs and encourage the preservation of local handicrafts.

Organic Fertilizer Project

The organic fertilizer project was formally established at a meeting held in February 2006. It was inspired by ongoing national discussions about the dangers of agrochemicals, attempts by local government agencies to promote organic farming, and specific concerns within Ban Tiam about declining soil fertility and rising fertilizer prices. The project was enthusiastically led by the village headman, seizing an entrepreneurial vacancy created by the sudden death of the village's volunteer "soil doctor" in late 2005. It was managed by a committee of eleven farmers. Members were required to buy a "share" worth one hundred baht to provide the group's initial working capital. Another twenty-four hundred baht was obtained when the members agreed to donate the wages they obtained from cutting firebreaks for the watershed protection office. This office later contributed eleven thousand baht to help the group buy land (from the chairman of the committee) and build a small "factory" for the production of fertilizer. Other funds for the purchase of equipment were obtained from the municipal administration and the Department of Land Development. The son of the former provincial assemblyman was appointed as an adviser to the group. He had excellent connections and had studied agronomy at a university in Chiang Mai. By early 2007 the group was producing compost using crop residue and chaff from the community rice mill. It had also started producing liquid fertilizer using crushed "golden apple" snails, which had infested the rice fields.[1] Many farmers within Ban Tiam were skeptical about the cost and technical viability of the fertilizer, but officials in the watershed protection office and Pad Siew Municipality considered the project to be successful in demonstrating Ban Tiam's collective solidarity and its environmental credentials.

Forest Protection Project

Residents of Ban Tiam have been involved in various projects in collaboration with forest regulators. For example, in 2005 they worked with the national park office to establish basic tourist facilities (toilets, tables, seats, and rubbish bins) at a popular recreational site on the river to the south of the village. The most concerted efforts in collaborative project development began in 2006 as a result of the close relationship that had been established among the headman, several of his friends, and the watershed protection office. The offering to the watershed spirit described at the beginning of this chapter was one component in this new phase of collaboration. Ultimately the watershed protection office did provide a fifty-thousand-baht grant to the newly formed watershed protection committee to support various environmental and livelihood initiatives within the village. The core objective was to establish a "community forest" in the mountainous area that lay immediately to the east of the village. This is an important area of forest, because the stream running through it is the source of the village's domestic water supply and it is vulnerable to flash flooding. When the grant was received there was some difference of opinion about how it should be used, despite the clearly stated community forest objective. The headman's brother (a small-scale contractor) proposed that they use the funds to contract out various minor construction projects. However, the headman was determined that it be used for more obviously communal purposes. Eventually much of the grant was used to fund tree planting in the newly established community forest and to support watershed protection activities such as cutting firebreaks in the forest (fig. 11). Surprisingly, a portion of the conservation grant was also used to purchase an area of privately owned agricultural land under which there was a substantial gravel deposit. The land was purchased so the gravel could be sold to road construction contractors, generating another source of funding for local development initiatives.

FIGURE 11. Tree-planting group working for the watershed protection project,
Ban Tiam, Thailand. (Photo by the author.)

Community Shop

Ban Tiam's community shop was established in 2005 with a grant of twenty-
nine thousand baht from the provincial Senior Citizens' Foundation. The
project proposal was prepared by the head of the village's senior citizens' welfare group, with considerable support from a member of the housewives'
group who worked in the district administration. In the planning stages,
there was considerable excitement about the prospects of the shop. There
were reports that another community shop, located in a considerably more
remote part of the district, had made an annual profit of one hundred thousand baht. I drove a small team of villagers to visit this famous shop, only to
find it closed because the manager was visiting friends in Chiang Mai. Ban
Tiam's shop was located in the village's newly constructed handicraft center,
which stood empty because most of the handicraft producers in the village
did not want to work or display their products there, largely because it was
built on a disputed piece of "public" land that had been unceremoniously

seized from a well-respected former headman. The establishment grant for the community shop was supplemented by the sale of ten-baht shares to members. When the shop opened in early April 2005 it traded well because prices on many items were a little lower than those charged by the other shops in the village. It did particularly well selling whiskey during the new-year (*songkran*) festival. Over the following months the amount of stock gradually increased, and in April 2006 it had a turnover of forty-eight thousand baht and eighty-four member households. The operating profit was around seven thousand baht for the month, but much of this was used up in meeting other "expenses," including a payment to the woman who staffed the shop and dividend payments to shareholders. Soon after, accusations of pilfering, incomplete stocktaking, and sloppy bookkeeping brought about the resignation of the attendant and the closure of the shop. It reopened in late 2006, now staffed by the daughter-in-law of the head of the senior citizens' welfare group.

Projects and Political Society

In his very influential book *The Anti-politics Machine*, anthropologist James Ferguson analyzes the effects of development projects in the small African country of Lesotho. He documents an internationally familiar litany of project failure and argues that development interventions have not delivered their intended improvements in livelihood and welfare. The projects have, however, been successful in extending state authority by implanting "specific bureaucratic knots of power" characterized by "an infestation of petty bureaucrats wielding petty powers."[2] The projects Ferguson examines were instrumental in the establishment of a new district center and facilitated the extension of administration, policing, and military force into an opposition stronghold. But, Ferguson argues, this political effect was obscured because development projects frame their interventions in technical terms. The development apparatus is an "anti-politics machine" because the extension of state power is packaged, in ideology and practice, as an expert-driven and neutral intervention designed to solve socioeconomic deficiencies. Another anthropologist, Tania Li, takes up a similar argument in her more recent study of development interventions in Indonesia. In *The Will to Improve*, Li argues that a wide range of development programs have operated by reducing complex social and political problems to a "knowable, manageable, technical domain."[3] The technical deficiencies within this domain—corruption, poverty, and environmental degradation—are addressed through expert-designed improvement schemes that shape the behavior of project beneficiaries, promote the expansion of capitalist social relations, and consolidate state authority. "Deficient subjects" are made governable through the implementation of standardized technical solutions. However, Li argues, this antipolitics machine of improvement operates imperfectly because development schemes also provoke attempts to manipulate, contest, and fracture their regulatory effects. State regulation encounters local resistance.

The projects in Ban Tiam I am considering are rather more mundane than most of those discussed by Ferguson and Li, but they, too, play a part in the extension of state power. Local projects reflect the policies of various Thai governments to promote infrastructure expansion, rural enterprise, sustainable agriculture, forest conservation, and good citizenship. Despite their local idiosyncrasies, many of the projects in Ban Tiam reflect nationally generic policy approaches to the challenges of combining livelihood improvement with environmental protection. The state resources that flow through projects provide a clear means for rewarding local behavior that is consistent with national policy. Projects also provide a forum for government officials to become involved in village affairs. Ferguson's metaphor of "infestation" is a little too melodramatic, but there is no doubt that, through projects, bureaucracy becomes entangled with the contested minutiae of village administration.

This extension of state power through development projects is important, but my primary interest is in exploring a different perspective, one that suggests a more nuanced mix of regulatory intent and local desire. This productive mix is an important feature of rural Thailand's new political society. Here the work of another anthropologist, Sherry B. Ortner, provides a useful complement to the ideas of Ferguson and Li. At the end of the last chapter, I discussed Ortner's concerns about ethnographically thin accounts that reduce cultural and political complexity to a rather simplified tussle between domination and resistance. One of her conceptual strategies to get away from this simplifying tendency is to draw attention to "projects," in the broadest sense of the word. Ortner describes projects as purposeful sets of activities through which people "seek to accomplish valued things within a framework of their own terms, their own categories of value."[4] In her account, these projects include political maneuverings, livelihood enterprises, and marriage arrangements. Cultivating contract crops or forming good relationships with local spirits could similarly be understood as projects through which Ban Tiam's residents pursue culturally meaningful forms of security and prosperity. Ortner suggests that the forms of "agency" involved in the pursuit of culturally framed projects are different from the forms of agency that lie along the familiar axis of domination and resistance. These projects are certainly not isolated from power relationships or structures of inequality, but they are not easily reduced to a tussle between those who seek to govern and those who seek to contest.

Much can be gained by taking Ortner's observations about projects, broadly defined, and applying them to the more specific domain of Ban Tiam's development projects. The regulatory intentions of some state-sponsored development initiatives are undeniable, but the forms of power and agency that these projects encapsulate are more multidimensional than the imagery of an expanding web of bureaucratic regulation suggests. In rural Thailand's middle-income economy, local projects are specific forms of enterprise in which administrative practices are productively bound with aspirations for development and the moral force of community. Far from being antipolitics machines, they are explicitly productive of politics and form a core institutional element of Ban Tiam's new political society. In some parts of the world, the withdrawal of the state from local service provision has prompted interest in the way the state uses community organizations as a site of "government at a distance," but in Ban Tiam projects persist in drawing the state into local fields of power and networks of exchange.[5]

Setting Projects in Motion

Before a project can be implemented it needs to be written. As in many ritual contexts, the beneficial flows of auspiciousness that projects encapsulate are initiated by the careful recitation of correct language. Writing a project (*khian khrongkan*) is highly skilled work and is usually undertaken by villagers with tertiary qualifications or, at least, substantial bureaucratic experience. Outside assistance is often sought. More complex project proposals, especially those that require the compilation of socioeconomic data, are usually written in collaboration with government officials. The project documents created are highly standardized and organized according to predictable categories: background, purpose, stages of implementation, period of operation, budget, and outcomes. They are carefully formatted and presented to maximize their official appearance. The language used is typically the universal language of development. Projects are proposed to "enhance village livelihoods and create alternative forms of income." They will "promote conservation of natural resources" and "develop the skills of project participants."

Where necessary, reference is made to specific policies, especially conservation policies and the delightfully vague sufficiency-economy philosophy of the Thai king, which has been taken up with royalist fervor by numerous government agencies. Writing a good project also requires statements about the solidarity, readiness and vitality of the recipient community. The formal purpose of the documents is usually to request funds, and requests for assistance are accompanied by itemized budgets and, where appropriate, a photocopy of the project's bankbook.

The bureaucratic mimicry involved in this correct recitation of words has its institutional counterpart in the process of project committee formation. Project proposals gain legitimacy from creating a plausible image of collective enterprise and united purpose. The individual aspirations of project leaders need to be placed in a context of collective endeavor. The communal orientation of projects is signaled most explicitly by the formation of project committees, typically at a public meeting. Committees have standardized positions: chairperson, secretary, treasurer, and often "advisers" who have the skills or status to provide advice or support to the project. There is usually a long list of general committee members, sometimes including almost all of those involved in the project. One of the primary tasks of the first committee meeting is to endorse a set of rules. These tend to have a strong financial focus, setting out the initial costs of joining the group (usually requiring the purchase of a "share" for around one hundred baht), the regular "deposits" required of group members (perhaps only ten baht per month), and the procedures for distribution of dividends and profits. Rules promote ongoing commitment ("anyone who misses more than three meetings will be excluded from project activities") and solidarity ("anyone damaging the image of the group will be expelled").

Another important component in the establishment of projects involves the active demonstration of capability, commitment, and solidarity. Project leaders draw potential grant providers into networks of exchange by showing that donor funds will be matched by the mobilization of labor and resources within Ban Tiam. They need to demonstrate that donors will be positioned within auspicious circuits of exchange that productively combine state subsidy with local sacrifice. A common strategy is for proponents of projects to mobilize labor to contribute to public events. The leader of the banana project, for example, organized some of her supporters to cook and serve food at a major festival staged at the district center. Members of the organic fertilizer project agreed to work with forestry officers on constructing firebreaks in the mountains to the west of the village. They were paid for their labor, but in a meritorious act of project building they donated their wages to enhance the initial capital of the fertilizer project. And, as described earlier, members of the watershed protection group made a special offering of a pig's head to the watershed spirit and renovated his rustic shrine, in order to signal that their proposed conservation project built on a genuine commitment to environmental protection. As one of them commented at the conclusion of the ceremony, "The watershed protection office wants to establish a demonstration project in this part of the district. They have chosen Ban Tiam because we have good communal attributes and we are close to a lot of forest. The villagers here cooperate well. And the municipality may also allocate more resources to this village. Ban Tiam is more ready than other villages [to implement projects]." These "good communal attributes" helped to justify a controversial wood-carving project that many in the village considered to be an elaborate front for the illegal sale of timber to furniture factories in Chiang Mai (fig. 12).

FIGURE 12. Wood carving, Ban Tiam, Thailand. (Photo by the author.)

In the spirit of the anthropological critique adopted by writers such as Ferguson and Li, it would be easy to read these various stages of project formation as the antipolitical implantation of specific types of bureaucratic practice that identify developmental deficiencies and propose standardized techniques to address them. Certainly, in writing formal proposals, establishing routinely structured committees, and demonstrating stereotypically good communal values, Ban Tiam's project proponents are creating a simplified and technically legible arena for state officials who are strongly motivated to find nonproblematic sites for the disbursement of their budget allocations. The important role of conventional forms of writing, not only in project proposals but also in the proliferation of project signs, minutes, accounts, and membership books, points to a desire for legibility and technical mastery. Political tensions are seemingly erased by the creation of a neutral domain of development activity. These are useful observations, but I find it more productive to read project formation as a ritualized performance that creates a localized field of auspiciousness in which power can flow between the various elements assembled. By conducting these rituals of project formation, Ban Tiam's project proponents are demonstrating that they are eligible members of community-based networks of development. Productive flows of power are set in motion by correct behavior. Standardized behavior may reflect a degree of bureaucratic incorporation, but it is also part of a ritually appropriate invocation of prosperity. The various stages of project formation—writing, assembly into committees, and sacrificial good works—carefully assemble bureaucratic technique and communal supplication into a single domain of development activity.

Capturing and Condensing Resources

Projects operate by aggregating and condensing material and symbolic resources from multiple sources. The word itself—*khrongkan*—conveys a sense of this aggregating function, with *khrong* meaning "framework," "skeleton," or "structure" and *kan* meaning "act" or "activity." So a *khrongkan* is a planned activity that draws together various elements into a coherent structure.

This aggregating function has a very practical motivation. Sources of money to support local projects have proliferated since the 1970s as the Thai state has moved from taxing the rural sector to subsidizing it. Over the last decade, Thailand's bold moves toward decentralization have pumped unprecedented budgets into subdistrict and municipal administrations. The budget of Pad Siew Municipality has increased to thirty million baht since its establishment in 1999. Local cash flows were enhanced by the Thaksin government's local economic development and poverty alleviation schemes. Ban Tiam has also benefited from the ongoing national priority accorded to forest conservation in the northern provinces. There are also numerous potential donors outside the formal government sector: the mayoral candidate who needs to demonstrate his commitment to village development, the construction contractor who supports local projects so he can mine gravel within the village territory, the Bangkok-based husband of a woman in the village who wants to improve the lives of his impoverished in-laws, a foreign researcher who makes a donation to the village in the vain hope that it will stem the constant pleas for support for specific projects, and the visitor to a nearby meditation temple who wants to enhance her store of otherworldly merit.

These multiple sources of funding are located in a socially and institutionally complex field with numerous government agencies, a tangle of acronyms, regularly updated administrative guidelines, and shifting interpersonal relationships. Modern rural society has had to develop mechanisms to domesticate this unruly domain and channel its multiple flows in desirable directions. Local development projects serve this purpose very well because they provide a relatively stable framework for condensing elements of this convoluted field of power into a single activity, which usually has a clear physical presence in the form of a building, an office, or, at the very least, a sign. Just as in dealings with the equally bewildering spirit world, it is important to create specific sites of exchange where external powers can be entangled in local livelihoods. As I wrote in the introduction, projects can be thought of as spirit shrines for the state.

Project proponents often anoint their schemes with generically auspicious names so that they can effectively capture and condense these multiple streams of financial support. Over the course of 2006 the "fertilizer group," for example, evolved into the "Committee to Promote Livelihoods and Development in Ban Tiam." Organic fertilizer was still its core business, but the more auspicious name—together with registration as an official "community corporation"—positioned the project committee to bid for other development projects in the Thaksin-government pipeline. The fertilizer group's name also sent a clear competitive message to the banana project, which was operating as the "Ban Tiam Development Group." Mrs. Bun, who ran the banana group, had been very successful in consolidating multiple sources of support. She had a part-time job in the district office and became close friends with the wife of the district head. This gave her good, and early, access to information about funding programs being implemented at the local and provincial levels. She was able to secure establishment funding from the district office, the municipality, the local member of parliament, and the provincial Office of Welfare and Community Development. Her husband's connections were also important. He was a retired policeman and had served with senior figures in the national police administration. In 2003, the national head of the police force donated ten thousand baht to support the banana project.

Projects are also effective vehicles for the consolidation of symbolic resources. I have already indicated that projects effectively combine elements of both community and bureaucracy. But there are other sources of symbolic value that can be drawn into their network. This symbolic aggregation is nicely illustrated by one of the main activities of the watershed protection project. In August 2006, the project committee organized a tree-planting day to mark the queen's birthday. The aim was to establish a "food bank" with trees that could provide traditional fruits and natural medicines. Villagers who came to help were paid 150 baht for their labor. Once again, the headman was unable to participate because he had to attend yet another of his project-related meetings outside the village. He arranged for Mayor Somsak to launch the day's activities. Resplendent in an improbably white uniform, Somsak spoke to the assembled villagers on a muddy track at the fringe of the forest. He spoke about the importance of honoring the queen, who is a champion of forest protection, and about the environmental benefits of tree planting. He linked this environmental objective to the need to develop the village and suggested that the municipality might be able to contribute funds to future projects. The project committee had prepared a large banner to mark the occasion. It read "Planting a Food Bank: Supported by the Project for Promoting Community Participation in Development, Ban Tiam Conservation Group." Before work started, a brief offering was made to the spirit of the mountain. The work proceeded quickly and efficiently, compromised only slightly by the fact that some of the villagers were more interested in collecting bamboo shoots than tree planting. When the work was completed, several of the participants assembled at the nearby district office, where they recited an oath of forest protection: "I will work to protect the natural resources of the nation to the best of my ability. I will work together with all parties to be the strength of the nation to prevent timber cutting, forest destruction, and the sale of illegal timber. If I violate this oath please bring me unhappiness and misfortune. If I adhere to this oath please bring health and prosperity to myself and my family."

All in all the tree-planting day was an impressive performance. Various elements of auspiciousness—royalty, environment, state, nation, community, family, supernatural authority, and local sustainability—were bound together in a single moment of project implementation. An official from the watershed protection office, who helped with the tree planting, expressed his delight at the commitment of the village and the strength of its environmental traditions.

Marking Boundaries

Another important feature of projects is that they provide a basis for demarcating and bounding flows of benefits. If a project is insufficiently bounded there is a risk that its material and symbolic resources will be too widely dispersed. In simple terms this bounding function is performed by the idea of the village community itself. The community represents a simplified institutional template in which projects are located, and it is community membership that defines the appropriate boundary of project activity. Projects that operate on a municipal or district level are viewed with suspicion—they are a sure recipe for the widespread dispersal of modest benefits. There was little interest in Ban Tiam when the municipality announced as early as 2004 that it was interested in developing a project to produce organic fertilizer, which it would sell from a newly constructed local produce shop. The feeling in Ban Tiam was that it was only through fertilizer production within the village itself that "benefits" (*prayot*) were likely to be generated. Similarly, there were strongly voiced concerns when residents of neighboring villages started buying shares in Ban Tiam's community shop, hoping for a dividend windfall from what was expected to be a lucrative venture. Committee members were pleased that the shop was generating interest outside the village, but they were concerned about the growing proportion of its profit that would be lost to Ban Tiam. These sentiments about the desirability of highly localized and bounded projects blend nicely with the views of many government officials that project funding is most effective when it is embedded in small-scale networks of cooperation.

The idea that projects exist for the benefit of the village community creates a clear symbolic boundary between Ban Tiam and other villages within the district. However, projects are also based on more narrowly drawn boundaries that lie within the village itself. They are initiated by specific groups within the village, they serve the economic and political interests of particular individuals, and they often challenge the position of others. There is a complex tangle of factionalism and interpersonal rivalry underlying many of these alliances, but there are some identifiable dynamics at work.

To start with, some projects involve a direct challenge to the commercial elite within the village. In 2006, a community rice mill was established with one of the Thaksin government's local development grants. This threatened the revenues of the two existing rice millers in the village and was resented by some of the non-rice-growing elite households because it offered them no direct benefit. A similar dynamic was evident in relation to the village credit fund. It was initially captured by one of the village's principal moneylenders—an affluent shopkeeper and successful farmer—but control was wrested away from him when it was alleged that he was using the communal funds to support his private moneylending business. The challenge to the commercial elite was clearest in relation to the community shop, which was established despite the fact that there were already six shops within the village. Both of the women who initiated the community shop had been involved in disputes with members of the commercial elite: one was bitterly resentful that her husband's cousin, a wealthy shopkeeper, had refused to give her financial assistance at a desperate time of family illness and crop failure; the other had been involved in a very public dispute with another shopkeeper, who she had accused of misappropriating community development funds. Several of those involved with the community shop were also personal enemies and political rivals of Mayor Somsak, a member of the village's most important shopkeeping family. Unsurprisingly, Somsak conspicuously failed to support the community shop. He refused to attend committee meetings, publicly questioned the need for the project, and argued that it would not be financially viable. This provided a useful opening for his main rival in the 2006 mayoral election, who energetically courted supporters of Ban Tiam's community shop, lauding it as a fine model for locally managed development. In return for his flattery, and modest financial support, he was fed a stream of information from Ban Tiam's malcontents about Mayor Somsak's inadequacies.

A second internal dynamic is that some projects seek to lessen the influence of the village's most important communal institution, the temple. As in many Thai villages, Ban Tiam's temple is a potent symbol of communal effort and merit making. The grandeur of its buildings—enhanced by seemingly never-ending renovations marked by elaborate festivals—reflects the virtue and prosperity of the village. The monks and novices present there are a focus for merit making and ritual activity. However the current abbot,

Tu Sonthi, is a divisive and controversial figure.[6] He achieved the position of abbot in contentious circumstances, leapfrogging over a more senior and very popular colleague who Sonthi accused of contributing to the death of the former abbot by placing a spiritually defiling pair of women's underpants under his pillow. This extraordinary incident split the village and resulted in Sonthi's popular rival leaving the village and taking up residence in a temple in a neighboring district. To this day there is a regular undercurrent of gossip about Sonthi's manipulative, overbearing, and autocratic style; his inappropriate personal habits; and his use of temple funds for personal benefit. For these reasons, a good number of residents are keen to establish alternative domains of communal activity that lie beyond his reach. A typical example of this occurred in 2005 when one of Ban Tiam's less successful farmers asked me to support a project he had initiated to purchase portable electric lighting that could be used at functions within the village. He told me that the temple already owned such lighting, but many villagers were tired of dealing with the often abusive abbot when they tried to borrow it, or any other communal equipment. He was also angry that the abbot was now charging for the use of the temple photocopier, despite the fact that it had been purchased through collective fund-raising. A more serious challenge came from the headman when he initiated a project to build a meeting hall outside the temple compound. He felt that holding meetings next to the temple gave the abbot too much influence, and he was keen that the village have a "second community center" located on neutral ground. In fact, the ground was not entirely neutral: it was an odd-shaped and hard-to-sell block of land owned by the former provincial assemblyman, and one of the headman's motives was to win favor with him by raising money to buy the land.

This intravillage demarcation of project boundaries is embedded in the institutional structure of projects. Projects usually have rules about membership, typically requiring an up-front payment (sometimes in the form of a share purchase), regular monthly contributions to help establish and maintain the project's financial resources, and regular participation in project activities. Project benefits often extend to nonmembers—anyone can patronize the community shop, anyone can sell snails to the fertilizer project, and the entire village benefits from watershed protection if it reduces flooding—but more specific benefits are limited to actual members. Many projects pay a "dividend" by distributing a proportion of the operating surplus to shareholding members. In some cases this may be just a token amount, perhaps 10 percent of the profits divided between all the members. But in other cases the dividend allocation is much more generous: the fertilizer project, for example, decided to distribute 40 percent of its annual surplus to shareholding members. Project members sometimes express concern that nonmembers will buy into projects once they see that they are successful, and some projects have rules that require higher levels of financial contribution from late joiners. In addition to dividends, active committee members usually receive special payments for their services to the project, and they are often eligible for generous reimbursement for costs incurred (such as when they have to travel to a meeting in Chiang Mai). The rules of the fertilizer project allocated 15 percent of its profits as a "bonus" for committee members, and 40 percent for other, nondefined "expenses." The village credit fund allocated 10 percent to committee members as payment for their services and another 15 percent for "allowances." Members of the community shop tried to minimize payments to committee members so that the dividend payments to general members could be maximized. Project members are also sometimes eligible to borrow small amounts of money from project funds, and it is not unknown for committee members to make temporary use of project budgets to support their private affairs. This is politely referred to as "rotating" the money.

Of course this businesslike style of operation—with shareholders, dividends, reimbursements, and bonuses forming a basis for a narrow demarcation of benefits—needs to be tempered by regular reference to the values of a broadly inclusive community. Even though they often reflect particular interests within the village, projects are not the same as private businesses in that they derive their primary legitimacy from combining personal and communal improvement. In case this is ever forgotten, projects will usually explicitly allocate a proportion of their operating surplus for community welfare purposes. In 2006, for example, the community shop contributed several thousand baht for the purchase of food packages for elderly people. This was an essential display of welfare, given that the project had been funded on the strength of a submission from the senior citizens' group. The village credit fund regularly allocated 10 percent of its surplus to support children in the village who are infected with the HIV virus. And the fertilizer project committee, having allocated itself a 15 percent bonus, chose to spend 5 percent of its surplus on "helping society."

The demarcation of projects, and the individual benefits that flow from them, is a fraught process, precisely because it can come into conflict with the moral value of a broadly inclusive community. Mrs. Bun's banana project nicely illustrates some of these dynamics. The banana project initially fell under the auspices of the village housewives' group, but after about a year it split off following concerns that Mrs. Bun's initiative was capturing funds that would normally have supported the core activities of the housewives' group. This split, and the location of the project's activities in Mrs. Bun's house, encouraged a view that the project was essentially a private business that only generated profits for Mrs. Bun and wages for a small group of her employees. In 2005, the housewives' group started making representations, both directly to Mrs. Bun and at village meetings, in an attempt to secure control of the banana-processing equipment that Mrs. Bun had bought with donor funds. Their aim was to move the equipment to the village handicraft center (yet another project!) where it could be used to provide income-generating activities for elderly residents. The head of the housewives' group told me that Mrs. Bun had fraudulently listed many project members on her application for funding in order to create a "false group" that would be attractive to potential donors. In fact, she argued, Mrs. Bun's project was an individual (*suan tua*) enterprise not a collective (*suan huam*) one. (This is a very important distinction in Ban Tiam's political society that I will discuss in detail in the next chapter.) She backed up her claim by arguing that members of the banana group (allegedly now just four or five people) no longer helped with communal activities, such as the preparation of food for festivals. Mrs. Bun refused to hand over the equipment and actually ran for election as president of the housewives' group when the position became vacant. She received only two votes but, despite the very public humiliation, was not deterred in her ambitions for higher political office.

The difficulties involved in establishing and maintaining a project charged with the moral value of collective enterprise were equally evident with the community shop. There were challenges to the claim of broad-based benefit from the outset, given the adverse commercial impact on other shopkeepers in the village. However, the project organizers argued that this negative impact on a small number of villagers was outweighed by the collective benefits of lower prices and dividend payments to project shareholders. These arguments, combined with the shop's promising financial performance in its early months of operation, were sufficiently compelling to attract almost two-thirds of the households in the village to join as shareholding members. However, the reputation of the shop started to unravel as rumors circulated that Paeng, the woman employed to work in the shop, was using it for personal gain. Paeng was accused of giving stock away to close friends, not entering all payments received in the account book, and only opening the shop when it suited her. When the shop became a favored drinking spot for Paeng's boyfriend and some of his colleagues from the Forestry Department, its communal reputation was damaged even further. Village confidence in the shop plummeted when the committee discovered that up to eight thousand baht was unaccounted for. Paeng blamed the committee's poor accounting and incompetent stocktaking. Some committee members accused Paeng of pilfering. Realizing that their dividend payments were likely to be minimal— and that there was a real chance of losing the value of their shareholdings— many member households shifted their custom back to the village's established shops. Ultimately Paeng resigned and moved to live outside the village with her boyfriend. After being closed for a period, the community shop reopened with a new employee, but its earnings were very modest. Much to the annoyance of the committee members, there was little support forthcoming when they sought a share of a village development grant provided by the Thaksin government to build a toilet next to the shop for the convenience of customers, staff, committee members, and, presumably, regular drinkers.

These various cases demonstrate a core tension that lies at the heart of project implementation: project boundaries are necessary to concentrate flows of benefits, but projects must also demonstrate a sufficient degree of inclusion and accessibility to retain the morally desirable aura of the collective. It is generally accepted that projects generate personal benefits and that those most closely associated with projects can expect the highest returns. But project leaders are vulnerable to charges of corruption, incompetence, and self-interest if an impression emerges that benefits are being distributed overly narrowly and that collective objectives are being ignored.

PROJECTS AND THE PRODUCTION OF POLITICS

It has become fashionable to argue that many development projects are failures and their significance lies in their ideological effects rather than their disappointing practical impacts. The experience of Ban Tiam's projects lends some support to this view. Many local projects have failed to achieve their ambitiously stated objectives. Support for the fertilizer project is very uneven: there are some enthusiastic producers of organic fertilizer, but it has had no significant effect in transforming agricultural practice within the village. Many of the trees planted by the watershed conservation project have died as a result of neglect. The "community forest" is really only a showpiece, with elaborate signage, rather than a source of valued forest products and medicinal herbs. The community shop limps along with very little custom, and it makes only a tiny contribution to the welfare of the elderly people it was established to support. And the banana project has generated much more acrimony than income. Given the time and energy that these projects absorb, it is hard to see how they could be justified in terms of their developmental outcomes.

Nevertheless, it would be a mistake to completely dismiss the practical benefits of these activities: local projects provide financial benefits for members, especially those who serve on project committees; they have generated some local employment; they have helped people to develop management skills; and they have provided some subsidized goods and services to Ban Tiam's residents. These benefits may seem to be financially insignificant, but in an economy based on diversification, small contributions supplement and broaden livelihood portfolios. As is evident in the cash-cropping sector, small experiments at the margin of the economy, even if most of them fail, can be important in identifying new forms of enterprise. This entrepreneurial understanding of projects is important, especially in an economy where private capital plays such a limited role. As was examined in chapter 2, business development in Ban Tiam is very limited and confined to relatively traditional rural pursuits such as shopkeeping, handicrafts, and some food processing. Projects can be seen as creating an artificial private sector where attempts at capital accumulation can be undertaken with minimal risk and the protective backup of communal participation. There are parallels with the local logic of contract farming, in that projects are a mechanism for drawing scarce capital into the village and combining it with underutilized labor resources. It is unsurprising that so many disputes are generated by the tendency of community development projects to develop into private ventures. In Ban Tiam, the local development project is an inherently unstable institutional form that straddles the very blurred line between private and communal benefit.

This is not just about business, narrowly understood. Projects also provide a vehicle for villagers to establish and demonstrate their leadership credentials. Mrs. Bun saw her banana project as a step along the path to political office, an ambition strengthened when a fortune-teller predicted that she would be elected to the municipal assembly within ten years. The two prime movers behind the community shop were both outspoken community activists who had clear ideas on how development activities within the village

should be managed. One was the wife of an unsuccessful candidate for headman in the previous village election; the other had hopes that one day she
might take on an assistant headwoman role. Ban Tiam's headman himself
saw local projects as an important way in which he could make his own mark
on the village's development. Strategically inspired by the king's "sufficiency
economy" philosophy, he had long discussions with me about Ban Tiam's
potential to make greater use of its natural resources by, for example, producing brooms out of a special type of grass that is abundant in the nearby forest.
He also emphasized the importance of generously funded project signs
that would appropriately honor project donors and committee members.
Within projects, ambitious villagers can demonstrate a form of leadership
that is not dependant on economic power or high-level political connections.
Small-scale projects establish a sphere of leadership and entrepreneurialism that lies outside the construction-shopkeeping-trading nexus dominated
by the village's elite. Involvement in projects requires no preexisting financial resources. In fact, strategic or opportunistic connections with a potential
donor can be more valuable in project development than a carefully accumulated stock of social or financial capital.

Projects are also sites where the state itself is refashioned, but this refash-
ioning is rather different from that described by some influential analysts
of the modern state. Ferguson's famous argument about development projects acting as an antipolitics machine—by presenting government intervention in neutral, technical, and apolitical terms—is part of an influential line of
thought that seeks to understand the state in terms of its ideological effects
rather than its institutional structures.[7] There is considerable variation in this
literature, but one common claim is that, despite its numerous intrusions
into everyday life, the state is imagined to be a rather autonomous and unified entity that is removed from the messy realities of social and political life.
This ideological effect occurs because there are common state practices—
typically those involving repetitive routines, standardized forms of discipline,
and the creation of universal citizenship—that create the impression of a
coherent and rational structure that is independent of individual action or
creativity. This seemingly autonomous and nonintrusive state implements
forms of remote and detached government by using cultural discourses and
social institutions to mold subjects who regulate themselves without the
heavy hand of bureaucracy.

The ideological effect of development projects in Ban Tiam is very different. These are certainly not antipolitics machines that create the impression

of a neutral and detached state. Projects are openly and explicitly productive of politics. Of course, some projects frame their objectives in the neutral and technical terms of modern bureaucracy. Ban Tiam's wordsmiths have mastered the international language and committee-based practice of development. Project committees, with their meetings, rules, and minute books, are certainly suggestive of a technical apparatus that implements projects to meet neutral and apolitical objectives. But project creation and implementation are auspicious performances that seek to conjure power not conceal it. Projects generate and maintain an indigenous model of power relations in which the developmental potency of the state is bound into locally auspicious networks of security and prosperity. In these auspicious enterprises, there is no distinction between the technical language of development and the language of power and politics. In Ban Tiam, the effect of projects is to draw state agencies into direct relationships of subsidy and support. Projects within Ban Tiam explicitly assert that local aspirations should be met not through technically neutral interventions but through the cultivation of specific, personalized, and communally embedded connections that draw resources into the village. Successful project proponents are not praised because they have developed a technically sound approach to development but because they have connections and have bought resources into the village that can then be used for a variety of communal and personal enterprises, whatever their specific technical purpose. Some of political society's most important expectations, desires, and disappointments about the intimate conduct of government are forged in the success and failure of projects.

6

Community, Legibility, and Eligibility

In mid-2004, Aunt Fon decided it was time that Ban Tiam's housewives' group (*klum mae ban*) obtain uniforms for its members. Like the many other such groups that exist throughout Thailand, Ban Tiam's *klum mae ban* is a vehicle for the expression of good housewifely values. Its members mobilize to prepare and serve food for funerals, weddings, temple festivals, and other civic occasions; they participate as a group in collective merit-making activities at the village temple; and they facilitate the implementation of local health and welfare activities. Aunt Fon decided it was appropriate that the members have a distinctive and elegant uniform to wear when they were representing the housewives' group. Some other villages in the district had already obtained uniforms, so why should Ban Tiam be left behind?

Aunt Fon was an active contributor to Ban Tiam's community development, and she was a keen player in its micropolitical landscape. She had recently become president of the housewives' group, and had been vice president for several years before that. She was a formidably good cook, an energetic organizer, and an enthusiastic networker. For several years, she had been head of the local health volunteers and delighted in showing me her large stock of condoms and passing on confidential information about the health status of other villagers. She was close to the village abbot, a confidant of the district agricultural officer, and a disciple of an influential nun who had established a large meditation temple in a neighboring village. Aunt Fon was a very capable masseuse, and some of her connections were built on a foundation of therapeutic muscle relief. During 2003, Fon had joined the network of the district's provincial assemblyman and accompanied him during his reelection campaign, cooking food for election meetings in villages throughout the district. This had brought her into close contact with organizers for Thaksin's Thai Rak Thai party, and by early 2004 she had signed up as a member and become one of the party's local organizers.

Aunt Fon's plan for the housewives' uniforms was straightforward. Relying on local idioms of patronage and political support, she was confident that she could secure funding from the local Thai Rak Thai member of parliament. At the very least, she expected, he would cover half of the cost. She would buy the cloth in Chiang Mai, one of the members of the housewives' group who had a dressmaking business would be paid to make the uniforms, and any outstanding costs would be met by each of the members in the form of a partial payment. Compared to many of the other projects that were being implemented in the village, this seemed a very simple affair.

But that's not how things turned out. A major problem emerged early on when funds from the Thai Rak Thai member of parliament were not forthcoming. This came as a shock. Quite apart from Aunt Fon's personal relations with local party players, Thai Rak Thai had actively used local housewives' groups as a vehicle for recruitment and electoral promotion. In fact, the district chairperson of the combined village housewives' groups was also the district secretary of the Thai Rak Thai party. It seemed very reasonable to assume that the housewives' uniforms would attract party patronage. So why wasn't the donation provided? One possibility is that the local member of parliament was concerned that direct support for Ban Tiam's housewives' group would attract allegations of vote buying from his political rivals. With a national election scheduled for early 2005 there was heightened sensitivity about vote buying and a risk of political disqualification if official complaints were made and proven. Discretion was not one of Aunt Fon's virtues, and there was little doubt that a donation from the local member of parliament would have been broadcast far and wide. It is also possible that the member of parliament was personally disinclined to become involved in this sort of patronage. He had a long career in public administration and was certainly not the stereotypical local patron who liked to openly splash his favors around. He preferred to do things through more formal channels.

The lack of financial support from Thai Rak Thai did not deter Aunt Fon. Displaying typical political pragmatism, she decided to approach the opposition candidate for support. As we will see in the next chapter, he was much better known as a dispenser of patronage, having supported numerous local projects during his previous terms as the local member of parliament.

However, Aunt Fon's request to the opposition candidate drew quick condemnation from some of the other opinion leaders in the village. There were already some well-established organizers for the opposition in Ban Tiam—including the village headman—and Aunt Fon's direct approach was seen as cutting across the political connections they were busily cultivating. They moved quickly to scuttle her request and refused to approach the opposition candidate themselves when asked to do so by other members of the housewives' group.

Despite this second setback, Aunt Fon was determined to proceed. But she needed cash to buy the cloth for the uniforms. She found a short-term solution for the problem by borrowing ten thousand baht from the village's domestic water supply group and an additional two thousand from the emergency welfare fund. Of course, in strict terms, both of these loans breached the rules of the relevant groups—and they highlighted Aunt Fon's skills of persuasion—but this informal "rotation" of funds is a common feature of local project administration within the village. Provided the loans are repaid quickly, they are not generally regarded as corrupt.

Fon then went to Chiang Mai, with two of her close colleagues from the housewives' group, and purchased the cloth for the uniforms. This generated a new set of problems. Back in Ban Tiam there were soon complaints about the cloth she had chosen. It was an orangey-pink color. Some considered it to be too orange; others thought it was too pink. Some wanted a completely different color. And others had hoped for a more traditional northern Thai look. Aunt Fon was criticized for not consulting widely enough on the cloth and only involving a small number of close friends in its selection. One group of housewives proposed returning the cloth and buying a completely different color, but their proposal came to nothing.

Soon after, work started on turning the cloth into uniforms. The dressmaker was a close ally of Aunt Fon and, no doubt, was due to make something of a killing from the 250 baht per dress that she quoted. But she, too, became disillusioned with the project when she found there were insufficient funds left to buy essential items such as thread, zippers, buttons, and additional cloth for lining and trim. She also had to make the dresses on the promise of payment for her labor, a promise that was looking somewhat tenuous because any funds recovered first had to be used to repay the water supply group and village welfare fund.

Eventually, with no financial options left, Aunt Fon decided that each member of the housewives' group would have to pay 500 baht for her uniform.

This decision turned smoldering discontent into outrage. In an economy in which the average payment for wage labor is about 140 baht per day, a payment of 500 baht represents a substantial outlay. Particularly galling was the fact that the payment was required in the latter months of the year, a period when rice growing—and thus exchange labor—dominates and there are relatively few local opportunities for paid employment. Aunt Fon was condemned for her mismanagement of the project. She had given her word that she would be able to obtain funding for the uniforms, but now she was imposing a heavy burden on almost every household within the village. She had "destroyed the credit" that the village had with political patrons and had bought disunity to the housewives' group and the village itself. The village headman started canvassing to replace her. Many of the housewives refused to hand over the required payment. The treasurer of the housewives' committee complained bitterly about the discomfort she and her assistant had experienced in going around the village collecting the much resented uniform tax.

The dispute rolled on for some weeks. Nevertheless, all the uniforms were made and, gradually, sufficient money was collected to repay debts and cover costs. But Aunt Fon's position as head of the housewives' group had become untenable. Complaints about the uniforms had escalated into broader complaints about her autocratic management style, her financial incompetence, and her spending of the group's funds in ways that benefited friends and relatives. The persistent criticism and gossip greatly upset Aunt Fon, and eventually she announced that she would step down from the presidency of the group.

The social drama of the housewives' uniforms can tell us a great deal about Ban Tiam's political society and, in particular, the role of community within it. To begin with, the conflict reflected the high degree of importance attached to projects as vehicles for improvement and connection. For some years, the housewives' group in Ban Tiam had been concerned about its inability to secure project funding. Its members often compared themselves unfavorably to groups in other villages that had strong connections with well-resourced patrons. If correctly managed, the housewives' uniform project could have drawn substantial resources—perhaps more than fifty thousand baht—into the group. Much of this would have been spent on producing the uniforms, but, as we have seen, project budgets are inevitably managed so that there are surpluses that can be put to both collective and personal benefit. The uniform project could have provided the group with a modest fund to support its social and welfare activities, and it also could have provided individual benefits in the form of inflated expenses and fees for service paid to committee members or their allies However, Aunt Fon failed as a project manager. The housewives' group only had three baht left in its bank account in the wake of the project. The prospects of individual benefits for committee members evaporated; instead, they were burdened with five-hundred-baht payments and, for some, the public humiliation of having to collect them from other households in the village. Fon had also compromised the finances and credibility of two other communal organizations—the water supply group and the village welfare fund—by borrowing funds that could only be repaid after a long and very public delay. Perhaps most damaging to her credibility as a project manager was the fact that Fon had failed to effectively manage relations with local political figures on both sides of the political divide. Her failure was not just her inability to manage a specific initiative, but it also undermined her reputation of competence in managing external connections in ways that would draw the material and symbolic benefits of development into Ban Tiam. In a political society built on direct and personalized relationships with sources of power, this was a highly culturally significant failure.

This is a familiar story, which illustrates some of the arguments about projects, patronage, and politics explored in the previous chapter. In this chapter I want to shift the focus to an issue that, so far, has been less explicitly addressed: community. One of Fon's driving motivations was her concern that Ban Tiam's community was insufficiently marked. She felt that the village's official leadership, which was exclusively male and, in her eyes, overly preoccupied with very concrete forms of development, was ineffective in promoting Ban Tiam's cultural identity. For Aunt Fon, the uniforms were a seemingly straightforward attempt to create a more explicit sense of village commonality and put this on public display on occasions of collective endeavor. This was a politically important effort given the modern state's administrative tendency to engage with clearly defined communities when implementing development programs. However, there is nothing straightforward about the construction of community, and Fon ultimately fell foul of one of the dilemmas of modern political society: while community provides a foundation of moral authority for the pursuit of development, it is a fragile, volatile, and capricious entity that often struggles to bear the weight of its own construction. The symbolic simplicity of community is all too easily caught up in the complex reality of village factionalism. Of all the domains of power and auspiciousness that the villagers of Ban Tiam seek to cultivate and domesticate, their own community may well be the most elusive.

THE SYMBOLIC CONSTRUCTION OF COMMUNITY

In order to understand how community is constructed, much can be gained by going back to a classic description of communal processes written by one of the founding figures of modern sociology, Émile Durkheim. In his examination of the religion of Aboriginal people in Australia, Durkheim was particularly interested in the phenomenon of totemism, whereby social groups have spiritual relationships with certain plant or animal species. Durkheim describes the totem as a condensed material representation of the diffuse moral force of the clan. In simple terms, the totem is a symbol of community. It is necessary to have a symbol because "the clan is too complex a reality to be represented clearly in all its complex unity."[1] For symbolic convenience, recourse is made to a totemic emblem. Durkheim points to two layers of simplification involved in this process. First, the clan is represented in the "simple, definite and easily representable" form of a plant or animal, in contrast to the complexity of the clan itself.[2] Second, the totemic species itself is represented by simple geometric figures on ritual objects and the bodies of clan members. In fact it is "the figurative representations . . . that have the greatest sanctity." The hold these representations have is automatic, a seemingly emotional response rather than a rational assessment of "useful or injurious effects."[3] Simplified symbols serve to both create and maintain collective sentiments, and they carry within them the condensed moral power of the collective.

A more recent contribution to this discussion is provided by Anthony Cohen in an important book, *The Symbolic Construction of Community*. Cohen starts out by arguing that community is imagined, even when it involves regular and highly localized contact. He rejects naive assumptions about the simplicity of face-to-face interaction and argues that people involved in direct sociality require symbols that provide a basis for understanding what they have in common, just like the totem in Aboriginal clans.[4] These shared symbols are socially orienting and serve to define social boundaries, marking out the community of "us" from "them." Cohen's second important insight is that these shared symbols of community are effective because they are vague. Unelaborated symbols are more capable of accommodating a diversity of meanings than are more detailed or specific symbols.[5] The high level of abstraction found in symbols of community means that they can provide a basis for general agreement and shared affection whereas argument and disagreement would probably break out if the symbols were explicitly linked to specific aspects of social or cultural life. In this sense, community exists in what has been called "an excess of banalities."[6]

So how is community symbolically constructed in Ban Tiam? Certain key terms play a very important role in this process. Interestingly, the modern Thai translation of *community—chumchon—*is infrequently used in Ban Tiam. As we will see, *chumchon* has a quite specific heritage in Thailand, and while it has made its way into local discourse it has not really captured the local imagination. There is, however, a more general term that appears to encapsulate much of the sentiment and sociality that we refer to as community. This term is *suan huam*, which can be translated literally as meaning "the group as a whole," "common," or "collective." Some of the modern force of *suan huam* (or *suan ruam* in central Thai) undoubtedly lies in its long history of use by the Thai state to encourage development "for the common good," but it has now become thoroughly integrated into local systems of representation and evaluation.[7] Within Ban Tiam there is an array of meanings associated with this term, but there is what might be called a core or simplified meaning that underpins the term's use. In this simplified sense, stripped of all ambiguity, the *suan huam* denotes a morally desirable domain of common endeavor. Activities falling within this *suan huam* domain include, for example, taking up positions on the village's various committees, attending meetings, contributing labor to public works, contributing to the management or maintenance of irrigation systems, assisting with the organization of public activities, participating in festivals and collective rituals, assisting with food preparation at funerals and other large gatherings, and voluntary work for the various village welfare associations. These *suan huam* activities are typically locally based and oriented toward the village (*ban*, another key term in discussions of community). Broadly inclusive kinship terms are also part of this constellation of meaning. The most common such term is *pho mae phi nong* (parents and siblings), which is often paired with *ban haw* (our village) to convey a general sense of localized solidarity and interdependence. *Suan huam* is also symbolically close to ideas about tradition (*prapheni*), and many *suan huam* activities are routinely justified in terms of their role in the maintenance of tradition. Conversely, one of the most common ways in which the decline of the *suan huam* is expressed is in terms of a decline in traditional practice.

The *suan huam* is a very special domain of activity, marked by moral desirability but practical ambivalence. Many of the projects examined in the previous chapter base their often fragile claims to legitimacy on the idea that they are contributing to morally valued *suan huam* pursuits. A useful way of understanding this moral dimension, and the tensions it creates, is by examining the distinction that villagers often draw between activities that carry the symbolism of *suan huam* virtue and those that do not. Consider this statement from Tor, one of Ban Tiam's assistant headmen:

> I do a lot of work for the community [*ngan suan huam*]. It takes a lot of time but my family doesn't get much benefit. The headman likes to come and ask me to help with village affairs but sometimes I have to tell him I can't. I've got debts. I have to send my children to school. So how can I sit around and make [organic] fertilizer like some of the others? They say that I don't make enough sacrifice [*sia sala*] but how can I? I just have too much work of my own [*ngan suan tua*] to do and I just can't fully contribute to the community.

Tor's reservations about the *suan huam* domain are based on the tension it creates with the private *suan tua* domain. As Tor's statement shows, the term *suan tua* refers to matters of the individual, household, and family. There is a commonly expressed sense in which *suan huam* activities are seen as diverting time, labor, money, and other resources away from this more private domain. As such, the *suan huam* has the moral force of altruism, and participation in *suan huam* activities is often spoken of as involving some level of sacrifice (*sia sala*). Here there are close parallels with the broader Buddhist emphasis on the moral value of the "selfless giving of gifts."[8] Those who sacrifice their *suan tua* pursuits are regarded as the appropriate occupants of leadership positions within the village, and, when criticized, village leaders often respond indignantly by referring to the extent of the sacrifices they have made for the *suan huam* or, like Tor, they excuse themselves on the basis of their heavy *suan tua* responsibilities. In anthropological terms the *suan huam* can be seen as a more or less "sacred" domain that is set off from the "profane" domain of day-to-day private concerns by the act of sacrifice.

This discussion of the cultural process of community creation can help us to understand why the housewives' uniforms were such a productive source of conflict. Put simply, the uniforms were culturally significant; they were totemic symbols of community that sought to condense Ban Tiam's social complexity into a simplified statement of uniformity. They condensed elusive

values of village unity and harmony into a seemingly straightforward material representation. At one stage during the dispute, when I was asked to
contribute money to help defray the cost of the cloth, a senior member of
the housewives' group told me that the uniforms would express the "real
identity" of the village and that the production of them was a genuinely communal activity, unlike many of the other projects, which were set up to generate individual (*suan tua*) benefits. More generally, the housewives' group
itself was saturated with *suan huam* symbolism. Indeed, one of the primary
purposes of the group was to extract housewifely energies from private pursuits within individual families and mobilize them for communal purposes.

Aunt Fon herself had been widely regarded as an exemplar of this form of
sacrifice. In the weeks leading up to her election to the position of president
of the housewives' group in early 2004, there was considerable discussion in
the village about the merits of the likely candidates. The two main candidates
were explicitly assessed in terms of their history of sacrifice for the *suan huam*.
Both contenders were what we would call "active in the community," but in
the view of key village opinion leaders only Aunt Fon was regularly involved
in a way that required sacrifice. She was renowned for her contribution to the
women's group and the health group and was a much sought after cook at
public gatherings such as weddings and funerals. These activities had brought
her little personal benefit as reflected in the parlous state of her own family's
economic position. As Fon herself once lamented, her active role as a village
housewife meant that she often neglected her role as a wife.

So far so good. Fon's strenuous efforts to obtain uniforms for the housewives' group were entirely consistent with the symbolic creation of community and with the moral desirability and personal sacrifice of *suan huam*
pursuits. But she soon fell foul of one of the core points of tension in rural
political society. This tension emerges out of what might be called the modern moral economy of the *suan huam*. As I have shown, in its most simplified domain of meaning the *suan huam* refers to activities that benefit a broad
group of people, ideally the entire village. But in its deployment in the modern world of community development—marked by the proliferation of projects—the *suan huam* is attached to more narrow fields of activity and benefit
based on often temporary coalitions and personalized connections. In this
more fragmented and highly politicized domain the relationship between
suan huam and *suan tua* also starts to shift and the clear distinction starts to
break down. In fact, as I described in the discussion of projects in chapter 5,
there is broad acceptance that many of those who are active in the *suan huam*

will gain some private benefit for themselves or their families, kin, and close friends. As such, while there is a flow of resources—labor in particular— from the *suan tua* to the *suam huam*, there is general acceptance that some level of benefit—cash, goods, status, or influence—will flow back in the other direction. The *suan huam* here is associated less with altruistic giving than calculated exchange. The key is to maintain this exchange at a level that is appropriate and, in particular, avoids overly explicit advantage at the expense of others. Understandably, this is a highly unstable and contested area of public life. In the absence of unambiguous sacrifice the boundary between the sacred domain of the *suan huam* and the profane domain of the *suan tua* becomes blurred. It is at this blurred conceptual frontier that conflict often erupts within Ban Tiam's political society.

There were several aspects of this moral economy that Aunt Fon's uniform project breached. First, her rather autocratic style created the impression that her *suan huam* efforts were excessively oriented toward her own self-aggrandizement and enrichment. Her forthright and assertive personal style made her a very effective operator in the public *suan huam* sphere, but it also directed critical attention toward her more private motivations. The moral authority of her sacrifice for collective enterprise was damaged by the perception that she was primarily interested in using her profile and connections to strengthen her family's economic and social status. Her personal ambitions were particularly resented by a faction of younger housewives in Ban Tiam who felt that they were carrying much of the group's organizational burden while Aunt Fon personally claimed much of the credit. Second, there was the specific concern that financial mismanagement and confusion would provide Aunt Fon with opportunities for excessive diversion of funds to herself and her friends. Concerns had already been raised about the travel expenses that Fon and her colleagues had claimed for the cloth-buying trip to Chiang Mai. This was a highly sensitive issue, as the previous head of the housewives' group had been forced to resign for making excessive personal use of the group's funds. Even Aunt Fon's allocation of five hundred baht to purchase grilled sausage from her sister's market stall—to provide snacks for a group of Ban Tiam's housewives who were traveling to a festival—was condemned as an act of nepotism. Third, and probably most damaging of all, the five-hundred-baht payment was not consistent with the locally calibrated balance between the *suan tua* and *suan huam* domains. Most members of the housewives' group accepted that some level of inconvenience and expense was required to achieve communal objectives, but when a significant cash payment was demanded, the *suan huam* intruded too much into the mundane world of household livelihoods. As a simplified symbol, the uniforms were powerful, but when they became caught up in the money politics of project implementation they became less compelling and much less desirable. This is a good illustration of one of the dilemmas of community: simplification is hard to sustain when the creation of convincing symbols involves the mobilization and distribution of resources. Disinterested moral virtue gives way to very interested calculations of costs and benefits.

FESTIVALS

The conflict about the housewives' uniforms came to a head in early November 2004, in the week or so before the *loi krathong* festival. *Loi krathong* is a famous Thai festival during which small banana-leaf trays (*krathong*) decorated with candles, incense, and flowers are floated (*loi*) on waterways to seek forgiveness from the goddess of the water for using and polluting her precious resource. Over the past few decades, encouraged by the promotional efforts of government agencies, *loi krathong* has become a busy and elaborate festival marked by public displays of local culture and competitions that reward the capable performance of traditional skills. In Ban Tiam, the entrance gateways to household compounds are decorated with coconut fronds, giant banana leaves, woven bamboo screens, and paper lanterns. A small cash prize is awarded to the gateway judged, by a small village committee, to be the most impressively decorated. In the village hall, carefully constructed *krathong* prepared by the young women are placed on public display. Before they are floated in the river that runs through the paddy fields (or in the irrigation canal for those who can't be bothered to take a long nighttime walk) they are judged by representatives of the housewives' group. Outside, temple novices and other young men launch delicate paper balloons into the night sky, held aloft by the hot air from a burning kerosene-soaked segment of banana stem hanging below them. Late at night there are fireworks displays, with Ban Tiam's arsonists competing with hopefuls from other villages. A potent mix of gunpowder, magnesium, iron filings, and other closely guarded mystery ingredients is packed into short, thick bamboo tubes, which are buried in the ground in front of the temple. When they are ignited, the ground vibrates as the minivolcanoes erupt, showering the crowd with white-hot fragments. The winner takes home five hundred baht for his trouble.

The climax of the *loi krathong* festival occurs the following evening when there is an elaborate procession through the streets of the district center. Each of the surrounding villages builds a float and parades behind it, assembling in an open square next to the municipal offices. In Ban Tiam the organizers hoped that the float, and the associated music, dancing, and costumes, would reflect the specific local identity and authentic cultural skills of the village. Aunt Fon's plan was that the Ban Tiam housewives would parade in their new orangey-pink uniforms, carrying lanterns made out of white tissue paper and bamboo. There were prizes on offer for the most impressive village, and the housewives of Ban Tiam hoped to defeat the women of Ban Noi, who were renowned float decorators but had, in years past, been spotted swigging whiskey as they paraded, without decorum, to the municipal hall.

Festivals are occasions when community is self-consciously created. The village itself is conspicuously displayed: special signs of welcome are erected; public spaces are hosed down and swept; stray vegetation that has found its way into the civilized space of the village is slashed and burned; stages are assembled from sheets of wood and metal drums; and the temple is decorated with ribbons, flags, lanterns, and lights. During the festivals, carefully rehearsed traditions that are said to reflect the shared cultural heritage of the residents are enacted: the orchestra performs northern Thai tunes, beautifully dressed and made-up young girls perform graceful dances, and acrobatic boys leap and gyrate with flashing swords. The *suan huam* collective is also expressed and created through the simple fact of assembly: community is created through proximity. Residents assemble for collective rituals and public entertainment; processions of merit makers parade noisily through the village; and ever-present loudspeakers unite participants in a cacophony of prayer, music, and the *suan huam* language of village, kinship, and tradition. At the larger festivals, public assembly often involves raucous, and often lewd, forms of public entertainment with singers and provocatively dressed dancing girls. Public moralists are sometimes prone to interpret this frivolity as an erosion of Buddhist piety, but it is a long-standing element in rural ritual that highlights its exceptional character.

Émile Durkheim understood what was going on during events like this very well when he wrote that ritual assembly creates a "sacred" state of collective concentration.[9] This state is sacred not because it is holy or revered but because it is set apart from the "profane" world of more scattered and independent day-to-day pursuits. A musical performer at Ban Tiam's great festival, held in March 2003 to celebrate the renovation of the main preaching hall, captured this Durkheimian point very effectively:

> Everyone please come. Come and form processions together. When we don't have festivals we don't see the faces of our relatives. Some people are trading, some people are working, coming and going. But today we will unite to make merit. We will have music. We will lift the low things up high. We will commit to making merit. . . . When we don't have a festival we don't meet. We are drunk with buying and selling and we don't meet. When we have a great festival we come together to meet. . . . Working hard for a living, working hard for whiskey. The grandmother is looking after the grandchildren. If we don't have a festival we don't have merit and we don't have music. Some people are relatives, but they don't visit each other. Now we have problems because we don't meet together. We can come together and have fun as brother and sister. Some people don't talk to each other, but today we will talk together nonstop. . . . We will be together as brothers and sisters, even though we are not born from the same stomach. We will come and help each other. We love unity.

The performer went on to praise the moral virtue of this collective spirit, comparing it to the world outside where young people abandon rice cultivation and their lineage spirits, where the boys dye their hair red, and where girls wear spaghetti-string tops and show off their pierced navels. In Ban Tiam, by contrast, "They have used their tradition to build a new preaching hall. The brothers and sisters from their various houses don't just disappear. They are good, clean hosts and help each other as a group to make merit. And they help each other to protect culture; they dance and have beautiful parades. When the faithful come to make donations they don't argue. Their parades are lots of fun. They are very good people. They don't play cards or have cockfights. They don't play 'high-low.' They are a model village. They even have a foreigner who has come to study them."

So festivals are occasions when a sacred and virtuous state of collective assembly is created. The housewives' uniforms, which were to be worn for the first time during the *loi krathong* festival, were one of many ways in which communal assembly, the temporary withdrawal from private pursuits, and the moral value of collective endeavor were signified. However, there is another important tension here that relates directly to Anthony Cohen's point about the hazards involved in elaborating symbols that function most effectively when they are vague. Festivals are wonderful opportunities for making simplified statements about the virtues of community and collective effort. But staging festivals that are both compelling and satisfying requires careful coordination and the mobilization of substantial resources. Here Durkheim's model of a seemingly spontaneous and clear-cut transition from the profane time of economic pursuit to the sacred time of ceremony starts to become more symbolically complex. As recent analysts of ritual as performance have argued, there are important logistical challenges involved in staging effective and compelling rituals.[10] In Ban Tiam, staging festivals inevitably involves the formation of committees to organize financial contributions from villagers and the mobilization of labor for the many tasks required. This mobilization is made difficult by the fact that festivals are also times when households have to invest time and labor in preparing for their own influx of guests. The bureaucratic elaboration involved in festival organization and the inevitable arguments about logistics, budgets, and labor contributions comprehensively entangle the simplified symbolism of the *suan huam* with the contested micropolitics of resource allocation. Attention, energy, and passion come to be focused on the *suan huam* as a domain of compulsion, negotiation, political promotion, and budgetary shenanigans. Put simply, during elaborate festivals like *loi krathong*, community strains under its own organizational weight.

The dispute about the uniforms was one component in the very typical process of contestation that arises when the simplified symbolism of festivals confronts their organizational reality. In this sense, festivals are similar to local development projects in that while the appeal to community serves a useful mobilizing and legitimizing function, it can fragment when dealing with organizational specificities. Aunt Fon was at the heart of some of these tensions. As the *loi krathong* festival drew near, several younger members of the housewives' group took out their frustrations about the uniforms by condemning Aunt Fon's autocratic organization of the festival itself. Fon wanted the village to produce a float for the major parade in the form of a small northern Thai house. Float design is a sensitive business, and there is vigorous competition with other villages in Pad Siew Municipality, spurred on by the lure of cash prizes. Fon felt that her innovative design would provide an ideal platform on which Ban Tiam residents could display their handicraft and construction skills. But others disagreed. As one woman said to me, "It's *loi krathong*, so the float must be a *krathong*." Rival designs were hastily drawn up on a blackboard in the village hall. Eventually Fon's plan was abandoned, and a *krathong*, resembling a giant lotus with huge pink petals, was produced (fig. 13). Another dispute broke out over the selection of the "princess" who would sit on top of the giant *krathong* as it was paraded through the streets. There was a strong rumor that Aunt Fon was planning to select the daughter of a close friend. There were calls for a more open and transparent selection process. Several other prepubescent claimants to the title were nominated. With ill feeling gathering pace, there was a real risk that many members of the housewives' group—especially some of its most active younger members— would boycott both the labor-intensive preparations and the *loi krathong* procession itself. On the first evening of serious work on the giant *krathong* only about twenty villagers came to help, despite several pleading announcements made over the public address system. Withdrawal of labor from a communal enterprise is a common strategy for expressing disapproval, not with the collective writ large (the simplified *suan huam*) but with particular people in it. In this case it was particularly crucial, as some of the women who were most annoyed about Fon's actions were also some of the most skilled in the handicrafts—typically involving the intricate folding and pinning of banana

FIGURE 13. Final preparations for the *loi krathong* procession. (Photo by the author.)

leaves—required to produce the cultural paraphernalia for the *loi krathong* procession. With tensions mounting, the village abbot was moved to intervene, calling for calm and solidarity in one of his sermons. Drawing from his rich stock of scriptural metaphor, he compared the housewives' group to a football team, saying that all eleven players needed to be on the field and playing for the team as a whole, not just for themselves. "Let's sort out the problems after *loi krathong*," he urged. "After that we can dissolve the housewives' assembly and elect a new one."

LEGIBILITY, ELIGIBILITY, AND THE STATE

Housewives' associations were first established in Thailand in the 1970s, as an initiative of the Thai government aimed at promoting women's participation in rural development.[11] This was part of a more general trend in government administration in Thailand, which emphasized "community" as a basis for security, welfare, and development. This morally desirable community has come to play an important part in the development of rural Thailand's modern political society.

According to the historian Craig J. Reynolds, the Thai word for community (*chumchon*) is a recent invention, having gained widespread currency only in the second half of the twentieth century.[12] He suggests that *chumchon* may have been the invention, in the 1930s, of an aristocratic wordsmith who brought together two preexisting words (*chum,* "to swarm"; *chon,* "living beings") to create a new term that referred to something like "the coming together of people." This was a rather mechanical coupling, but *chumchon* was to take on much more alluring connotations when the Thai bureaucracy adopted it in the 1950s and 1960s. As the Thai government's interest in community development flourished in the postwar era, the idea of *chumchon* brought together disparate agendas of cultural modernization, economic development, and national security into a simplified symbolic framework. Strong local community came to be seen as a defense against the spread of communism, the undesirable flip side of communal sentiment. American aid money and counterinsurgency advisers, often working through the powerful Ministry of Interior, encouraged community development initiatives within the Thai bureaucracy. In 1962, a Department of Community Development was established, complete with its own mouthpiece, the *Community Development Bulletin.* As Reynolds writes, "[C]ommunity (*chumchon*) acquired an identifiable history in the Thai bureaucracy in the name of administrative

units charged with managing rural development programs, training officials
and youth, improving the well-being of the community, rural productivity,
family income and village industry, as well as health services, and education.... The aims of these programs were strategic as much as for the better-
ment of society."[13]

This legacy has continued to the present day, nurtured by several new ideological influences. Between 1970 and 2000, Thailand received over US$13
billion in international aid, much of it directed to rural development.[14] Officials in the many Thai government agencies that partnered with these aid
initiatives quickly learned to adopt the new international orthodoxy of community participation. This was a timely strategy for the Thai government as
it attempted to neutralize the political potency of farmers' organizations
by appropriating their language of local rights and empowerment. Interest
by academics and NGOs in "community culture" also contributed to this
discursive evolution of ideas about *chumchon*. According to the proponents
of community culture, locally specific forms of social organization, economic
activity, and cultural practice provided a more sustainable basis for rural
development than the single-minded pursuit of market opportunity. Some of
these alternative ideas were crystallized in the sufficiency-economy philosophy of the Thai king, which gained popularity in the wake of the 1997 financial crisis. According to the king's theory, rural communities should prioritize
subsistence production and localized exchange in order to develop sustainable livelihoods that are not overly exposed to the hazardous excesses of
the market. In all their different ways, these approaches propose community
as an antidote to the amoral individualism of the modern market and to the
social disruption and environmental destruction that the individual pursuit
of prosperity produces. As a result of these various influences, development
has come to be ideologically embedded in strong communities with virtuous
leaders and vibrant traditions.

In Ban Tiam, the word *chumchon* is infrequently used except when referring
to specific administrative structures to which the term has become attached.
However, although the word itself may not have gained much local currency, official ideas about *chumchon* have become productively entangled
with local ideas about *suan huam* values of collective endeavor and individual sacrifice. As in many parts of rural Thailand, the villagers in Ban Tiam
now clearly recognize that engagement with state development initiatives
requires some commitment to the symbols and institutional forms of community. They understand that grants won't be made without representative

committees, resources won't be allocated unless they are for the benefit of a group, and project proposals will be all the more compelling if they are rooted in commonly held traditions. As we have seen, projects are usually the preferred vehicle for this productive linking of community and development. Community-based projects have become iconic of development, even if their contribution to livelihood improvement is often quite modest. There is a commonly observed dilemma here: participation in development often requires sacrifices for the *suan huam* that divert time and money away from personal livelihood pursuits that are often more lucrative. Yet, despite the regular grumbling about the level of sacrifice required to support collective endeavors, the community remains a morally valued site of development. It is commonplace for people in Ban Tiam to make comments along the lines of "If we don't have unity we can't have development"; "We are a strong community with strong traditions, and that's why the government wants to invest here"; and "If we don't learn to manage our conflicts better, we will lose our development projects."

The symbolic cross-fertilization between local performances of community and government administration is particularly evident during festivals such as *loi krathong*. These festivals have become an important occasion for interaction between the modern state's community development agenda and more localized expressions of unity, communal devotion, and the virtue of *suan huam* pursuits. In addition to the long-standing practices of private feasting, public Buddhist ritual, and sacrificial merit making, modern festivals often involve massed assembly in the presence of government officials, usually on the grounds of provincial, district, or municipal offices or at the homes of local notables. Particularly important assemblies occur during the new-year celebration when the traditional practice of respectful visits to village elders is now routinely extended to government officials, ranging from the headman and his assistants to the local member of parliament and the provincial governor. During village festivals, groups of villagers make respectful visits to the village leaders where they present them with gifts and receive food, drink, motivational words, and election promises in return. At the larger district and provincial events, large crowds gather in front of government officials and their entourages, who are auspiciously displayed on vinyl couches beneath the shelter of canvas awnings. Emerging from the shade, the officials deliver cliché-laden speeches about the desirability of harmony and cooperation, the preservation of local traditions, the importance of environmental protection, and the insight and wisdom of the king's approach to rural development. Those who are facing upcoming elections may use the occasions to emphasize the contributions they have made to local development and to not so subtly hint at the generous size of future budget allocations.

On the final evening of the 2004 *loi krathong* festival, after a long parade through the streets, the residents of each village assembled in front of a large stage erected by the municipal administration. There were cultural performances, a display of locally produced fireworks, and a long address from an exceptionally nervous Mayor Somsak, who was wearing an iridescent pink shirt. "I am glad to be presiding at the *loi krathong* festival today," he proclaimed. "This is our old tradition and needs to be preserved for later generations. We need to light lanterns for three days and three nights and dress in local costumes. It is our common responsibility to preserve this tradition. I thank everyone who has been involved in organizing this event, including every public office and village in the municipality. We all have the responsibility to continue this old tradition." These were fine words, but there were complaints from Ban Tiam because they were assembled closest to the increasingly rancid toilet block throughout the proceedings, surely a disrespectful way to treat the village that, after all, was the mayoral home.

In many respects these events are clearly an example of governing practice, whereby the population is disciplined, demarcated, categorized, and rendered legible in the eyes of a supervisory state. This is particularly evident at the larger events where the administrative structuring of the population is very clearly marked. The representatives from each village assemble in a neat row, usually headed by a young, attractive, and elaborately dressed woman carrying the village sign. Ethnic distinctions are highlighted with costumes and carefully prepared banners declaring local identities. Village-specific traditions are proudly displayed during the cultural shows. Local legends are recalled in costumes, dances, and carefully built displays. On these ritual occasions, the rural population is, quite literally, laid out in a culturally legible grid for the inspection and appraisal of government officials. The modern developmental vision, based on ideas of communal solidarity under the leadership of the state, is publicly enacted. Such assemblies are the ritual counterpart of the techniques of demarcation, registration, and enumeration that the modern state uses to define appropriate targets for administration and development by placing people in identifiable collectivities. As James C. Scott has famously argued, it is through such processes of "simplification"—and remember that symbols of community are usually simplified symbols—that the state renders the population legible for the business of government.[15] Confronted with the bewildering complexity of the social system, the state mobilizes the local population to represent itself in simplified totemic form.

These are important observations, but an emphasis on the technology of government provides an incomplete interpretation of the political dynamic underlying these assemblies. Alongside the state's desire for legibility, we have to consider the desire of the governed population for eligibility: eligibility for grants, services, development, and political representation. One of the modern objectives of the symbolic construction of community is to create an entity that is an eligible participant in the new fiscal relationship that has emerged between the subsidizing state and the rural economy. The formation of modern community is not a strategy to preserve convoluted institutional forms that will bamboozle tax collectors and cadastral surveyors; rather it is a strategy to present the state with a simplified framework for disbursement of its development resources. In this sense, festival assemblies in the presence of government officials are ritualized processes of reciprocal recognition. The local social system is stripped of its complexity and represented in clear governmental categories, while the state is represented as a benevolent supporter of local livelihoods and traditions. This ritual relationship is underlined by the exchange of gifts. Villagers bring food, samples of local produce, betel nuts, fermented tea, alcohol, and contributions to officially sponsored projects (fig. 14). Sometimes the offerings made by the villagers are strikingly similar to the offerings made to guardian spirits. At the new-year celebrations in 2008, a group of villagers presented the district officer with a traditional set of tribute objects—small "trees" displaying wax flowers, candles, betel nut, and fruit. In return the state provides food prizes for the best cultural displays and direct handouts of cash or other essential items (such as blankets) to the elderly and socially disadvantaged. If the weather is particularly hot, fire engines may be mobilized to rain refreshing water on the patient crowds. The *loi krathong* procession took place at night, so escaped the dousing, but the distribution of cash was a highlight of the evening. Ban Tiam picked up a prize for its musical performance, but, unfortunately, the major prize for the best float and procession went to its rival, the village of Ban Noi. Its dragon-style float was certainly impressive, but surely, some argued, Ban Noi's heavy reliance on foam cutouts was contrary to the traditional spirit of *loi krathong*.

In most general terms, the housewives' uniforms can be seen as quite literally embodying this ritualized approach to local state formation. They were a deliberate attempt to make the village of Ban Tiam more legible to the

FIGURE 14. Presenting gifts of garlic to the district head, Pad Siew District, Thailand. (Photo by the author.)

community development gaze of state agencies and officials. Dressing up in generically distinctive uniforms is an important component of the collaborative rituals of governance that punctuate the Thai calendar. The modern administrative and fiscal dimensions of this practice are new, but it reflects the long-standing use of textiles to mark community membership and make "outward expressions of allegiance" to traditional chiefs.[16] It was the mismanagement of this exercise in social legibility and eligibility that, more than anything else, bought about Aunt Fon's demise. As development has come to be embedded in the normative context of community, ritualized displays of village-based solidarity, cooperation, and tradition are important components in the contemporary currency of stateship. Fon's failure to deal effectively in this symbolic currency was, ultimately, more significant than her shortcomings in actual financial management. Her failure to deliver timely, affordable, and unifying uniforms for the housewives' group compromised Ban Tiam's ongoing attempts to present itself as an eligible recipient of government administration, service provision, and classification. In Ban Tiam's modern political society this was a fatal flaw.

THE ENDURING BUT FRAGILE COMMUNITY

The geographer Jonathan Rigg is an astute observer of rural transformation in Southeast Asia. In a series of publications he has shown that rural livelihoods have become increasingly diversified and multisited. The modern mobility of labor, capital, and ideas has broken down old distinctions between rural and urban areas. One consequence of this, according to Rigg, is a reduction in the importance of community as external economic and social connections shift identities and aspirations away from the village. In a recent article written with co-researchers, he illustrates this erosion of community in a cluster of villages in Thailand's central plains.[17] The article documents the social and economic changes that have occurred in these villages following the establishment of a large industrial estate nearby. This has brought about a dramatic decline in the importance of agriculture, rising land prices, and an influx of migrant workers who live in dormitories established by enterprising locals. These villages "are now 'connected' in a manner that would have been inconceivable a few decades ago." These connections have improved physical access and created better opportunities for employment and enterprise. They have also created modern "desires, aspirations, norms, expectations and outlooks . . . which are profoundly different from those they have displaced."[18] And, perhaps most important, modern connections have reduced the relevance of community:

> Informants told us that with road development, came *kwaam charoen*, or "progress," and this led to rifts between households in the village and also caused the village "community" to be socially and physically divided. Roads replaced canals, and road transport replaced travel by foot and boat. No longer did villagers have to pass fellow villagers' houses as they walked to the fields or to the market. Over time, villagers lost touch with their community as an entity; strangers, previously so quickly and easily noticed, can today walk through the village undetected and unheralded. Fences and iron window gratings have become essential to protect the inhabitants and their wealth from thieves and other criminals. . . . [I]t is becoming more and more difficult to think of these villages as "communities" in the sense that there is a historical

and social covenant that links the people who live in the geographical space we call Tambon [Subdistrict] Khan Haam.[19]

Rigg and his coauthors are certainly not alone in describing the decline of rural community in the face of modernization and commercialization. Indeed, this anxiety has been one of the enduring preoccupations of modern social science, and it has featured prominently in accounts of the dissolution of the peasantry. But there are also more optimistic perspectives, which point to the political and social resilience of rural community. One line of thinking is that the elaboration of symbols of communal attachment can be a defensive response to the experience of modernity. Community is one aspect of the emphasis on boundaries that occurs as contact between different worldviews intensifies. In Thailand this is the defensive or resistant local community of civil society activism, community culture, and sufficiency economy. In this chapter, however, I have focused on another way in which community can endure in a context of modern interconnection. I have argued that a particular type of community is shaped at the intersection between local values and state development policy. Modern rural community is a symbolically constructed domain where external powers are drawn in and combined with local ideas about sacrifice and the moral virtue of communal pursuits. This modern community is a symbolically simplified domain of reciprocal recognition where the state and the population mutually create governmental categories that are both legible and eligible.

This may seem like a rather utilitarian, perhaps even cynical, use of community. Sometimes this is surely the case. But it would be a mistake to ignore the moral content that makes appeals to community compelling. As Partha Chatterjee notes, "[T]here are many imaginative possibilities for transforming an empirically assembled population group into the morally constituted form of a community."[20] In Ban Tiam, this moral content is not associated with the modern word for community, *chumchon*, but with *suan huam*, the collective. In its simplified form, the *suan huam* is a domain of altruistic sacrifice for the common good. It is morally contrasted with the more private and self-interested *suan tua* domain. As a vague and simplified symbolic representation, the *suan huam* encourages a sense of localized belonging that forms a basis for various types of cooperative enterprise. In the contemporary middle-income context of state support, the modern development enterprise has been culturally embedded in this cooperative domain. Development has taken on some of the sacred aura of the collective. It is no coincidence that, on the occasion of his ordination, the controversial village abbot took on a new name, one that means "patient and gentle leader of development." At a major festival held in 2003 to celebrate extensive temple renovations, a performer sang his praises, very clearly illustrating the symbolic intersection among *suan huam* virtues, the avowal of *suan tua* pursuits, and the moral virtue of community development:

> Our abbot is a virtuous and kind man. He has the patience to develop the temple. Even when it's rainy or windy, he does not give up. He has many followers from many villages, and they respect him highly. He lives in the temple and uses donations to develop it. He thinks constantly about construction and renovation. And he doesn't take any money at all out of the temple. He doesn't concern himself with commerce. He is a man with a lot of money. But he uses the money for the renovation of the temple. He doesn't take the money for any other purpose. He uses it to restore the preaching hall of the temple.

Of course, the social and economic changes described by Rigg and his colleagues make *suan huam* mobilization more challenging in practical terms, but the increasingly exceptional nature of communal assembly also reinforces its moral value. As the events in Ban Tiam show, the *suan huam* is a constantly challenging work in progress. It is an elusive sentiment that is easily lost in the tangle of micropolitics. The symbolic construction of community is made particularly challenging by the fact that it is constantly caught up in the complex transactions that are woven through rural political society. The simplified symbolic space of community has become crowded with development projects, categories of administration, and desires for productive relationships with the state. Community is both energized and compromised by the trappings of modern political society. Effectively deployed, simplifying symbols are compelling, but they are undermined by elaboration. In the symbolic domain the sacred relies on simplification and unelaborated imagery. In political society, as Aunt Fon found, the devil is in the detail.

7

The Rural Constitution

So far in this book, my exploration of Ban Tiam's political society has addressed "political" issues in broad terms. I have examined political society as being made up of specific contexts in which people cultivate connections with sources of power in the spiritual, commercial, and bureaucratic world. In this chapter I move to a much more familiar version of political behavior: that which is associated with elections and party politics. Many commentators are inclined to see this domain of activity as being very different from the more informal and socially embedded forms of political behavior that I have considered so far. For political scientists, electoral contests are a central element in a more formal "political society" in which organized political parties aggregate the views of citizens into policies that are implemented by winning control of the legislature. Anthropologists, and others similarly attuned to the grass roots, often tend to see party-dominated elections as a procedural exercise that has little meaningful relationship with local power dynamics. But in examining relationships with power in Ban Tiam, the formal-informal distinction that underlies these perspectives is not particularly useful. Candidates in Thailand's formal elections cannot escape the informal political culture in which they are embedded. Local political culture and formal electoral culture are closely woven together. This political culture is poorly understood, largely because existing approaches to rural electoral behavior often resort to either disparagement of the ignorance and parochialism of downtrodden rural voters or wishful thinking about nonelectoral social movements that will challenge the hegemony of capitalism and the state.

Discussions of rural political culture have taken on a particular salience in Thailand in recent years. Following the overthrow of Thaksin Shinawatra's government in September 2006, the coup makers based their claim to legitimacy on the argument that the Thaksin government's electoral mandate was illegitimate because it had been bought from an unsophisticated and easily manipulated rural electorate. The denial of electoral legitimacy was fundamental in justifying the removal of a government that had garnered strong electoral mandates. And, with a further election scheduled for late 2006, those seeking to defend the coup relied heavily on the argument that the electorate was in no position to make a reasonable judgment about the Thaksin government's well-publicized faults. Faced with the likelihood that Thaksin's party would win yet another election, the coup makers argued that the army's intervention was the only way to resolve deep political divisions. The fact that the electorate continued to support Thaksin was, in the eyes of many of his opponents, clear evidence of voter irrationality and the ongoing failure of the electoral process.

There is nothing new about this argument, nor about its use in justifying military interference. Political commentators have regularly asserted that the Thai populace, and especially the rural populace, lacks the basic characteristics essential for a modern democratic citizenry and that deficiencies need to be overcome via elite-led education. Accounts of the deficiencies of the voting population often focus on three perceived problems, which draw on well-established discourses about patronage, apolitical peasants, and the dangers of money politics.[1] First, uneducated rural voters are parochial and have little interest in policy issues. Lacking a well-developed sense of national interest, they vote for candidates who can deliver immediate benefits. Second, given their poverty, lack of sophistication, and disinterest in policy, they are readily swayed by the power of money. Vote buying is said to be endemic. Cash distributed by candidates, through networks of local canvassers, is said to play a major role in securing voter loyalty. And third, rural electoral mobilization is achieved via hierarchical ties of patronage whereby local influential figures can deliver blocks of rural votes to their political masters. Studies documenting the political rise of provincial businessmen and godfathers have added considerable strength to this patron-client model of rural political behavior. Within this model there is very little sense of an economically and politically engaged rural electorate that plays an active role in evaluating the personal and policy merits of candidates.

The literature on rural political behavior in Thailand, and elsewhere in the region, provides two main alternatives to this negative perspective on rural political culture. One perspective emphasizes rural people's nonelectoral political mobilization, in cooperation with civil society organizations, to resist the incursions of both state regulation and market commercialization. This approach emphasizes nonelectoral civil society's struggles against infrastructure development, heavy-handed conservation policies, and the commoditization of local resources. Rural people's involvement in protest movements and advocacy coalitions, their commitment to alternative forms of resource management, and their vigorous promotion of local knowledge are regarded as providing a more meaningful basis for political involvement than the occasional expression of opinions via the ballot box.

Does this civil society perspective provide a sound basis for a reappraisal of local political culture? I don't think so. Partly my view is influenced by the specific situation in Ban Tiam itself, where grassroots advocacy organizations have had a very low profile. But there are more fundamental issues involved. In rural Thailand, participation in these types of organizations is, in overall demographic terms, very modest, and their influence outside specific sites of high-profile resource conflict is very limited. More important, many of the rural advocacy campaigns waged by civil society organizations are based on what I have called a "limited legitimacy," which relies on an imagery of local cultural identity, self-sufficient agriculture, and ecologically friendly lifestyles.[2] This is an empowerment framework that is largely disconnected from the livelihood aspirations of Thailand's commercially connected middle-income peasantry, and it struggles to account for rural electoral support for policies that promote external inputs into local economic development. Faced with the middle-income peasantry's apparent betrayal of communitarian values, civil society advocates tend to resort to the standard imagery of a rural populace seduced by money politics and manipulated by the electoral process.

A second alternative approach to rural political behavior focuses on "everyday politics" rather than organized social movements. The concept of everyday politics draws on James C. Scott's famous study of the "weapons of the weak," discussed at the end of chapter 4, which directed attention to the informal, day-to-day, and often surreptitious ways in which people engage with prevailing structures of power and systems of resource distribution. The political scientist Benedict J. Kerkvliet uses this general approach in his study of the subtle and unspectacular politics of daily life in a rural village in the Philippines.[3] Kerkvliet's aim is to counter the prevailing view in the

Philippines—and in Thailand as well—that political behavior is to be understood in terms of the operation of hierarchically organized "factions" that mobilize voters to serve the electoral purposes of the elite. Adopting a broad and inclusive perspective on what is regarded as political behavior, Kerkvliet writes about the unorganized forms of "everyday politics" that tend to fall beneath the radar of much conventional political analysis. This broader view of political society embraces the "debates, conflicts, decisions, and cooperation among individuals, groups, and organizations regarding the control, allocation, and use of resources and the values and ideas underlying those activities."[4] These debates and values are explored via the informal and everyday politics of complaint, theft, gossip, avoidance, sabotage, denunciation, and, at times, outright protest. A key dimension of this analysis is a concern with the alternative sets of values that inform day-to-day political action. Building on Scott's earlier analysis of "moral economy," Kerkvliet identifies a range of values related to assistance, basic needs, security, and dignity that "interact" and "tussle" with the values that underpin capitalist property and market relations.[5] In a later study of everyday politics and the demise of collectivization in Vietnam, Kerkvliet found that these seemingly inchoate political values and actions transformed government policy because they directly influenced the many state officials who interacted with peasants and also because everyday political actions affected economic outcomes that mattered to national leaders.[6]

An emphasis on everyday politics is an approach that I find much more promising in exploring the role of elections in rural Thailand's political society. Its strength lies in its focus on localized day-to-day debates about resource allocation and political values rather than the more exceptional cases of mobilization under the banner of civil society organizations. It also directly challenges the view that rural voting behavior can be understood in terms of an uninformed and unintelligent peasantry mobilized to serve the political interests of elite patrons. The concept of everyday politics places local political values at the center of analysis and invites exploration of how these values have shifted since the moral economy values of the subsistence-oriented peasantry were proposed by Scott. However, I propose a modification to Kerkvliet's approach: I am less inclined than he is to draw a distinction between "everyday politics" and the formal politics of electoral contests.[7] The regularity of elections and the density of participation in electoral matters render the distinction untenable. In Ban Tiam there were thirteen local and national elections between early 2004 and the end of 2010.[8] Voter turnout is

usually high (around 80 percent) and, more important, there are a considerable number of people in the village (by my count at least twenty) who are
active in this "formal" political arena. Given this temporal and social density
of political participation, discussions about elections, candidates, policies,
and campaigns are a regular feature of day-to-day life. Electoral contests are
embedded in local social relationships and are played out through a myriad
of everyday interpersonal interactions. In Ban Tiam there is a very blurred
line indeed between the seemingly official world of party membership, political rallies, and ballots and the many day-to-day social contexts in which
power is invoked and evaluated.

The local values that inform the everyday politics of elections can be usefully thought of as a "rural constitution."[9] In the most general terms, constitutions regulate the exercise of government: they define government structure,
attribute roles, and distribute power. As a result they authorize the legitimate
use of government power and constrain its illegitimate manifestations, often
providing a range of protections for the governed population. While most
attention focuses on the formal constitution, political advocates and constitutional scholars recognize that written charters are situated within a broader
field of tradition, morality, and cultural orientation. This contextual framework is what I am referring to as the rural constitution.[10] In Ban Tiam's rural
political society this uncodified set of political values regulates, constrains,
and legitimates the exercise of political power. It sets out the desired type
of political representative, proposes ideal types of political behavior, and
proscribes various forms of abuse of public office. This constitutional role is
evident both in local government elections and in electoral assessments of
the national government.

LOCAL ELECTORAL CULTURE

Localism

Unlike some versions of localism promoted by civil society organizations,
Ban Tiam's localism does not seek to resist the state. Rather, it seeks to draw
the state into a socially and culturally legible frame of meaning. What is
important in Ban Tiam's localism is that political society's relations with the
state are mediated by appropriately embedded local actors.

One of the most commonly expressed aspects of Ban Tiam's rural constitution is the view that it is better to elect a local than a nonlocal person. This
is usually expressed as a preference for candidates from *ban haw*. Literally,

ban haw can be translated as "our village," but *ban* is a delightfully malleable word and its spatial referent of belonging can readily adjust to the different scales of electoral competition. In local government elections, localism provides an explicit framework for political discussion and debate. Candidates are readily assessed in terms of the strength of their local linkages, which are highly legible and amenable to commentary within the electorate. The importance of localism is enhanced by the fact that state investment in rural development and the decentralization of a large portion of government finances to local government has heightened budgetary competition between villages. As one villager told me, seeing the municipal assembly fall under the control of another village would be like "waiting for an air drop of food and then watching the parachute float down on the other side of the hill."

In fact Ban Tiam has been a successful contender in these local resource contests. The previous subdistrict head was a Ban Tiam resident, and he went on to become the district's provincial assemblyman, a position he lost in the election of early 2004 (fig 15). Most of his supporters in Ban Tiam expressed their support for him in terms of their desire to "help" someone from the same village. As Grandmother Hong said just before the provincial assembly election, "I'm helping one of us; whatever happens he's one of us." When Mayor Somsak, another Ban Tiam resident, stood for reelection in 2006 he derived considerable support from the view that it was only logical to vote for a fellow villager. He was also able to expand the range of his localist support as a result of close kinship connections in at least two other villages in the municipality. By contrast, other mayoral candidates were weakened by perceptions that they were insufficiently locally embedded. This clearly applied to one candidate who was a former government official and had been posted to the area for only three years. But even long-term residents could be judged as non-local. One mayoral candidate, Dr. Tanet, had distributed aprons advertising one of his businesses to vendors in the market. When I asked one of the small restaurant owners if her apron signaled support for Tanet she responded that "he came and gave them out, so we decided to wear them. He is standing for election to be mayor. But I don't know if he will get elected. He is not a local. He has lived here for twenty years. Most people know him. But he is from somewhere else."

Some of the subtleties and shifting coordinates of localism were demonstrated by the Senate election of 2006. Of all the elections discussed, this was the least local and posed particular challenges for a localist approach to electoral decisions. There were thirty-nine candidates for the five provincial

FIGURE 15. Vote counting in the 2004 provincial assembly election, Pad Siew District, Thailand. The three baskets are for "no vote marked," "spoiled votes," and "formal votes." (Photo by the author.)

seats, and only a small number of them had tenuous ties to the local area. A typical comment in the lead-up to the poll was that there "wasn't even one person standing from Pad Siew District, only people from other places." Without the orientation of local affiliation many voters indicated that they had difficulty making a choice, and a good number spent a long time reading the board outside the polling booth where the candidates' profiles were displayed. Some village officials predicted a large number of spoiled or frivolous votes, and, possibly, a low voter turnout. In fact, the vote went relatively smoothly—although the informal vote was somewhat higher than usual—but the officials' comments did reflect some anxiety about the socially and spatially disconnected nature of the candidates.

Voters are flexible and pragmatic, and sentiments of local belonging are highly malleable. Overall the Senate results from Ban Tiam accorded with a broadly defined localist logic. Two candidates each received thirty-eight of the votes cast in the village. One of these was predicted to do well because he was well known, as the younger brother of a former member of parliament for the province (he was also said to be Thaksin's man). The other was a former resident of the district and a former provincial assemblyman. As the only candidate who had lived in Pad Siew District he could have been expected to poll better, but preelection sentiment was that his connections to the district had been very limited in recent years and his work as an assembly-man had produced no real local benefits. The next most strongly supported candidate (thirty-six votes) was a generous supporter of a nearby temple. Her recent history of merit making in the area was highly regarded, as was her close connection with a senior opposition party figure. Other candidates receiving local support were also locally situated in various ways: one had local business connections through his moneylending activities ("good con-nections, lots of money, but perhaps not trustworthy"); another hosted a popular radio show ("lots of people here know him so they will want to help him"); and another, with a "famous" surname, had good connections among the district's cockfighting fraternity (and he had supported the construction of a cockfighting facility in a neighboring district). Interestingly, Thaksin's sister-in-law, who carried the famous Shinawatra surname but had no signifi-cant local connections, received only three of Ban Tiam's votes.

One of the underlying motivations for what I am referring to as localism is a desire for political legibility. As I argued in the previous chapter, it is not just the state that seeks to create simplified and legible structures of gover-nance. As part of the ongoing process of reciprocal recognition, electors themselves seek to locate political candidates in a simplified framework of inside (ban haw) versus outside. This is a morally charged framework in which the spatially flexible concept of ban haw is associated with suan huam values of approachability, social familiarity, linguistic ease, and commitment to local institutions. But localism does not provide a simple template for political decisions. Partly this is because it operates in ambiguous ways and there are competing claims to varying degrees of localness. Within Ban Tiam there is real concern that the large number of politically engaged people will split the local vote and reduce the political influence of the village in munici-pal affairs. Quite simply, there are too many locals to choose from. Another key factor mitigating the purchase of localist values is that local legibility also often involves an intimate awareness of the human frailty of electoral contenders. The symbolic force of the simplified ban haw categorization can be attenuated when it is set alongside the reality of interpersonal dis-putes, jealousy, resentment, and gossip. Unsavory rumors swirled around one prominent local politician: his family members had been involved in a violent brawl, he regularly used his official car for private business, and he had been arrested for marijuana possession but managed to bribe his way out of a formal charge. The local reality of interpersonal conflict and character assassination opens up fissures that can provide a basis for nonlocalist forms of political orientation. In brief, localism provides one flexible framework for political decision making, but local social life is simply too complex for it to be used as a one-dimensional template for political action.

Support

Many accounts of localism in Thailand focus on the role of local resources and locally oriented livelihoods in acting as a buffer against the disruptions caused by the external economy. These versions of localism do not necessarily advocate disengagement from external economic systems, but they often argue for "looking inwards for a basis to resist the destructive forces of globalization."[11] Again, the form of localism that I am describing has a rather different emphasis: it is based on maximizing support provided as part of the Thai state's long-term fiscal transformation, from taxing the rural economy to subsidizing it. In Ban Tiam locally embedded political representatives are not valued simply because they embody local resources or capabilities but also because they are more likely to direct externally derived resources to locally valued initiatives. They are culturally and socially familiar figures with whom villagers feel relatively confident to negotiate for material benefits. Securing access to external resources is a key element of Ban Tiam's outward-oriented localism.

In Ban Tiam's rural constitution there is a strong expectation that political representatives will financially support their constituency. In discussions of Thailand's political system, the issue of financial support is clouded by the specter of vote buying. I have no doubt that political candidates make direct cash payments to voters in Ban Tiam—even I was a beneficiary of Thaksin's munificence (one hundred baht) when I attended a Thai Rak Thai party meeting. But it is important to place direct cash handouts to electors in the broader context of the array of material assistance that is expected of political representatives and other well-resourced people seeking to demonstrate their social standing and embeddedness in local circuits of exchange. In general terms, direct assistance from candidates and elected representatives is consistent with the view that leaders should "nurture" their followers. The word that is often used in these contexts is *liang*, which has a broad range of meanings ranging from the care that parents provide for a child to the provision of food at a festival or the support that a businessman provides to his employees and clients. Political leaders, like other sources of power, are domesticated by idioms of nurture and reciprocal support. The instrumental language of vote buying is often misleading when it is used to describe these idioms because, in anthropological terms, they are part of a gift rather than a commodity relationship. Gifts create enduring, incalculable, and multistranded relationships whereas commodity exchanges are one-off transactions. In Ban Tiam culturally valued forms of material assistance provided by political leaders include personal loans, donations to temples, support for household rituals, payment of (appropriately inflated) expenses for attendance at meetings, payment of children's educational expenses, provision of low-cost transport services, and support for budgetary shortfalls in local development projects. Here are four brief examples:

- Prior to Ban Tiam's headman election in early 2004, a group of women was invited to represent the village at a cultural festival in a neighboring subdistrict. Transport was provided by one of the candidates, Jakkrit, who owned one of the few pickup trucks in the village. He also provided modest support to cover the women's expenses for the day, but they considered this inadequate. He was accused of being stingy, and the other main candidate was approached for a contribution. He refused, saying it could be regarded as vote buying.
- In March 2004 Ban Tiam held a great festival (*poi luang*) to celebrate the renovation of the temple's preaching hall and kitchen. A substantial portion of the festival's expenses were covered by the richest man in the village who was also the district's representative on the provincial assembly. The great festival was timed to take place just after the election for the new provincial assembly, in which he was seeking reelection. He came under some pressure to provide the donation because his main electoral rival had supported Ban Tiam's participation in a district-level festival held a few months earlier.
- Aunt Fon, who we met in the previous chapter, obtained a personal loan from the Thai Rak Thai candidate in the national election when she experienced financial difficulties as a result of crop failure. The local rumor was that this was an important factor in her becoming a canvasser for the Thai Rak Thai party. Later she received a mobile phone for her efforts, but this came to grief when her husband drunkenly dropped it into the toilet.
- Khruawan was a candidate in the 2006 Senate election. For some time she had been building up connections in Pad Siew District by patronizing highly regarded temples and supporting religious construction projects. In November

2005, I attended a major temple festival in a village about ten kilometers from Ban Tiam. Khruawan was the major sponsor of the festival, but her donation was actually presented to the temple by the district's new provincial assembly-man. I was told that Khruawan was simultaneously making donations in every district of the province.

These various forms of assistance are locally assessed in terms of a range of interlinked political values that address issues of personal status, capabil-ity, and morality. There is a widespread view that those with an established financial position are in the best position to hold political office. In part this is due to the obvious personal financial demands made on local and national politicians. Being a politician involves the building of charisma and frequent material demonstrations "that they have not forgotten the villagers." This is an expensive process, requiring regular investment in the form of donations, loans, and attendance at many social events. The preference for politicians with established financial positions is also informed by the common view that they are less likely to corrupt public monies than those who are less affluent. One villager, clearly rating affluence above local connections, spoke enthusi-astically about the credentials of one of the mayoral candidates: "He is a good and fair man. I don't think he would cheat with money because he already gets paid a lot, about forty thousand [baht per month]. He is not likely to want to cheat more. Some people say that he is an outsider, but this is not important because a person from outside doesn't have an opportunity to favor anyone. And he is well educated."

Political representatives are also expected to demonstrate an appropriate level of sacrifice for the broader community. Many types of sacrifice are locally expected: participating in committees, assisting with the implementa-tion of development projects, making representations on behalf of less capa-ble villagers, and active involvement in village festivals. Provision of financial assistance is a highly visible way of demonstrating personal sacrifice, espe-cially in the busy preelection environment when time constraints limit other more-time-consuming forms of participation. But there is a caveat here. An appropriate demonstration of sacrifice requires that there is a perception that the funds being used are private rather than public. Of course, there are numerous ways in which candidates attempt to blur this distinction (espe-cially incumbents who already have access to various budgetary allocations), but a widespread perception that public funds are being used to create an impression of personal sacrifice is likely to generate some electoral backlash.

A commitment to local development is another important element in the rural constitution's positive evaluation of support. A standard mode of justifying or challenging a candidate's credentials is the extent to which he or she has brought, or will bring, development to the local area. The importance of this value is reflected in the ubiquity of terms such as *phatana* (development), *jaroen* (prosperity), and *kaw na* (progress) in local campaign material. The incumbent candidate, Mayor Somsak, emphasized his development achievements in the campaign songs he broadcast before the March 2006 municipal election: "The municipality has moved forward. The roads are good; the work is finished. We have lights on both sides of the road. We have water to drink and water to use. The water supply system has provided water to houses near and far. We will continue to expand it. Rich and poor are equal. Mark my words, the work we have done is not insignificant. We will continue to move forward and work together so everyone can be happy and secure."

The discursive force of development in electoral culture is complex. On the one hand it fits readily with the image of the generous and good-hearted patron who is sacrificing for the benefit of the broader community. Financial donation prior to the election is a demonstration of the candidate's willingness and capability to direct development resources to constituents. Personal sacrifice, community development, and the moral virtue of the *suan huam* collective are symbolically linked. But, at the same time, the common emphasis on progress and development can move local discussions of support into a somewhat different domain of social meaning. In broad terms a distinction is emerging between forms of benevolent assistance that are expressed in highly personalized patron-client terms and forms of development assistance that are linked to more socially inclusive discourses of progress, administration, and broad-based access. Whereas personal generosity is highly valued in relation to the former, the latter places primary emphasis on the ability to effectively mobilize government resources and direct them to the projects that have proliferated in the local area. Once again, projects can be seen as a somewhat transitional form, midway between the personalized benevolence of patrons and the universal provision of benefits to all citizens.

Some of the dimensions of the local emphasis on both benevolent support and community development can be explored in relation to the election for mayor, which took place in 2006. As I have already explained, the incumbent, Somsak, was one of Ban Tiam's prominent residents with extensive kinship connections within the village and a high economic and cultural profile.

His younger sister was elected head of the village's housewives' group a few months before the municipal election, and his key running mate was the brother of the village headman.[12] But this substantial social capital did not translate automatically into electoral support. Overall, there was recognition that Somsak had contributed to local infrastructure development, even if this had been slower than some villagers had hoped. This was most visible in the conversion of many of the village's rutted dirt lanes into smooth concrete strips, and there were numerous other small construction projects that had received municipal allocations. But there were some complaints that one of the key beneficiaries of this development was his son-in-law, who had received many of the construction contracts. Somsak was also criticized for not mobilizing assistance quickly enough when the village experienced flash flooding and for not taking sufficient action to prevent the flood in the first place. And perhaps most damaging was the view that he had not used enough of his reportedly substantial salary to support local projects, despite building himself a grand new house. For one villager, his failings were highlighted when he responded to a request for budgetary support from members of an irrigation group by asking them to submit a formal written proposal to the local government planning committee. In brief, while Mayor Somsak may have been a reasonably good, if somewhat plodding, developer, he lacked some of the key characteristics of the quick-acting benevolent patron.

Somsak's main electoral rival, Dr. Tanet, provides an interesting contrast. He was from outside the district (although he had lived there on and off for twenty years), and his social distance from the population was signaled by the ubiquitous use of his professional occupational title. But he had gained a reputation as a locally influential "Mr. Fixit," personally supporting a number of local projects, enterprises, and welfare activities. For example, when he was told about the irrigation group's request he immediately "pulled money out of his own pocket" and handed it to Chusak, the group's deputy head. "Compare this to Mayor Somsak," Chusak said. "When he does help us he uses the government's money, not his own, and it comes too late." This act of patronage and personal sacrifice was sufficiently impressive for Chusak to sign up as a local canvasser for Dr. Tanet. It was widely reported that Dr. Tanet also distributed satellite dishes to key supporters (and was somewhat bemused to receive one of the dishes back after the election along with a request for repairs under warranty). And he also expressed keen interest in providing support for Ban Tiam's community shop, cleverly exploiting Mayor Somsak's lack of support for this particular project given that two of his close relatives were village shopkeepers. Overall, Dr. Tanet's reputation was that of a well-connected and wealthy man who could quickly mobilize funds to address local needs and desires.

But the demonstration of an ability and willingness to provide financial support is not without electoral risks. Dr. Tanet's generous displays of financial assistance generated some feeling that his campaigning was too "strong" and insufficiently linked to broader development goals. A number of voters expressed the view that he would win the election with money and suggested that there were likely to be "dirty stories" in relation to his campaign. One resident of Ban Tiam suggested that someone who had invested so much in cultivating local support would want it back, plus profit, if he won. There were also allegations about vote buying directed particularly at Dr. Tanet's vigorous campaigning in a large upland minority village located near Ban Tiam. But possibly most damaging was the fact that his demonstrations of local support were undermined by his history of acquiring land and houses through foreclosure on unpaid debts. One woman advised her mother, "Don't vote for that shit. He has grabbed land all over the place." This was combined with a feeling that he was seeking election so he would be in a position to upgrade the land titles on many of his holdings in the area. In other words, for some voters, Dr. Tanet's demonstrations of personal sacrifice and benevolence were simply not credible given what was regarded as an established personal history of self-interest and excessive private benefit.

Administration

The concern about the inappropriate use of financial influence points to another key aspect of the rural constitution, one that, to some extent, challenges a political emphasis on the localist provision of support. This alternative perspective places a primary emphasis on good administration and takes on self-consciously modernist connotations. Local advocates of this position often present themselves as a "new generation" and not infrequently make explicit reference to the general principles of participatory democracy and the need to move beyond old-fashioned systems of patronage and local "dictatorship" (*phadetkan*).

This perspective places considerable emphasis on educational qualifications. This is a clear challenge to localist values. Most locally embedded politicians are of a generation in which few rural people progressed beyond the middle years of primary school. For some voters this is seen as a limitation in terms of administrative and legal competence. This issue gained some currency in the mayoral election, with some arguing that Mayor Somsak's limited education (fourth grade) meant that he was incapable of effectively reining in officials within his administration, most of whom held bachelor's degrees. Other, better-educated candidates, who also had more formal experience in public administration, were seen as better able to "reduce the role" of nonelected officials. There was particular concern about Mayor Somsak's ability to manage one particular official—a gun-toting local strongman who was widely rumored to have enriched himself through manipulation of construction contracts. Of course, this view did not go unchallenged, and Mayor Somsak responded by drawing on localist sentiments about the remoteness and impracticality of knowledge acquired through formal education: "Dr. Tanet may have university degrees, but that doesn't mean he can manage the work. Just sitting at a desk in an air-conditioned office giving orders is one thing, but he can't get out and walk in the paddy fields. How will he help the villagers? There are lots of people who think like this. That's why they will vote for me."

Apart from the desirability of educational qualifications, there are a number of other elements in the modernist emphasis on strong administration. These include an ability to speak well at meetings, to make quick decisions, to manage budgets effectively, and to represent the locality energetically in meetings with high-level bureaucrats and politicians. Perhaps most important of all is the fact that administration, and specifically the implementation of development projects, is transparent. Mayor Somsak's campaign slogan—"Aiming for development, honest, transparent, accountable"—tapped into one of the most common preoccupations of local political discourse. For some, this emphasis on transparent administration qualifies the electoral value of development. In this alternative framing, rapid development can be portrayed as rushed and unaccountable expenditure, often on projects of dubious economic value. Development can also be framed as a form of electoral manipulation. High levels of spending on local projects, especially in the months leading up to an election, can be regarded as a blatant attempt to secure votes. Supporters of Dr. Tanet were at pains to point out that Mayor Somsak had spent over eleven million baht in the final months of his tenure, building on their critique that he was a less than competent administrator for whom development amounted simply to approving projects and pouring concrete.

And, of course, the discourse of transparent administration is linked to explicit concerns about corruption (*corupchan*). One of the most damaging aspects of corruption is that it can undermine the electorally important image of personal sacrifice for the common good. For politicians this is a subtle and potentially hazardous moral economy. Sacrifice in the form of diversion of resources from the private to the collective domain is a highly valued electoral asset. At the same time, as in the world of development projects, there is a common expectation that there will be some flow in the other direction, and it is regarded as quite normal for political representatives to derive some private benefit from public office. Elected leaders have to manage this balance carefully, given that the gray area of exchange between collective and private benefit is a very common site of conflict in rural political society. Concerns about inappropriate behavior are likely to be most electorally potent when there is a perception that collective resources are being used for private benefit in a way that directly disadvantages others. A classic example of this occurred in Ban Tiam when an early contender in the village headman election was ruled out on the basis of allegations that he had used his position on various village committees to divert communal funds to support his private moneylending business. The fact that communal funds were being used to extract punitive rates of interest from fellow villagers was, for many residents, a blatant breach of the moral economy of exchange between the collective and private spheres. It was corrupt.

EVERYDAY POLITICAL VALUES AND THE THAKSIN GOVERNMENT

In the 2001 national election, which brought Thaksin Shinawatra's Thai Rak Thai party to power, his candidate in Ban Tiam's constituency won with 48 percent of the votes cast. In the 2005 election the Thai Rak Thai vote climbed to 66 percent. This was part of the most resounding election victory ever experienced in Thailand, with Thai Rak Thai winning 377 of the 500 seats in parliament. It was the first time in Thailand's modern political history that a single party had won an absolute majority. Another election was held in April 2006, after Thaksin dissolved parliament in the face of growing antigovernment protests in Bangkok. The opposition Democrat Party, recognizing that it had no chance of victory, boycotted the election. Even without an effective opposition, Thaksin took a hit in the polls. Discontent with his government was reflected in Ban Tiam's constituency, as in many other parts of Thailand. Compared with his 2005 landslide, the local Thai Rak Thai candidate's vote was halved, with almost 60 percent of the electorate not voting, casting spoiled ballots, or registering a "no vote" (fig. 16). In other

FIGURE 16. Thaksin Shinawatra at a 2006 campaign rally in northern Thailand. (Photo by Nicholas Farrelly.)

words, during the period of Thaksin's tenure there was considerable varia-tion in the level of his electoral support in national elections. Local elections also cast doubt on the common image of Thaksin's electoral hegemony. In the provincial assembly election of 2004, the incumbent candidate, who had strong backing from Thaksin's party, was soundly defeated. And in the vigor-ously contested mayoral election the pro-Thaksin candidate, Dr. Tanet, fell short by the slimmest of margins (three votes) despite his well-resourced and high-profile campaign to unseat Mayor Somsak. So, rather than assuming uniform and unwavering rural electoral support for Thaksin, readily mobi-lized via financially lubricated networks of patronage, it is more useful to examine how the Thaksin government was evaluated in terms of the rural constitution's local political values.

Localism: "The Prime Minister Is from Chiang Mai"

In the national election of 2005, localism played an interesting, but politi-cally ambiguous, role. Thaksin is from Chiang Mai and is, in the eyes of many voters in the region, one of *ban haw*. One of the popular Thai Rak Thai slogans, regularly printed in the distinctive northern Thai idiom, reflected this sentiment: "The people of Chiang Mai are proud. The prime minister is from Chiang Mai. Thai Rak Thai is the only party." Part of the local political identity of Pad Siew District was that it had become part of the Thai Rak Thai heartland, and there was a common extension of the *ban haw* category to include Thaksin's party. This commonly expressed sentiment was nicely summarized by a local party canvasser: "Thaksin's policies develop Chiang Mai. And we are Chiang Mai people. So why wouldn't we vote for him? Northerners have to help northerners, and then Thai Rak Thai will win. We have to help Thaksin because the southerners will vote Democrat; they won't vote for a northerner. If Thai Rak Thai win then the budgets will come here. Otherwise they will be canceled."

The common contrast with the Democrat south is morally charged, with the southern region often viewed as an undesirable place characterized by religious cleavage; ongoing violence associated with the Muslim insurgency in the far south; and, in the lead-up to the 2005 election, the inauspicious misfortune of the tsunami, which killed over five thousand people. At a speech in the district center the Thai Rak Thai candidate made much of the contrast between the "good-hearted" people of Chiang Mai and the Democrats of the south. In response to a question about agricultural extension he enthusiastically promoted the virtues of rubber, claiming that Thaksin had destroyed the Democrat-imposed southern monopoly on the cultivation of rubber, providing a new source of lucrative income for farmers in the north and northeast. Initial tests, he suggested, had shown that northern farmers could produce even higher quality rubber than their southern counterparts!

So localist sentiment certainly acted in Thai Rak Thai's favor, and it was actively cultivated during the 2005 election campaign. But this was not without complexities when we come to consider the candidates themselves. The Thai Rak Thai candidate (the incumbent, first elected in 2001) may well have been a Chiang Mai man, but this was not a key point of local discussion. What was more relevant was that his long career in public administration, combined with a somewhat bookish, formal, and aloof style, clearly marked him in nonlocal terms. Regular comments were made that he had a very low profile in the district, that his main interests lay in other parts of the constituency, and that he did not communicate easily with farmers. His main opponent, who had previously served as a member of parliament and was now running for the newly formed Mahachon Party (an ally of the Democrats), was well known and locally popular.[13] He came from a neighboring district (where many in Ban Tiam had relatives) and was renowned for his informal, friendly, and avuncular style. At the election rally he held in the Pad Siew District center he impressed the large crowd with his entertaining command of informal northern Thai. He was even able to address some comments to upland minority villagers in their own language, a smart move in a region where linguistic wordplay is an exceptionally popular pastime. He explicitly played up his localist credentials, emphasizing that the election was about choosing a local representative rather than choosing a party (the Thai Rak Thai campaign message was exactly the opposite). The preelection sentiment was that the localist credentials of the opposition candidate might well result in his victory, and while he lost heavily in the overall count I have no doubt that he attracted substantial support in Ban Tiam, where some of the most influential opinion leaders (including the headman) were keen supporters.[14]

Support: "Good in Some Respects"

Thai Rak Thai had a rather mixed record in terms of the rural constitution's valuing of financial support. There was considerable grumbling about the limited local involvement of the Thai Rak Thai candidate, and there were also complaints about the paltry payments received for attendance at party meetings. Within Ban Tiam, the local party canvassers were accused of making only halfhearted attempts to mobilize villagers to attend various party events, thus denying them potential income. Some even suggested that incompetent village-level canvassers had been deliberately recruited so that district-level party workers could pocket a greater share of the electoral benefits. Overall, despite some specific acts of personal support, the Thai Rak Thai candidate did not have a reputation for high-profile generosity, especially after his refusal to fund Ban Tiam's housewives' uniforms. In fact it was the locally embedded opposition candidate who was more readily associated with the rural constitution's values of benevolent patronage. His active engagement in Pad Siew District had earned him the affectionate (and, for some, slightly mocking) title "the honorable tent" (*sor sor tent*), referring to the large number of canvas awnings (printed with his name) that he had donated to local organizations during his previous tenure as local representative in the national parliament. At his election rally *sor sor tent* could also claim that he had contributed to various local projects, most notably the construction of the district's only hydroelectric project and the new agricultural cooperative building. His benevolent profile was enhanced by the commonly expressed local view that "Mahachon is much more generous than Thai Rak Thai" in paying for attendance at rallies and party meetings.

But Thai Rak Thai's disadvantage in relation to the personal characteristics of its candidate was outweighed by the strong local endorsement of the official support provided under Thaksin's policy initiatives. Here his government was regarded as having performed very strongly: "They have helped us in many ways. Thaksin has many projects that bring benefits to farmers. The old government did not help us like this." Particularly strong support was expressed for Thaksin's local economic development initiatives, especially the village credit fund and the so-called SML (Small-Medium-Large) program.[15] In Ban Tiam, despite some problems, the million-baht village credit fund operated successfully with relatively high rates of repayment. It had also managed to increase its original capital stock as a result of members' regular deposits and the purchase of member shares. The SML grant funded the construction of a village rice mill, which offered cheaper rates than the privately owned village mills. A number of farmers in Ban Tiam also took the subsidized cattle provided under the "one million cows" program: "People still like Thaksin a lot. The project for raising cattle tries to fix the problem of poverty by creating income for villagers." And about twenty households participated in income-generating activities provided as part of the government's poverty alleviation campaign. There was also very strong local support for the government's health policy, which provided hospital treatment for only thirty baht.

Electoral support for the various government initiatives was enhanced by the perception that they had been implemented very quickly and in a manner that largely bypassed the local bureaucracy. The rapid pace of Thaksin's financial assistance was a key point of contrast with previous governments. The SML scheme was a regularly cited illustration. It was promised in the campaign for the February 2005 election, and by June 2005 the village had received the money and was in a position to decide which project would be implemented. Although there was considerable local debate about how the money would be spent, the policy of village-level decision making and implementation was seen as a welcome departure from the usual administrative practice of submitting funding requests to high-level authorities. The eventual decision was to construct a community rice mill, and it was completed by early 2006, little more than a year after villagers had first heard about the new program. Overall, there was a strong feeling that Thaksin's development policies were "the real thing"—rather than just words—and proof of their success lay in the fact that other parties were starting to copy them.

However, it would be very misleading to suggest that Thai Rak Thai was invulnerable on the issue of support. In fact, there was persistent local criticism that Thaksin's government had offered insufficient support to the agricultural sector. Examination of government spending on agriculture shows that this criticism had some foundation in fiscal reality. Under Thaksin, there was no real growth in government spending on agriculture and, as a percentage of agricultural GDP, it declined from 14.6 to 8.4 percent.[16] Nationally, agricultural incomes grew solidly during Thaksin's term in office, but the state's relative contribution to that income was declining.

The local political impact of this trend needs to be understood in terms of the considerable agricultural uncertainty faced by Ban Tiam's farmers. As discussed in chapter 4, during the early years of the Thaksin government, many Ban Tiam farmers experienced large declines in the yield of garlic, their main cash crop. Of course, the primary causes of this reduction in yield—disease, bad weather, and soil-fertility decline—were unrelated to government policy. However, the government was not completely blameless on the garlic woes, and a good number of farmers linked the steep drop in the price of garlic in 2004 to the government's free-trade agreement with China. The garlic adjustment scheme allayed some of the discontent, but its effectiveness was reduced by the modest level of payments and the administrative bungling and delays that marked its implementation. Even more damaging, in the long term, were emerging perceptions that the government had done little to address the overall agricultural malaise, that it was pushing farmers into the arms of the private sector rather than expanding state-funded extension services, and that some of the agricultural support programs (especially the livestock initiatives) were tokenistic and unviable. The voters of Ban Tiam drew an implicit contrast between the government's strong performance on local enterprise and development projects and its poor performance in relation to broad-based support for the agricultural sector. These sentiments were passionately expressed by Daeng—a local organizer for Thai Rak Thai—when he was responding to reports that provincial officials would be coming to the village to check the accuracy of farmers' claims under the garlic substitution scheme (discussed in detail in chapter 4):

Why should they come? Really, farmers who grow garlic don't get anything anyway. You have to invest a lot in fertilizer, and I don't want to be in debt. But we have to do it, because there is no alternative income. Garlic is high risk but gives a good return. If we are lucky we may be able to get out of debt.

The government helps a little, but everyone is in debt. Why is the price of fertilizer and fuel going up? But the money to help us and the prices for our crops don't go up, they just go down. Just look at it! For the rice I lost [in the floods in the 2005 wet season] I only got three hundred baht. If I had not lost that rice and been able to sell it I would have got several thousand. But, the government is not completely bad. Some of the other projects are OK, and quick. But their commitment and spending on agriculture is small, and the farmers are still in trouble. No end in sight! I am still in debt. Everyone is in debt. Have a look at the rich farmers in the village. Even they are in debt. We work every day but don't have enough money to pay off our debts. See if you can find a house in the village that is not in debt. Since this government came a lot of things have gotten better, such as the thirty-baht health care scheme. And the [Thaksin] government has started to help us, but not enough and not transparent.

Similar disillusionment was voiced by Bunyuan, another struggling garlic farmer:

The things we have to buy, even instant noodles, get more expensive every day. Look at the price of fuel. If the prices of our crops went up too it wouldn't be a problem, but with the garlic price so low it's just impossible. We have to invest more all the time, but the price we get just goes down. I wish the government was not just interested in developing the city. Out here in the countryside the grass roots are still undeveloped. They are only interested in us when they come looking for votes because they want us to be a strong voting base for their party. But once they are elected into government they just go back and worry about the needs of the city. Thailand is a country that is only really growing in the city.

And this from Mrs. Somporn, the owner of one of the village's small noodle shops:

Thai politics is terrible. I don't like Thaksin. He has given money to the villagers, but I have not seen any of them get rich, just further into debt. They just bring budgets and give loans to the poor people, who then go and support them. But it's the money of the government, not Thaksin's own money. Farmers are in trouble; all the crop prices are going down. I stopped farming a few years ago. Running a restaurant is better.

In these statements we see some related lines of critique coming together. There is a healthy cynicism about election campaigns and the generous promises of support that are made during them. There is also a broader concern about policy failure, ranging from the specifics of crop-price support to the more general challenge of promoting balanced regional development within the country. Somporn's impassioned statement about the link between agricultural decline, government policy and indebtedness expresses one of the key socioeconomic concerns in Ban Tiam. A debt repayment moratorium introduced by the Thaksin government in 2001 was appreciated, but it provided temporary relief rather than addressing the debt problem itself. Some felt that Thaksin's million-baht village credit fund had merely increased indebtedness.

Administration: "I Call Him Sapsin"

There is no doubt that many of Thaksin's personal qualities were highly valued according to the rural constitution's measures of strong administration. He had a record of extraordinary business success, he was a very capable public speaker and a charismatic media performer, and he had excellent educational qualifications. Particularly important in local perceptions was the fact that Thaksin could speak English well—a key cultural marker of social connection, sophistication, and intellect. These attributes meant that Thaksin could effectively represent Thailand internationally. "Thailand is famous now," Ban Tiam's assistant headman told me, and "everyone has heard of Prime Minister Thaksin."

There was one particular aspect of his administration that contributed to the Thaksin mystique and reinforced the image that he was a national leader who could operate effectively on the world stage. Local supporters regularly cited the fact that Thaksin had cleared the International Monetary Fund (IMF) debt that had been Thailand's national burden in the wake of the Asian financial crisis in the late 1990s. This had enhanced Thailand's international status, improved the country's credit rating, and enabled the government to better support its own population. Some even suggested that Thaksin's success in settling the IMF debt was an indication that, given time, he would be able to deal with the problem of household debt. This electorally beneficial blurring of national and private debt was nicely expressed by the owner of one of Ban Tiam's small shops: "In the past any Thai child that was born was sixty thousand baht in debt. But now the IMF debt is gone, and Thailand's newborn can rest easy. And money is coming into the village. Thaksin has done a good job. As for the other side—I've seen nothing."

Another factor that acted strongly in Thaksin's favor was his penchant for high-profile campaigns (or "wars"). The ambitious targets and tight deadlines of these campaigns clearly captured the local imagination. The most prominent of these was the so-called war on drugs, during which there were reported to have been over two thousand extrajudicial killings of alleged drug dealers in a nationwide crackdown. As in other parts of Thailand, this heavy-handed campaign attracted significant local support. It was regularly cited as evidence of Thaksin's effectiveness and his strong and decisive leadership. It tapped into profound local anxieties about the spread of amphetamine use among young people and was also consistent with local sentiments, which continue to value direct action against alleged criminals. Consider the comments of Uncle Man, who checked himself out of hospital on election day in 2006 so he could cast his vote in favor of Thai Rak Thai even though there was no opposition candidate: "The thing I like most about Thaksin is the war on drugs. There has been a real benefit. In the past there were a lot of people on drugs, a lot of young people in this village. Just a couple of years ago, some young people came and tried to steal computers from the school. They were kids from our village. I didn't want to get involved. I am old, and they might kill me. Our village set up a 'night patrol' committee. It was a secret committee. They got people in several villages. Now it is quiet, and I feel much safer."

Set against these positive features of Thaksin's administrative record were common concerns about his corruption. Thaksin's extraordinary wealth and his various business dealings and manipulations while in government made him vulnerable to the charge that he was "greedy," "cheated" too much, and surrounded himself with bad people. These were commonly expressed views, although for many they were not electorally potent given the view that, although he had "helped himself," Thaksin had also "shared" the benefits with rural people: "He cheated a bit, but it's not a big deal. He cheated, but he also gave money to the villagers." In other words, his diversions from the public domain to his private domain were not seen as having directly disadvantaged rural voters. But this rationale was not universal, and some countered by pointing out that Thaksin's apparent generosity to the poor was not genuine, as it had come from government money rather than his own private funds: "Talking of Thaksin, I call him *sapsin* [property]. I don't like the way he has cheated so much money. My relatives in Bangkok don't like him at all and never agree with his actions because he just throws money away. The money that Thaksin uses is the country's money. It is not money from his pocket. He has lots of money, but we never see him make donations. When he dies will he be able to take it with him?"

For some voters Thaksin's corruption and maladministration were high-lighted by the controversial April 2006 general election. As a result of the boycott by opposition parties, Ban Tiam's electorate only had one party standing—Thai Rak Thai. Some argued that the election itself was a waste of money ("the country's money, the money of every villager") and that the electorate was being taken for granted by offering it no electoral choice: "I think they should delay the election. Because doing it like this is not fair to all parties. I don't like Thaksin's government because it has cheated a lot and 'eaten' too much. But here we only have Thai Rak Thai, and this district is a vote base for them. Personally I would like another government to run the country."

In the end, the constituency's voting turnout in the 2006 election was only 66 percent, and more than a third of those who did vote decided to cast an informal ballot or formally registered a "no vote." There was clearly consid-erable disillusionment with the Thaksin government.

The 2007 National Election

Following the coup of September 2006, the appointed government of former army supremo Surayud Chulanont undertook to organize an election within twelve months. This election was held, a few months late, on 23 December 2007. By this time, Thaksin's Thai Rak Thai party had been dissolved by the Constitutional Court and over one hundred of its most senior figures banned from politics for five years. Thaksin himself was living in exile in London. A new party, the People Power Party (PPP), had been formed to replace Thai Rak Thai. It was led by Samak Sundaravej, a controversial and pugnacious politician who was infamous for his role, as interior minister, in a bloody crackdown on student protesters at Bangkok's Thammasat University in October 1976. The main opposition party, the Democrats, was now led by the urbane, Oxford-educated, and youthful Abhisit Vejajiva. For those who backed the military coup, the election was a crucial test to determine if they had succeeded in neutralizing Thaksin's formidable electoral power.

At a national level there was strong criticism of Samak and the PPP for being "proxies" for Thaksin. The image of Thaksin as a cashed-up, behind-the-scenes power broker was used to challenge the legitimacy of the PPP as a genuine political party. However, within Ban Tiam the proxy charge was not a significant electoral liability. The April 2006 election had given voters a chance to register their unhappiness with Thaksin, but following the coup much of his electoral magic seems to have been restored. In Ban Tiam, the PPP's popularity derived principally from the fact that it was regarded as the legitimate inheritor of Thaksin's legacy. One woman concisely summed up a common feeling in the lead-up to the election: "We don't like the gray-headed man [Samak, leader of the PPP], but we will vote for him because he is Thai Rak Thai." Another man commented, "I don't care who Thaksin's representative is. I will vote for him." Many voters in Ban Tiam saw the 2007 election as an opportunity to restore a government committed to Thaksin's policy agenda. Some voters even openly welcomed the prospect that a Samak government would seek to bring Thaksin back to Thailand, although several feared that this could result in further conflict or even Thaksin's assassination. Despite the vocal condemnation of Thaksin's "irresponsible" populist programs by the postcoup government, there was still considerable local support for the thirty-baht health scheme, the village credit fund, and local economic development schemes. Thaksin had succeeded in creating an enduring impression that his government was the first to genuinely address the needs of the rural economy. One of the members of the community rice mill committee summed this up nicely: "The money that is still coming to the village is a result of Thaksin's government. When the Democrats were the government the villagers didn't get anything. The Democrats have been around since I was a child, and I haven't seen the country change. Thaksin was prime minister for just a short time, and everything changed. He helped us a lot, but now he can't even come back to Thailand."

These views were certainly not universal. In the rather polarized political context there appeared to be a sharpening of support for the Democrats. In Ban Tiam, some voters took the view that the Democrats were the appropriate party to lead Thailand out of a period of political chaos, especially now that Thaksin and members of his family had abandoned the country. They saw Abhisit's relative youth as signaling a new start for Thailand. This was a potent signal when contrasted with Samak's long and very checkered political history. Support for the Democrats was particularly evident among a few high-profile members of Ban Tiam's commercial elite, including Mayor Somsak himself. Some of these more vocal Democrat supporters felt that they had benefited very little from Thaksin's policies, and some local initiatives—the community shop, the village credit fund, and the SML funding for a community rice mill—were a direct challenge to their business success. At the other end of Ban Tiam's social spectrum, the Democrats' electioneering claim that "the people must come first" tapped into a feeling that Thaksin, as a wealthy businessman, was only really interested in helping Thailand's business elite. Some poor villagers were also very attracted to the Democrats' "people's agenda" of free school education, universal health care, and income support. The appeal of Democrat promises was, however, diluted by the common argument that the Democrats could not be trusted because they had blatantly copied their policies from the Thaksin government. Thaksin's political allies capitalized on this sentiment, producing campaign posters featuring the slogan "Anyone can talk, but those who both talk and act are in the People Power Party."

Given changes to the electoral rules introduced by the postcoup government, results are available for individual polling stations.[17] The postcoup 2007 Constitution provided for multimember constituencies (four hundred members of the national parliament) and a "party list" vote (eighty members, ten from each of Thailand's eight regions). Under the new arrangements Ban Tiam's expanded constituency was to elect three members. In Ban Tiam's polling station, the PPP attracted about 53 percent of the constituency votes cast, and the most popular three candidates were all from the PPP. Ban Tiam's party list vote for the PPP was almost exactly the same, suggesting that in Ban Tiam the appeal of particular local candidates did not play an important role on this occasion. The Democrats attracted about 28 percent of the vote in Ban Tiam. Nationally, the PPP fell just short of an absolute majority in the parliament but was able to form a government with the support of all the other parties except the Democrats. The new PPP government lasted less than one year, falling in the wake of the street protests organized by the anti-Thaksin yellow shirts, their occupation of Bangkok's international airport, and, finally, the Constitutional Court's dissolution of the PPP as a result of electoral misconduct by one of its executive members.

ELECTIONS AND POLITICAL SOCIETY

The rural constitution represents an emerging agreement between Thailand's middle-income peasantry and the state about the nature of government. It embodies the middle-income peasantry's aspirations for productive connections with sources of power. Specifically, the rural constitution seeks to regulate and guide the new fiscal relationship with the state, characterized by wide-ranging support for the rural economy. Through the everyday politics of discussion, gossip, and debate the rural constitution enmeshes government in local economic and political values. Elected representatives are expected to have strong local connections so they can be effective and accessible brokers between the village and the state. They are also expected to be generous in their provision of gifts, both to symbolically reinforce their legitimacy and to practically demonstrate that they are capable of initiating and maintaining flows of subsidy. There is also an emerging emphasis on capable and transparent administration, often drawing on explicitly modernist values of effective government. Corruption is evaluated in terms of a carefully assessed balance between personal gain and public benefit. All these various elements are refracted in complex and sometimes contradictory ways and do not provide a ready template for political decision making. Rather, they provide a broad framework in which local political evaluation takes place.

In proposing this rural constitution I want to avoid creating a mirror image of the negative portrayals of rural electoral behavior with which I began this chapter. It would be stretching the argument too far to argue that all rural electors are careful and rational decision makers who painstakingly assess candidates against a range of clearly defined criteria. Mrs. Priaw told me that she voted for Thaksin because she did not know who else to support. Miss Noi went to vote because her parents and relatives told her to, but she voted informal because she did not know any of the candidates. And Num, a young government employee, was a member of Thai Rak Thai but not sure why because he did not derive any personal benefits from it. As in any electoral system there are a good number of people who vote (or not) on the basis of disinterest, disengagement, or disillusionment.

Nor do I intend to argue that vote buying and the activities of party canvassers have no influence on electoral behavior in Ban Tiam or elsewhere in rural Thailand. But I do insist that these specific institutions need to be placed in the much broader context of the everyday values that inform rural Thailand's political society. As I have indicated, cash distributed by candidates and their canvassers is subject to evaluation and critique within the broad framework provided by the rural constitution. Gifts of cash and other goods are part of a political culture that values personal sacrifice, embeddedness in networks of exchange, and conspicuous displays of willingness and ability to channel resources toward local development. Both insufficient generosity and conspicuous extravagance are likely to attract censure. Party canvassers are similarly evaluated. In Ban Tiam one of the key Thai Rak Thai canvassers was widely regarded as a man who "talked too much, a lot of it rubbish." His somewhat dubious leadership status was underlined when, in late 2004, he was dumped as head of the village's largest irrigation group due to his inattention to the smooth running of the system (largely because his own fields lay at the head of the irrigation canal). Aunt Fon, who we met in the previous chapter, was another important Thai Rak Thai canvasser. Her fall from grace, as a result of the debacle caused by the housewives' uniforms, also came in late 2004. By the time of the general election in February 2005, both of Thai Rak Thai's local canvassers had suffered serious blows to their credibility as a result of their failure to successfully manage communal undertakings.

In Ban Tiam's political society, the electoral process is socially embedded in complex and overlapping networks of relationships. The rural constitution provides the normative framework for this embedding. Rural Thailand now has a diverse economy and a complex administrative structure, with an array of organizations involved in various aspects of government. There is no neat hierarchy of political patrons and vote-offering clients. Rather, there is a "diverse society of ill joined actors" in which personal connections overlap, compete and draw people in different directions.[18] Max Gluckman's classic anthropological analysis of "custom and conflict in Africa" shows how a complex network of conflicting loyalties prevents feuds from degenerating into outright conflict.[19] In the same way, rural voters in Thailand find themselves linked in multiple ways to local figures on all sides of political contests. There is no ready-made social basis for political mobilization into clearly defined electoral entourages. In this socially complex environment, the rural constitution is drawn on to provide an informal framework for specific electoral allegiances.

Conclusion

Political Society, Civil Society, and Democracy

The national-level conflict that has convulsed Thailand over the past decade owes much to the emergence of rural Thailand's new political society. Rural people have mobilized to defend the direct relationship they have established with the Thai state over the past forty years. This is not the old-style Southeast Asian peasantry of rebellion, revolution, or resistance. Contemporary rural politics is driven by a middle-income peasantry with a thoroughly modern political logic. The strategy of this modern peasantry is to engage with sources of power, not to oppose them.

Half a century ago, 96 percent of Thailand's rural dwellers were living in poverty. As a result of rapid economic growth and diversification, the official rural poverty rate has plummeted to about 10 percent. Life expectancy has increased, infant mortality is close to first-world standards, and primary schooling is near universal. Ban Tiam is only one of Thailand's seventy thousand villages, but its middle-income status is broadly representative of this dramatic national improvement in the quality of life of rural residents. For the majority of the rural population in Thailand, as in Ban Tiam, subsistence rice farming, commercial agriculture, and extensive off-farm employment is combined to produce levels of household income and consumption unthinkable a few decades ago. In Thailand's modern rural economy, fear of outright subsistence failure is no longer a core driver of political activity.

However, while Thailand has been very successful in managing absolute poverty, it has a less impressive record on relative poverty. Livelihoods in the rural north and northeast have certainly improved, but levels of income and rates of growth lag well behind those found in central Thailand, Bangkok, and parts of southern Thailand. In Ban Tiam the average household income is 125,000 baht per year, while in Bangkok it is close to 470,000.[1] One important reason for this inequality is that Thailand has maintained a relatively large agricultural workforce that is much less productive than its industrial workforce. The Thai peasantry has been remarkably persistent. There has been productivity growth in the agricultural sector, and this has made an important contribution to Thailand's dramatic reduction in rural poverty, but productivity in industry has increased much more rapidly, and from a much higher base. A worker in industry contributes 8.5 times as much to GDP as a worker in agriculture. As Ban Tiam's recent experience shows, nonagricultural employment has helped to increase the incomes of peasant households, but due to the low level of rural enterprise, jobs are most often available in the less productive parts of the nonfarm economy.

Thailand's governments have been only too aware of the disparity problem and the political hazards of rural disadvantage. For the past half century, attempts to promote rural development have been the central feature of the relationship between the Thai state and the peasantry. These attempts certainly did not start with the populism of Thaksin Shinawatra. His policy initiatives were consistent with a long-term trend that has gathered pace since the communist threat emerged in the 1950s and newly assertive farmer's organizations moved onto the national stage in the 1970s. In simple terms the Thai government, like governments in many other developing countries, has moved from taxing the rural economy to subsidizing it. Government funding in the form of infrastructure, price supports, economic development, health, welfare, and education has become an integral part of the complex livelihood mix pursued by peasant households throughout rural Thailand. Ban Tiam's irrigation infrastructure, community-based projects, agricultural subsidy schemes, and ever-active construction sites are local manifestations of the Thai state's high-profile presence in the rural economy.

The origins of Thailand's current political tension lie in the dilemmas of this transformed fiscal relationship. State investment, combined with wide-ranging support for the tenure of smallholders, has enhanced agricultural incomes and created numerous sources of nonfarm employment in the construction sector, local development projects, and government agencies. However, the overall impact of this state support for rural Thailand has been to help develop and maintain a middle-income peasantry rather than fundamentally transform it. The government's performance on agricultural productivity has been lackluster by the standards of many of its regional neighbors, and, more important, it has had limited success in developing nonfarm rural enterprise. As a result, the government's massive investment in the rural economy has helped to maintain a large rural population that, despite significant livelihood improvements, is insufficiently productive to fully meet the aspirations that economic growth has aroused. There is a strong political expectation that the state will improve its efforts to enhance rural livelihoods, reduce inequality, and provide a secure backup when experimental engagements with private capital fail. Rural political society in Thailand is not driven by a peasantry that is staging a rearguard action against dissolution but by a peasantry that is assertively negotiating the terms of its persistence. The central element in the political strategy of this middle-income peasantry is to weave the power and resources of the state into the economic and social fabric of village life. As we have seen in Ban Tiam, this strategy is part of a broader orientation toward power—also evident in dealings with capricious spirits and unpredictable corporations—that seeks to domesticate power in the pursuit of safety, security, and prosperity.

Thaksin Shinawatra cleverly capitalized on the dilemmas that have emerged in Thailand's modernization. His unprecedented political success owes much to the fact that he shaped his policies around rural aspirations for productive connections with sources of power. He recognized that decades of rural economic growth and diversification had produced a very different type of peasantry. It was a peasantry for which the most important challenges were diversifying livelihoods, increasing productivity, limiting exposure to debt, and maintaining the flow of government support for the rural economy. There was nothing particularly new about Thaksin's emphasis on rural modernization, but he packaged it in a way that was very attractive to an economically sophisticated electorate: rural households can turn their assets into capital, villagers can manage agricultural credit, farmers can implement infrastructure projects, and local hospitals can provide universal health coverage. He cashed in on the new social contract, which embodies the notion that the state should play a direct and active role in supporting the rural economy. This social contract has been developing since the 1970s, but it took Thaksin to turn it into a core political asset.

The coup of September 2006 severed Thaksin's electorally successful engagement with rural Thailand's sprawling political society. Thaksin's rural support base had elected him three times: in 2001, 2005, and 2006. Defenders of the coup argued that electoral endorsement had been devalued by money politics. They resorted to old ideas about the moral preeminence of virtuous power embodied in the king and his military, judicial, and bureaucratic network. They refused to acknowledge that a vigorous electoral culture had developed in rural Thailand through which voters evaluate, applaud, and critique the government's implementation of its new social contract. It was no accident that the postcoup government made the king's sufficiency economy philosophy the centerpiece of its political platform. Sufficiency economy is the antithesis of political society. Its heavily moralistic emphasis on the virtues of local knowledge, subsistence production, and limited exchange forms a stark contrast with political society's pragmatic judgments about nonlocal connections, commercial engagement, development projects, and state subsidies. Of course, there was no real economic substance to the coup makers' sufficiency economy pitch: their economic agenda was business as usual, apart from a sharp increase in military spending. Their intention was to ideologically undercut Thaksin's cultivation of rural political society by arguing that his policies had eroded the authentic morality of rural culture by promoting immoderate economic expectations. This resonated with the anticapitalist and antiglobalization agenda of some civil society organizations that had emerged from the social movements of the 1990s, and some of their leaders took up the anti-Thaksin cause with a passion.[2] Political society was under concerted attack.

Rural political society's defense of its relationship with the state has been an important factor energizing the violent confrontations on the streets of Bangkok and the strong support shown for Yingluck Shinawatra in the election of July 2011. Rural people are demanding an active role in the political process. They are rejecting a system in which their votes can be overruled when they elect governments that are unpalatable to powerful forces in Thailand's palace network, the military, or the political elite. Rural Thailand cares about election results because elections have become an important mechanism through which people evaluate and domesticate the power of political leaders. Some commentators complain that the red-shirt protesters have no clear policy agenda; the 1970s grievances about landlessness, indebtedness, and onerous rents have hardly featured.[3] Others seek to discredit the red-shirt protests by pointing to vastly improved standards of living in rural areas, as if it is only the abjectly poor who have a right to political mobilization.[4] These are outdated assessments based on old-fashioned stereotypes of peasant protest. For Thailand's middle-income peasantry, specific policies are less important than a secure relationship with the state. Thaksin's clever promotion and timely implementation of specific policy initiatives were certainly important in galvanizing rural support, but even more important was the strong sense that electoral force had shifted the nation's most important power bargains away from Bangkok and toward the rural electorates of northern and northeastern Thailand. The red-shirt protesters have been defending political society's direct transactions with power in all its regular and irregular forms and rejecting the view that economic development and other matters of state should be guided by the elite embodiments of virtuous power located in the nation's capital.

IS POLITICAL SOCIETY CIVIL?

In the introduction to this book, I referred to the strong distinction that Partha Chatterjee draws between civil and political society. At one level, Chatterjee is making a demographic distinction. The formal associations of civil society are found mostly among middle- and upper-class residents in India's expanding cities: civil society is "restricted to a small section of culturally equipped citizens."[5] By contrast, the informal connections of political society are most evident in the larger, and much more marginal, population of farmers, slum dwellers, petty traders and small-scale entrepreneurs. Chatterjee argues that this pattern is a result of the uneven distribution of full citizenship rights. Civil society flourishes where basic rights to association, property, free speech and assembly are guaranteed. Legally protected citizens are empowered to form organizations "based on equality, autonomy, freedom of entry and exit, contract, deliberative procedures of decision making, recognized rights and duties of members, and other such principles."[6] However, a large proportion of the population in India lacks the infrastructural rights, or the cultural legitimacy, that give rise to civic associations. Urban squatters have no tenure rights, day laborers have no employment security, small enterprises operate without proper licensing, sidewalk vendors face the constant risk of expulsion, and poor farmers are subject to the whims of their overlords and resource-hungry corporations. Because members of these population groups are often disadvantaged by official rules and regulations, they direct their political efforts to a gray area of manipulation, appropriation, and interpersonal negotiation. These unconventional and colloquial strategies form the basis of political society. The strategies are often irregular, or even illegal, but the state engages with them in order to meet basic standards of welfare, limit social conflict, and win electoral favor. Political society is the domain of these populations (not citizens) who seek to creatively engage with state administration and welfare on the most favorable possible terms.

Like most social scientists who break new conceptual ground, Chatterjee is inclined to overstate the distinction he draws between civil and political society, and he has been criticized for doing so.[7] In fact, civil society advocacy and development organizations are active in many of the more marginal social locations where Chatterjee locates political society. Some of these may reflect elite paternalism, but it would certainly be a mistake to describe all of them in these terms. Conversely, personalized and informal manipulation of government is certainly not the sole prerogative of the lower classes. The middle class can be as dexterous with social connections as the subaltern. One useful suggestion coming out of commentary on Chatterjee's work is that rather than seeing civil and political society as demographically distinct, it is probably preferable to see them as different styles of political agency that are drawn on by different groups at different times.[8] This moderating comment is particularly important when applying arguments about political society to the rather different context of middle-income rural Thailand. There is no doubt that many of Thailand's middle-income peasants confront varying degrees of economic, cultural, and political marginalization, but it is also clear that their basic rights, such as rights to property, are much more secure than they are among some of the groups that Chatterjee considers in India. The political society of rural Thailand is based less on the absence of formal rights and more on the efforts of groups that have achieved some degree of economic and legal security to further improve their position.

So, in terms of political style, does the distinction between civil society and political society stand up in relation to the various relationships with sources of power that I have examined in this book? An influential definition of civil society provided by the political scientist Larry Diamond is a useful place to start in answering this question: "Civil society is conceived here as the realm of organized social life that is voluntary, self-generating, (largely) self-supporting, autonomous from the state, and bound by a legal order or set of shared rules. It is distinct from 'society' in general in that it involves citizens acting collectively in a public sphere to express their interests, passions, and ideas, exchange information, achieve mutual goals, make demands on the state, and hold state officials accountable."[9]

Ban Tiam's political society differs from this in some important respects, which I will highlight below, but there are also clear commonalities. In Ban Tiam the networks of political society regularly draw villagers into civic activities involving the mobilization of groups and the conspicuous deployment of symbols of community. Diamond tells us that the collective mobilization of civil society is pluralist, diverse, and partial, with different groups representing different interests.[10] This is certainly the case in Ban Tiam where population mobility, livelihood diversification, and bureaucratic expansion have created an enormous number of crosscutting networks and groups associated with the worship of spirits, the cultivation of cash crops, the implementation of development projects, and the mobilization of support for political leaders. These relationships are not necessarily "bound by a legal order or set of shared rules," but there are often broadly understood sets of values that inform evaluations of appropriate and inappropriate behavior. These values, as in civil society, provide a moral basis for residents of Ban Tiam to express their passions, make demands on the state and other powerful entities, and, when expectations are not met, demand accountability. Other desirable functions of civil society are also evident in political society's networks: they promote political participation and the development of leadership skills, educate people about political processes, contribute to self-help and local welfare, promote crosscutting alliances that blur social and political polarization, and provide forums for debate, monitoring, and critique.[11] The sharp dichotomy Chatterjee draws between political and civil society becomes rather blurred in practice.

Nevertheless, it would be a mistake to lose sight of two important points of distinction between civil and political society. The first relates to the degree of institutionalization. In Diamond's terms, civil society is a *"realm of organized* social life" that is *"distinct* from 'society' in general." There is a common view that civil society is made up of groups that are organized on a relatively formal basis: clubs, associations, NGOs, advocacy groups, religious organizations, and charities. Indeed, the presence of stable and enduring associations that play a role in aggregating interests and instructing their members about civic life is seen as one of the key contributions of civil society to democratic consolidation. These formal associations draw people out of their atomistic private spheres into a more transparent public sphere of civic engagement, accountability, and trust.

The political society I have described in Ban Tiam is much less marked by formal associations. Of course they are not completely absent—the village housewives' group, the committees that are established to implement local development projects, and even the lineage clusters that enter into reciprocal dealings with *pu nya* spirits—but many of the groups that operate in political society's pursuit of livelihood, security, and prosperity are unstable, highly personalized, and have very situationally specific goals. The distinction between

the private domain and the public domain is most commonly marked symbolically, especially by using the language of sacrifice for collective benefit,
rather than via the elaboration of formal institutions. In fact I interpret many
acts of institutionalization within political society as ritualized acts that seek
to draw sources of power into intimate domains rather than attempts to create a sphere of activity that is structurally distinct from the private realm. To
pick up some rather old sociological terminology, many of the clusters of
enterprise that form in political society are best regarded as "action sets" or
"quasi groups" that coalesce around specific, and often time-limited, objectives.[12] Action sets in Ban Tiam's political society are fragile and flexible; they
are based on pragmatic connections rather than formal rights of association.

The second important point of distinction between civil and political society concerns the relationship with the state. There is common agreement
on the definitional point that civil society is a domain that is autonomous
from the state; it is a "distinct sphere" and an "arena of governance in its
own right."[13] The formal associations of civil society form a mediating layer
between society in general and the bureaucratic structures of the modern
state. Autonomy is important in establishing civil society's pluralist credentials and providing room for expressions of opinion and forms of organization that are free from administrative or policy constraints. Associations that
fall under the influence of the state, or are initiated by it, are, at best, regarded
as degraded forms of civil society. More authentic versions of civil society are
often, to some extent at least, oppositional to the state. In some cases, civil
society opposition may be modest and reformist, attempting to nudge state
policy in desired directions or providing services that make up for the deficiencies of the state. In other contexts, civil society organizations may seek
to protect society from the interference of the state, perhaps by establishing
relatively independent domains of governance and resource management.
At the more radical end of the spectrum, civil society may operate as an arena
of resistance, struggle, or even rebellion where the state is directly challenged
by counterhegemonic political and economic visions.

Here we have a clear point of difference between civil and political society.
The productive intersection between the welfare and subsidy programs of
the state and the aspirations of the middle-income peasantry is a central component of the political society I have described in Ban Tiam. As the state has
expanded its administrative reach and shifted its orientation from taxing the
rural economy to supporting it, these productive nodes of intersection have
proliferated. Unlike civil society, political society places no particular moral

value on autonomy. Quite the opposite: political action, in the broadest sense of the term, is valued precisely when it draws the state—and other nodes of power—into systems of reciprocal exchange. In political society the function of boundaries, such as the symbolic marking of community, is not to shut out external influence but to condense and concentrate it within localized systems of exchange. This is not a matter of the undesirable capture of formerly autonomous civic associations by external agents but of the highly desirable entangling of these agents within local networks. The modern state has become particularly vulnerable to entanglement as its administrative expansion has created a vast army of officialdom that is regularly prone to local fraternization.

I want to emphasize this distinction between political and civil society, but I don't want to overstate it. While the relationship with the state highlights some important institutional and philosophical differences between civil and political society, there are similarities in relation to certain objectives. As indicated above, the autonomous activities of civil society range from those that might be described as more "resistance focused" to those that are more "civic focused."[14] The distinction with political society is most apparent at the resistance end of the spectrum where the relationship with the state clearly takes an oppositional form. But, in Larry Diamond's terms, many civil society organizations are involved in a "positive engagement" with the state, even while they remain formally autonomous from it.[15] It is at this more reformist end of the civil society spectrum that objectives start to merge with those of political society. These common objectives include policy concessions, financial support, bureaucratic sensitivity to social values, and accessible political leaders. The unorthodox and even illegal methods used within political society may be different from those employed within civil society, but some of the desired outcomes are very similar.

Given these points of similarity and difference, to what extent can Thailand's rural political society perform the democratizing functions often attributed to civil society?

POLITICAL SOCIETY AND DEMOCRACY

In a recent book, the political scientist and historian Paul Ginsborg argues that modern democracy is in crisis. *Democracy: Crisis and Renewal* asserts that that the problems facing modern democracy are about quality rather than quantity. Despite democratic setbacks in countries such as Thailand,

Bangladesh, and Kenya, there are now more democratic countries than there have ever been. However, Ginsborg argues, within democratic countries the political process is becoming increasingly hollow. Many people feel that politics occupies a "privileged and remote sphere" in which political parties serve the interests of big business and where cronyism, clientism, and corruption are rampant. The general public has responded with "extraordinary passivity and disinterest," withdrawing into the self-interested private sphere of consumption and television viewing.[16] This disillusionment with democracy is reflected in low voter turnout in electoral contests. In the European Parliament elections of 2004, less than half of the electorate voted in many Western European countries. In Eastern Europe the situation was even worse: 39 percent in Hungary, 28 percent in the Czech Republic, and only 17 percent in Slovakia. "Although there are many reasons for these figures," Ginsborg writes, "there is one that all shared—the feeling among large swathes of the European electorate that participation in the democratic process had little meaning."[17]

For Ginsborg, and many other commentators on modern politics, the remedy for this democratic malaise is a reinvigoration of civil society. According to this view, civil society provides an essential infrastructure of association, civic education, and citizen participation for the consolidation and effective operation of democracies. Representative systems of government need to be combined with forms of deliberation, participation, and monitoring so that "voting-centric" democracies develop into more inclusive "talk-centric" democracies.[18] Ginsborg argues that "active and dissenting citizens" need to be drawn out of their private sphere of consumption and conformity into "thriving networks of autonomous organizations."[19] His favorite case study is the participatory budgeting process adopted in the Brazilian city of Porto Alegre. A series of meetings, at various spatial scales, are held in which citizens (and their delegates) contribute to the formation of the city's spending program. In 2002 over 30,000 of the city's 1.3 million residents participated in the process. Final budgetary decisions in Porto Alegre are made by elected representatives, but their power and responsibility are "modified, enriched and institutionally constrained by the deliberative and participatory activity that is taking place around them."[20]

So where does political society fit into this tale of democratic "crisis and renewal"? To a significant extent it simply slips below the radar. The pessimistic approach adopted by Ginsborg and others is informed by an image of an institutionally disengaged and consumption-obsessed electorate that only occasionally emerges from its private sphere to cast desultory and conformist votes. Electoral democracy is hollow because voters choose representatives who act on their behalf with little direct accountability until the next election. Participatory democracy, by contrast, involves active citizens: joining organizations, attending meetings, forming committees, building civil society. Whereas the electoral citizen is a passive recipient of government largesse—and vulnerable to the inducements of populist demagogues like Italy's Silvio Berlusconi and Thailand's Thaksin—the participatory citizen is critically engaged in the budget process itself.

The problem with this dichotomous vision of democratic alternatives, and its enthusiastic celebration of one particular style of political action, is that it overlooks the vast substratum of political behavior that takes place within political society. Debate, discussion, and dissent about power and the allocation of resources—in other words, politics—take place within an intricate web of day-to-day interactions that few would associate with Ginsborg's more institutional vision of civil society. Critically engaged political orientations are not only forged within formal associations or structured arenas for participation. For a great many people they emerge out of highly localized and often very personal encounters with power in its many forms. In Ban Tiam, capricious spirits are domesticated, arrogant company representatives are berated, ineffectual officials are condemned, failed projects are subject to relentless gossip, and benevolent politicians are endorsed. This is the engine room of political consciousness. Many of the interactions within this complex field of power draw on sets of values that attempt to address the tricky balance between private and collective interests. In this world, there is no clear distinction between a politically apathetic private domain and a public domain of civic engagement. Rather, political society straddles the private-public divide both by drawing power into intimate domains and by strategically promoting private sacrifice for collective benefit.

Of course, there is a risk of romanticizing political society. This is not my intention. It is clear that political society has a dark side. Chatterjee acknowledges that "political society will bring into the hallways and corridors of power some of the squalor, ugliness and violence of popular life."[21] In Thailand, concerns about the squalor of local political culture coalesce around the image of the local strongman, who uses coercion and financial inducement to consolidate political power. These provincial businessmen-cum-politicians enrich themselves by capturing government contracts and corruptly appropriating funds destined for local development. One of the enduring themes of modern Thai political commentary has been that democratic values are undermined by electors who are willing to go along with the abuses of strongmen in order to avoid recriminations and obtain a paltry share of the benefits. In Ban Tiam's dealings over projects, subsidies, festivals, and elections there is no shortage of petty corruption, favoritism, factionalism, character assassination, illegality, and, at times, downright thuggery. The nationwide campaign of extrajudicial killings that the Thaksin government used to deal with alleged drug dealers won widespread local support, with firm and protective government action trumping due legal process. The practices and values of political society are sometimes far from edifying, and this gives plenty of ammunition to those who argue that Thailand's balance of power needs to be shifted in a more civil and virtuous direction.

Nevertheless, a realistic view of political society's shortcomings does not justify rejection of its democratic potential. As Chatterjee argues, "[I]f one truly values the freedom and equality that democracy promises, then one cannot imprison it within the sanitized fortress of civil society."[22] In the Thai context, I propose three reasons why this incarceration would be unjustified. First, political society is very diverse as a result of the economic, administrative, and supernatural diversity of rural society. While some relations within political society may be corrupt or abusive, they exist within a wide network of relationships, some of which can provide a basis for critique and promoting alternative styles of political behavior. A diverse political culture certainly contains some very unattractive elements, but, as in the natural world, diversity is also a basis for political resilience and adaptation. Second, despite some of the stereotypes of rural people's acceptance of corrupt practices, actions in political society are subject to judgment and evaluation. Local political society is pragmatic and flexible, but it is also experimental and evaluative. The rural constitution contains a range of informal precepts against which political action is assessed, and there is good evidence that civil society's concerns with transparency and sound administration are steadily being drawn into local networks of appraisal. Values matter in political society. Finally, and most important, political society may well provide a more realistic basis for dealing with the realities of contemporary politics. In Thailand there is a powerful elite discourse, drawing on carefully cultivated royal imagery, about the need for "good men" to guide the political process. Some of the most prominent civil society figureheads are among the royal network of good men who are regularly called on in times of crisis to provide wise and ethical counsel. Political society lacks this elite preoccupation with goodness, and its political values are not based on the assumption that good government can only be provided by good men. Evaluations of power within political society are more multidimensional and realistic; they are concerned with channeling power in desired directions, negotiating deals, and striking a reasonable balance between private and public benefit. This template is certainly a lot more ragged than the purist appeal to absolute goodness but it is more likely to be able to deal with the warts-and-all realities of political life.

Some survey research in Thailand suggests that political society may not be all that bad at promoting democratic values. A recent survey of fifteen hundred voters in twenty-seven provinces conducted by the Asia Foundation found a high level of interest in politics, widespread experience of free speech, and very considerable political tolerance.[23] Importantly, 83 percent of respondents disagreed with the statement "[I]t makes sense to follow the recommendations of local leaders when deciding who to vote for," 90 percent felt that family members should make their own choices about voting (rather than following the advice of the household head), and 91 percent said that religious leaders have little or no influence on their voting. There was concern about vote buying, with 58 percent saying that voters in the area could be influenced by it, but 84 percent thought that it was reasonable to take money from a party and then vote for whoever one likes. Other surveys, undertaken as part of the ongoing Asian Barometer project, also found that satisfaction with democratic processes is very high in Thailand, in fact considerably higher than in other democratic countries in the region.[24] These surveys have also found that support for democracy is higher in rural Thailand than it is among the Bangkok middle class, contrary to the common view that the civil-society-oriented middle class is a strong defender of democratic values.

Rural political society is certainly not perfect, but its everyday role in the democratic life of the nation warrants much more respectful attention. Discussions of options for democratic strengthening, in Thailand and elsewhere, will be enriched when they are able to recognize the diversity of commonplace political practice that legitimately informs democratic decision making. Without this respectful engagement with informal—and sometimes unattractive—political culture there is a real risk that those who write about democracy's contemporary crisis of participation will unwittingly encourage the view that votes cast in elections can be discounted because they represent only fleeting and superficial engagements with the political process. In fact, elections are just one of the ways in which rural people in Thailand seek to marshal power in the pursuit of security and prosperity. The visit to the ballot box is just one moment in an ongoing process of culturally informed judgments about the nature of power, in its many forms. Genuine democratic consolidation needs to take this rural political judgment seriously, even when—in fact especially when—it does not fit within the familiar templates of patron-client relations, class struggle, or civil society mobilization.

Notes

INTRODUCTION

1. Anek Laothamatas, "A Tale of Two Democracies: Conflicting Perceptions of Elections and Democracy in Thailand," in *The Politics of Elections in Southeast Asia*, ed. R. H. Taylor (Washington, D.C.: Woodrow Wilson Center Press, 1996).

2. "Red Rage Rising," *Bangkok Post*, 13 March 2010.

3. Partha Chatterjee, *The Politics of the Governed: Reflections on Popular Politics in Most of the World* (New York: Columbia University Press, 2004).

4. James C. Scott, *The Moral Economy of the Peasant: Rebellion and Subsistence in Southeast Asia* (New Haven, Conn.: Yale University Press, 1976), 1.

5. Eric R. Wolf, *Peasants* (Englewood Cliffs, N.J.: Prentice-Hall, 1966), 2–4; Teodor Shanin, "Introduction," in *Peasants and Peasant Societies*, ed. Teodor Shanin (Harmondsworth: Penguin, 1971), 14–15.

6. Michael Kearney, *Reconceptualizing the Peasantry: Anthropology in Global Perspective* (Boulder, Colo.: Westview Press, 1996), 141; Chris Baker, "Thailand's Assembly of the Poor: Background, Drama, Reaction," *South East Asia Research* 8, no. 1 (2000): 26.

7. Lucien M. Hanks, "Merit and Power in the Thai Social Order," *American Anthropologist* 64, no. 6 (1962); Lucien M. Hanks, "The Thai Social Order as Entourage and Circle," in *Change and Persistence in Thai Society: Essays in Honor of Lauriston Sharp*, ed. G. William Skinner and A. Thomas Kirsch (Ithaca, N.Y.: Cornell University Press, 1975).

8. Lauriston Sharp and Lucien M. Hanks, *Bang Chan: Social History of a Rural Community in Thailand* (Ithaca, N.Y.: Cornell University Press, 1978), 46.

9. Hanks, "The Thai Social Order as Entourage," 207.

10. Herbert P. Phillips, *Thai Peasant Personality: The Patterning of Interpersonal Behavior in the Village of Bang Chan* (Berkeley: University of California Press, 1965), 38, 39.

11. Ibid., 143.

12. Stephen B. Young, "The Northeastern Thai Village: A Non-participatory Democracy," in *Modern Thai Politics*, ed. Clark D. Neher (Cambridge, Mass.: Schenkman Publishing, 1979).

13. Clark D. Neher, "The Politics of Change in Rural Thailand," *Comparative Politics* 4, no. 2 (1972): 201.

14. Ibid., 216.

15. Ibid., 205–6.

16. Michael Moerman, "A Thai Village Headman as Synaptic Leader," in *Modern Thai Politics*, ed. Clark D. Neher (Cambridge, Mass.: Schenkman Publishing, 1979).

17. The collection edited by Ruth McVey is an important contribution to discussions of provincial strongmen and vote buying: *Money and Power in Provincial Thailand* (Copenhagen: Nordic Institute of Asian Studies, 2000).

18. Anek, "A Tale of Two Democracies," 223.

19. Michael J. Montesano, "Market Society and the Origins of the New Thai Politics," in *Money and Power in Provincial Thailand*, ed. Ruth McVey (Singapore: Institute for Southeast Asian Studies, 2000); Yoshinori Nishizaki, *Political Authority and Provincial Identity in Thailand: The Making of Banharn-Buri*, Studies on Southeast Asia (Ithaca, N.Y.: Southeast Asia Program, Cornell University, 2011).

20. Anek, "Tale," 206–8; Daniel Arghiros, *Democracy, Development and Decentralization in Provincial Thailand* (Richmond: Curzon, 2001), 114, 125.

21. Peter F. Bell, "'Cycles' of Class Struggle in Thailand," in *Thailand: Roots of Conflict*, ed. Andrew Turton, Jonathan Fast, and Malcolm Caldwell (Nottingham: Spokesman, 1978), 60.

22. Andrew Turton, "The Current Situation in the Thai Countryside," in *Thailand: Roots of Conflict*, ed. Andrew Turton, Jonathan Fast, and Malcolm Caldwell (Nottingham: Spokesman, 1978), 121.

23. Ibid., 133.

24. Ibid., 125.

25. Katherine A. Bowie, *Rituals of National Loyalty: An Anthropology of the State and the Village Scout Movement in Thailand* (New York: Columbia University Press, 1997).

26. Andrew Turton, "Limits of Ideological Domination and the Formation of Social Consciousness," in *History and Peasant Consciousness in South East Asia*, ed. Andrew Turton and Shigeharu Tanabe (Osaka: National Museum of Ethnology, 1984).

27. Andrew Turton, "Thailand: Agrarian Bases of State Power," in *Agrarian Transformation: Local Processes and the State in Southeast Asia*, ed. Gillian Hart, Andrew Turton, and Benjamin White (Berkeley: University of California Press, 1989).

28. Philip Hirsch, *Development Dilemmas in Rural Thailand* (Singapore: Oxford University Press, 1990).

29. James C. Scott, *Weapons of the Weak: Everyday Forms of Peasant Resistance* (New Haven, Conn.: Yale University Press, 1985).

30. Somchai Phatharathananunth, *Civil Society and Democratization: Social Movements in Northeast Thailand* (Copenhagen: Nordic Institute of Asian Studies, 2006), ix.

31. Baker, "Thailand's Assembly of the Poor."

32. Ibid.; Bruce D. Missingham, *The Assembly of the Poor in Thailand: From Local Struggles to National Protest Movement* (Chiang Mai: Silkworm Books, 2003).

33. Somchai, *Civil Society and Democratization*, 16.

34. Chatthip Nartsupha, *The Thai Village Economy in the Past* (Chiang Mai: Silkworm Books, 1999).

35. Nicholas Farrelly, "Tai Community and Thai Border Subversions," in *Tai Lands and Thailand: Community and State in Southeast Asia*, ed. Andrew Walker (Singapore: National University of Singapore Press, 2009).

36. Chang Noi, "A New Cold War Underway in Thailand," *The Nation*, 29 November 2007; Sonthi Boonyaratglin, "Sarup Kan Banyai Phiset, 26 Kanyayon 2550" [Summary of the special lecture, 26 September 2007] (secret Thai government document circulated by e-mail, 2007).

37. Attachak Sattayanurak, "Let's Reassess the Issue of Class," *On Open*, 30 April 2010, accessed 15 November 2010, http://www.onopen.com/attachak/1-04-30/5360; Kengkij Kitirianglarp, "Kan Tosu Khrang Ni Khue Songkhram Thang Chonchan Thi Pranipranom Mai Dai" [The fight this time is class war without compromise], *Prachatai*, 31 March 2010, accessed 12 November 2010, http://www.prachatai3.info/journal/2010/03/28605.

38. Niels Mulder, *Everyday Life in Thailand: An Interpretation* (Bangkok: Duang Kamol, 1979), 25.

39. Benedict R. O'G. Anderson, "The Idea of Power in Javanese Culture," in *Culture and Politics in Indonesia*, ed. Claire Holt, Benedict R. O'G. Anderson, and James Siegel (Ithaca, N.Y.: Cornell University Press, 1972), 7.

40. Nicola Beth Tannenbaum, *Who Can Compete against the World? Power-Protection and Buddhism in Shan Worldview* (Ann Arbor, Mich.: Association for Asian Studies, 1995).

41. Ibid., 79.

42. Nancy Eberhardt, *Imagining the Course of Life: Self-Transformation in a Shan Buddhist Community* (Honolulu: University of Hawai'i Press, 2006), 83–84.

43. One excellent example is Shu-Yuan Yang, "Imagining the State: An Ethnographic Study," *Ethnography* 6, no. 4 (2005). I also find Peter Evans's work on "synergy" very useful: "Government Action, Social Capital, and Development: Reviewing the Evidence on Synergy," *World Development* 24, no. 6 (1996): 1121.

44. Chatterjee, *The Politics of the Governed*.

45. This notion is rather different from the concept of "political society" used by some political scientists to refer to "the arena where citizens are represented and their views, therefore, are aggregated and packaged into specific policy demands and proposals." Goran Hyden, Jusius Court, and Ken Mease, *Political Society and Governance in Sixteen Developing Countries*, World Governance Survey Discussion Papers, no. 5

(London: Overseas Development Institute, 2003), 2. This more formal political society is seen as being made up of political parties, the electoral system, and the legislature.

46. Chatterjee, *The Politics of the Governed*, 116.

47. Partha Chatterjee, "Peasant Cultures of the Twenty-First Century," *Inter-Asia Cultural Studies* 9, no. 1 (2008): 125.

48. Ibid.

49. Chatterjee, *The Politics of the Governed*, 41.

50. Mayfair Mei-Hui Yang, "The Gift Economy and State Power in China," *Comparative Studies in Society and History* 31, no. 1 (1989): 50.

51. Chatterjee, *The Politics of the Governed*, 47–48.

52. Kasian Tejapira, "Toppling Thaksin," *New Left Review* 39 (May–June 2006): 14.

53. John Holt, *Spirits of the Place: Buddhism and Lao Religious Culture* (Honolulu: University of Hawai'i Press, 2009), 175.

54. A. Thomas Kirsch, "Complexity in the Thai Religious Sytem: An Interpretation," *Journal of Asian Studies* 36, no. 2 (1977): 262.

55. Holt, *Spirits of the Place*, 236.

56. R. E. Elson, *The End of the Peasantry in Southeast Asia: A Social and Eocnomic History of Peasant Livelihood, 1800–1990s* (Houndmills, Basingstoke: Macmillan, 1997), xii.

57. Anthony P. Cohen, *The Symbolic Construction of Community* (London: Tavistock, 1985), 16.

58. Chatterjee, *The Politics of the Governed*, 56.

CHAPTER 1. THAILAND'S PERSISTENT PEASANTRY

1. V. I. Lenin, *The Development of Capitalism in Russia* (Moscow: Progress Publishers, [1899] 1960), 174.

2. E. J. Hobsbawm, *Age of Extremes: The Short Twentieth Century, 1914–1991* (London: Michael Joseph, 1994), 292.

3. Kearney, *Reconceptualising the Peasantry*, 3.

4. Elson, *The End of the Peasantry*, 241.

5. Deborah Fahy Bryceson, "The Scramble in Africa: Reorienting Rural Livelihoods," *World Development* 30, no. 5 (2002).

6. Ibid.

7. Deborah Fahy Bryceson, "Disappearing Peasantries? Rural Labour Redundancy in the Neo-liberal Era and Beyond," in *Disappearing Peasantries? Rural Labour in Africa, Asia, and Latin America*, ed. Deborah Fahy Bryceson, Cristóbal Kay, and Jos E. Mooij (London: Intermediate Technology Publications, 2000), 309.

8. Warwick E. Murray, "From Dependency to Reform and Back Again: The Chilean Peasantry during the Twentieth Century," in *Latin American Peasants*, ed. Henry Veltmeyer and Tom Brass (London: Frank Cass, 2003), 211.

9. Deepankar Basu, "Some Comments on Partha Chatterjee's Theoretical Framework," *Radical Notes Journal*, 31 October 2008, accessed 29 August 2010, http://

radicalnotes.com/journal/2008/10/31/some-comments-on-partha-chatterjees-theo
retical-framework/.

10. Andrew Robinson, "Review of the Politics of the Governed: Reflections on
Popular Politics in Most of the World by Partha Chatterjee (2004)," *Contemporary
Political Theory* 7, no. 1 (2008).

11. GDP per capita data (current $US) is from the World Bank's World Develop-
ment Indicators Online for 2009, accessed 9 November 2010, http://data.world
bank.org/data-catalog/world-development-indicators. The average for all middle-
income countries is $3,344. Historical GDP data for Thailand is from the same source.

12. Land use data are from Alpha Research, *Thailand in Figures* (Bangkok: Tera
International, various years).

13. Office of the National Economic and Social Development Board, *Gross Regional
and Provincial Products, 2008 Edition* (Bangkok: Office of the National Economic and
Social Development Board, 2008).

14. Benchaphun Ekasingh et al., *Competitive Commercial Agriculture in the Northeast of Thailand* (Chiang Mai: Faculty of Agriculture, Chiang Mai University, 2007), 6.

15. Bidhya Bowornwathana quoted in Richard F. Doner, *The Politics of Uneven
Development: Thailand's Economic Growth in Comparative Perspective* (Cambridge:
Cambridge University Press, 2009), 26.

16. Sectoral GDP and labor force data are from the World Bank's World Development Indicators Online, accessed 22 June 2010, http://data.worldbank.org/data-cata
log/world-development-indicators.

17. Data from Food and Agriculture Organization of the United Nations (FAO-
STAT), trade, commodities by country: Thailand, accessed 22 August 2010, http://
faostat.fao.org.

18. Data on poverty are from Medhi Krongkaew, Suchittra Chamnivickorn, and
Isriya Nitithanprapas, "Economic Growth, Employment, and Poverty Reduction Linkages: The Case of Thailand" (Issues in Employment and Poverty Discussion Papers,
no. 20, International Labour Organization, 2006); United Nations Development Program, *Human Security, Today and Tomorrow: Thailand Human Development Report,
2009* (Bangkok: UNDP, 2010); Peter Warr, "Boom, Bust, and Beyond," in *Thailand
Beyond the Crisis*, ed. Peter Warr (London: Routledge, 2004).

19. Kym Anderson and Will Martin, "Distortions to Agricultural Incentives in
China and Southeast Asia" (Agricultural Distortions Working Papers, no. 69, World
Bank, 2008), 2.

20. Office of the National Economic and Social Development Board, "Phak Phanuak Kho: Kan Khamnuan Sen Khwam Yakchon" [Appendix C: The calculation of the
poverty line], in *Rai-Ngan Kan Pramoen Khwam Yakchon Pi 2551* [Report of poverty
assessment in 2008] (Bangkok: NESDB, 2008); World Bank, *Thailand Economic Monitor, April 2005* (Bangkok: World Bank, 2005), 8–10.

21. Data for these three indicators are from the World Bank's World Development Indicators Online, accessed 16 September 2009, http://data.worldbank.org/

data-catalog/world-development-indicators. The figures for life expectancy and infant mortality are for 1960 and 2007; the figures for primary school completion are for 1975 and 2007.

22. Peter Warr, "Thailand's Crisis Overload," *Southeast Asian Affairs* 2009 (2009): 334.

23. Average income figures are from National Statistics Office, *Report of the 2007 Household Socio-economic Survey* (Bangkok: National Statistics Office, 2007), table 1. Regional rural income figures are from the basic needs survey for 2008: Department of Community Development, *Rai-Ngan Khunaphap Chiwit Khong Khon Thai Pi 2551: Chak Khomun Khwam Champen Phuenthan* [Report of Thai People's Quality of Life in 2008: From Basic Needs Data] (Bangkok: Ministry of Interior, 2008).

24. Office of the National Economic and Social Development Board, "Appendix C."

25. Percentage estimates are derived from table 2.

26. Data cited in this paragraph are from National Statistics Office, *Sathiti Khomun Khwam Yakchon lae Kan Krachai Raidai, 2531–2552* [Data on poverty and income distribution, 1998–2009] (Bangkok: Office of the National Economic and Social Development Board, 2010).

27. United Nations Development Program, *Sufficiency Economy and Human Development: Thailand Human Development Report, 2007* (Bangkok: UNDP, 2007), 23. The World Bank's World Development Indicators Online (accessed 20 June 2011, http://data.worldbank.org/data-catalog/world-development-indicators) places Thailand's 2009 Gini coefficient at 54, compared with 46 for Malaysia, 37 for Indonesia, and 44 for the Philippines (2006 figure). The higher the Gini coefficient, the higher the level of inequality.

28. Borwornsak Uwanno, "Thai Political Situation: Wherefrom and Whereto" (paper presented at the panel discussion "Thai Political Situation: Wherefrom and Whereto?," cohosted by the Royal Thai Embassy and the SOAS Thai Society, School of Oriental and African Studies, London, 29 January 2010), 3. There is good evidence that disparities in wealth, rather than income, are significantly greater. See Chang Noi, "Politics and Thailand's Wealth Gap," *The Nation*, 2 November 2009. For other discussions of inequality in Thailand, see Yukio Ikemoto and Mine Uehara, "Income Inequality and Kuznets' Hypothesis in Thailand," *Asian Economic Journal* 14, no. 4 (2000); and Erik Martinez Kuhonta, "The Political Economy of Equitable Development in Thailand," *American Asian Review* 21, no. 4 (2003).

29. United Nations Development Program, *Human Security*.

30. Data on the contribution of agriculture to GDP are from the World Bank's World Development Indicators Online, accessed 22 June 2010, http://data.worldbank.org/data-catalog/world-development-indicators. Thailand's 2008 percentage is broadly similar to that of Indonesia (14 percent), the Philippines (15 percent), Malaysia (10 percent), and China (11 percent) but much less than that of Laos (35 percent), Cambodia (35 percent), and Vietnam (22 percent). In South Korea agriculture comprises only 3 percent of GDP.

31. Data on the percentage of the labor force in agriculture are from the World Bank's World Development Indicators Online, accessed 22 June 2010, http://data .worldbank.org/data-catalog/world-development-indicators. Thailand's percentage is similar to that of China (44 percent), Indonesia (41 percent), Cambodia (40 percent), and the Philippines (36 percent) but significantly higher than that of Malaysia (15 percent) and South Korea (7 percent) and significantly lower than that of Vietnam (58 percent). For discussion of Thailand's relatively slow movement of labor out of agriculture, see Ammar Siamwalla, Suthad Setboonsarng, and Direk Patamasiriwat, *Thai Agriculture: Resources, Institutions, and Policies* (Bangkok: Thailand Development Research Institute Foundation, 1991); and Teerana Bhongmakapat, "Income Distribution in a Rapidly Growing Economy of Thailand," *Chulalongkorn Journal of Economics* 5, no. 2 (1993).

32. United Nations Development Program, *Human Security*, 10.

33. Yujiro Hayami, "An Emerging Agricultural Problem in High-Performing Asian Economies" (Policy Research Working Papers, no. 4312, World Bank Development Research Group, Trade Team, 2007).

34. Ibid., 7–8.

35. International Rice Research Institute, "Table 3: Paddy Rice Yield (t/ha), by Country and Geographical Region, 1961–2007," *World Rice Statistics* (2008).

36. Doner, *The Politics of Uneven Development*, 37.

37. Peter Warr, "Productivity Growth in Thailand and Indonesia: How Agriculture Contributes to Economic Growth" (Working Papers in Economics and Development Studies, no. 200606, Department of Economics, Padjadjaran University, 2006).

38. Figures for Thailand and other countries are derived from sectoral GDP and labor force data from the World Bank's World Development Indicators Online, accessed 22 June 2010, http://data.worldbank.org/data-catalog/world-development-indicators. Of course, these are indicative figures only, as official labor force surveys do not capture the labor of migrant workers (thus probably understating the agricultural labor force in Thailand given the large number of Burmese laborers, although it is highly uncertain how this shadow labor force is distributed between agriculture and industry). At the same time there may be some overestimation of the agricultural labor force with some rural labor classified as agricultural, even though it is also involved in other activities.

39. National Statistics Office, "The Labor Force Survey, Whole Kingdom, Quarter 4, Oct.–Dec. 2006, Table 14," National Statistics Office, Bangkok, 2006.

40. Hayami, "An Emerging Agricultural Problem," 5.

41. Ibid., 6, 8.

42. Anne O. Krueger, "Political Economy of Agricultural Policy," *Public Choice* 87, no. 1/2 (1996).

43. Michael Lipton, *Why Poor People Stay Poor: A Study of Urban Bias in World Development* (London: Temple Smith, 1977).

44. David Burch, "Globalized Agriculture and Agri-Food Restructuring in Southeast Asia: The Thai Experience," in *Globalization and Agri-Food Restructuring: Perspectives from the Australasia Region*, ed. David Burch, Geoffrey Lawrence, and Roy E. Rickson (Aldershot: Avebury, 1996), 326; W. M. Corden, "The Exchange Rate System and the Taxation of Trade," in *Thailand: Social and Economic Studies in Development*, ed. T. H. Silcock (Canberra: Australian National University Press, 1967), table 7.6. Quotation from T. H. Silcock, "The Rice Premium and Agricultural Diversification," in *Thailand: Social and Economic Studies in Development*, ed. T. H. Silcock (Canberra: Australian National University Press, 1967), 232.

45. Brewster Grace, "Recent Developments in Thai Rice Production," *American Universities Field Staff Report, Southeast Asia Series* 23, no. 3 (1975): 5.

46. George Rosen, *Peasant Society in a Changing Economy: Comparative Development in Southeast Asia and India* (Urbana: University of Illinois Press, 1975), 154.

47. Anderson and Martin, "Distortions to Agricultural Incentives," 60.

48. Unichi Yamada, "Capital Outflow from the Agriculture Sector in Thailand" (Policy Research Working Papers, no 1910, World Bank, 1998), table 2.

49. Tyrell Haberkorn, *Revolution Interrupted: Farmers, Students, Law, and Violence in Northern Thailand* (Madison: University of Wisconsin Press, 2011), 52.

50. Office of the National Economic and Social Development Board, *The First Economic and Social Development Plan, Second Stage, 1964–1966* (Bangkok: NESDB, 1964), chapter 6.

51. Benchaphun et al., *Competitive Commercial Agriculture*, 47.

52. Shinichi Shigetomi, "Thailand: Toward a Developed, Rice-Exporting Country," in *The World Food Crisis and the Strategies of Asian Rice Exporters*, ed. Shinichi Shigetomi, Kensuke Kubo, and Kazunari Tsukada (Chiba: Institute of Developing Economies, 2011), 86.

53. Kym Anderson and Ernesto Valenzuela, "Estimates of Global Distortions to Agricultural Incentives, 1955 to 2007," World Bank, 2008, accessed 1 October 2010, http://cies.adelaide.edu.au/agdistortions/database/report/.

54. Kei Kajisa and Takamasa Akiyama, *The Evolution of Rice Price Policies over Four Decades: Thailand, Indonesia, and the Philippines* (Tokyo: Foundation for Advanced Studies on International Development, 2003), 21.

55. Agricultural budget figures for 1960 to 1986 are from National Statistics Office, *Statistical Yearbook, Thailand* (Bangkok: National Statistics Office, various years). Budget figures for 1987 to 2008 are from Alpha Research, *Thailand in Figures*. Irrigation funding figures are from Bureau of the Budget, *Rairap Raichai Priapthiap Ngoppraman Pracham Pi* [A comparison of the government's anuual revenue and expenditures] (Bangkok: Bureau of the Budget, various years).

56. Somporn Isvilanonda and Nipon Poapongsakorn, *Rice Supply and Demand in Thailand: The Future Outlook* (Bangkok: Thailand Development Research Institute, 1995), tables 2.2 and 2.4.

57. Waleerat Suphannachart and Peter Warr, "Research and Productivity in Thai Agriculture" (Working Papers in Trade and Development, no. 2009/11, Arndt-Corden Division of Economics, College of Asia and the Pacific, Australian National University, 2009).

58. Benchaphun et al., *Competitive Commercial Agriculture*.

59. Paul Cohen, "The Politics of Economic Development in Northern Thailand, 1967–1978" (PhD thesis, University of London, 1981), 149–50; Turton, "The Current Situation in the Thai Countryside," 113–14.

60. Bank for Agriculture and Cooperatives, *Annual Reports* (Bangkok: BAAC, various years); Somporn and Nipon, *Rice Supply and Demand in Thailand*, 16.

61. Tomas Larsson, "Security and the Politics of Property Rights in Thailand" (manuscript, Department of Politics and International Studies, University of Cambridge, 2010), 3.

62. National Statistics Office, *The 2003 Agricultural Census* (Bangkok: National Statistics Office of Thailand, 2003).

63. Shenggen Fan, Somchai Jitsuchon, and Nuntaporn Methakunnavut, "The Importance of Public Investment for Reducing Poverty in Middle-Income Countries: The Case of Thailand" (Development Strategy and Governance Division Discussion Papers, no. 7, International Food Policy Research Institute, 2004), 52.

64. Terry B. Grandstaff et al., "Rainfed Revolution in Northeast Thailand," *Southeast Asian Studies* 46, no. 3 (2008): 297.

65. Fan, Somchai, and Nuntaporn, "The Importance of Public Investment," 38.

66. Ibid., 13.

67. United Nations Development Program, *Human Security*, 152.

68. Alpha Research, *Thailand in Figures*.

69. Piya Hanvoravongchai and William C. Hsiao, "Thailand: Achieving Univeral Coverage with Social Health Insurance," in *Social Health Insurance for Developing Nations*, ed. William C Hsiao and R. Paul Shaw (Washington, D.C.: World Bank, 2007), 137.

70. Ibid., 140.

71. Alpha Research, *Thailand in Figures*; National Statistics Office, *Statistical Yearbook*.

72. World Bank, *Thailand Social Monitor: Improving Secondary Education* (Washington, D.C.: World Bank, 2006), 45–47.

73. Fan, Somchai, and Nuntaporn, " The Importance of Public Investment," 47.

74. World Bank, *Thailand Social Monitor*, 23.

75. Bureau of the Budget, *Comparison*; National Statistics Office, *Yearbook*.

76. Gerald W. Fry, "Decentralization as a Management and Development Strategy: A Thai Case Study," *Asian Journal of Public Administration* 5, no. 2 (1983): 51.

77. National Statistics Office, *Statistical Yearbook*.

78. Fumio Nagai, Kazuyo Ozaki, and Yoichiro Kimata, *JICA Program on Capacity Building of Thai Local Authorities* (Tokyo: Japan International Cooperation Agency, 2007), 6, 14.

79. Larsson, "Security and the Politics of Property Rights," 2.

80. Ibid., 27.

81. Andrew Walker and Nicholas Farrelly, "Northern Thailand's Specter of Eviction," *Critical Asian Studies* 40, no. 3 (2008).

82. World Bank, *Thailand Economic Monitor*, 10–11.

83. World Bank, *Thailand Social Monitor*.

84. James C. Scott, *The Art of Not Being Governed: An Anarchist History of Upland Southeast Asia*, Yale Agrarian Studies (New Haven, Conn.: Yale University Press, 2009), 7.

85. Kevin Hewison, "Neo-liberalism and Domestic Capital: The Political Outcome of the Economic Crisis in Thailand," *Journal of Development Studies* 41, no. 2 (2005): 325.

CHAPTER 2. BAN TIAM'S MIDDLE-INCOME RURAL ECONOMY

1. Ban Tiam basic needs survey data were obtained from the Department of Community Development in Chiang Mai. Regional data are from Department of Community Development, *Report of Thai People's Quality of Life in 2008*. The poverty line for northern Thailand comes from National Statistics Office, *Sathiti Khomun Khwam Yakchon lae Kan Krachai Raidai*, 2531–2552 [Data on poverty and income distribution, 1998–2009].

2. Jonathan Rigg et al., "Reconfiguring Rural Spaces and Remaking Rural Lives in Central Thailand," *Journal of Southeast Asian Studies* 39, no. 3 (2008): 372.

3. Office of Agricultural Economics, *Basic Data on Agricultural Economics, 2009* (Bangkok: Ministry of Agriculture, 2009).

4. This is based on an estimate of about 150 kilograms of milled rice per person per year. Somporn and Nipon, *Rice Supply and Demand in Thailand*, 62. I have assumed, based on local information, that about 2 kilograms of unmilled rice are required for each kilogram of milled rice.

5. International Rice Research Institute, *Background Paper: The Rice Crisis—What Needs to Be Done?* (Los Banos: IRRI, 2008).

6. Benchaphun Ekasingh et al., "Rabop Kan Phalit Lae Phalittaphap Nai Kan Chai Thi Din Khong Kasettrakon Changwat Chiangmai Chiangrai Lae Lamphun" [Production system and productivity of land use by farmers in Chiangmai, Chiangrai, and Lampun provinces] (paper presented at the conference Su Rabob Ahan Thi Plotphai Sang Mulakha Phoem Lae Chai Sapphayakon Yang Yangyuen [Toward a safe food system, added value, and sustainable use of natural resources], Pang Suan Kaew Hotel, Chiang Mai, 2004), 60.

7. Annual rice consumption is assumed to be about 1,050 kilograms (unmilled) per household (see note 4; 150 kilograms per person of milled rice is equal to about 300 kilograms of unmilled rice, multiplied by average household size in Ban Tiam of about 3.5 = 1,050 kilograms). Of course, some households produce more than they

consume, but many other households produce less or none at all. Over the period of research the average price of rice was about 7 baht per kilogram, making the total value of consumption about 7,350 baht. Taking a conservative estimate of average household income in recent years of 100,000 baht (the 2009 average was 125,000), the value of rice production represents only 7.35 percent.

8. Farmers were asked to subjectively rate the yield of their crop as very bad, bad, average, good, or very good.

9. Livestock raising and fruit orchards are supplementary sources of agricultural income for many households but major sources of income for very few. I estimate that about 10 percent of households also derive some income from the sale of timber cut illegally in the neighboring national park.

10. National Statistics Office, *The 2003 Agricultural Census*, table 7.

11. Department of Community Development, *Report of Thai People's Quality of Life in 2008*, 123.

12. Anna L. Paulson, "Insurance Motives for Migration: Evidence from Thailand" (working paper, Kellogg Graduate School of Management, Northwestern University, 2000), 8; Sauwalak Kittiprapas, "Social Impacts of Financial and Economic Crisis in Thailand" (report, East Asian Development Network Regional Project on the Social Impact of the Asian Financial Crisis, 2002), 15.

13. National Statistics Office, *Northern Region Industrial Survey* (Bangkok: National Statistics Office, 2007), 161.

14. These data were provided to me by the late Larry Sternstein. I have not been able to confirm who compiled the data, but they appear to be from a nationwide survey of industrial establishments. Each establishment is listed, with its village location, the nature of its activity, and the number of employees. I have been able to approximately date the local data from the dates of closure of some of the main enterprises.

15. This is a rough estimate based on fragmentary data on provincial, district, and municipal populations.

16. Daniel Arghiros and Joanne Moller, "Thai Rural Enterprise Development Strategies in the 1990s: A Critical Appraisal," *Sojourn: Journal of Social Issues in Southeast Asia* 15, no. 2 (2000).

17. The SML scheme provided grants of 200,000 baht for villages with a population of less than 500 people, 250,000 for villages with a population of 501 to 1,000, and 300,000 for villages larger than 1,000.

18. Yoko Ueda, *Local Economy and Entrepreneurship in Thailand: A Case Study of Nakhon Ratchasima* (Japan: Kyoto University Press, 1995), 87.

19. Doner, *The Politics of Uneven Development*, 11–14.

20. Ibid., 3.

21. Somporn and Nipon, *Rice Supply and Demand in Thailand*, 53.

22. Jonathan Rigg, *Living with Transition in Laos: Market Integration in Southeast Asia*, Routledge Contemporary Southeast Asia (London: Routledge, 2005), 120.

23. Keijiro Otsuka and Takashi Yamano, "Introduction to the Special Issue on the Role of Nonfarm Income in Poverty Reduction: Evidence from Asia and East Africa," *Agricultural Economics* 35, no. 3 (2006): 396.

24. Turton, "Local Powers and Rural Differentiation," 81–82.

CHAPTER 3. DRAWING POWER INTO PRIVATE REALMS

1. *Larb* is a classic northern Thai dish made from finely chopped meat (sometimes raw) mixed with chilies and a variety of herbs.

2. This general discussion of *pu nya* spirits draws on observations in Ban Tiam along with a review of previous research on them, especially Paul Cohen and Gehan Wijeyewardene, eds., "Spirit Cults and the Position of Women in Northern Thailand," special issue, *Mankind* 14, no. 4 (1984).

3. Gehan Wijeyewardene, "Matriclans or Female Cults: A Problem in Northern Thai Ethnography," *Mankind* 11, no. 1 (1977): 19.

4. Mary R. Haas, *Thai-English Student's Dictionary* (Stanford: Stanford University Press, 1964), 621.

5. Paul Cohen and Gehan Wijeyewardene, "Introduction," "Spirit Cults and the Position of Women in Northern Thailand," special issue, *Mankind* 14, no. 4 (1984): 250–51.

6. Wijeyewardene, "Matriclans or Female Cults," 20.

7. Cohen and Wijeyewardene, "Spirit Cults and the Position of Women," 298.

8. For Chiang Rai: Andrew Turton, "Matrilineal Descent Groups and Spirit Cults of the Thai-Yuan in Northern Thailand," *Journal of the Siam Society* 60, no. 2 (1972): 272. For Chiang Mai: Jack M. Potter, *Thai Peasant Social Structure* (Chicago: University of Chicago Press, 1976), 146. For Lampang: M. V. McMorran, "Northern Thai Ancestral Cults: Authority and Aggression," "Spirit Cults and the Position of Women in Northern Thailand," special issue, *Mankind* 14, no. 4 (1984): 309. For Nan: Richard B Davis, *Muang Metaphysics: A Study of Northern Thai Myth and Ritual* (Bangkok: Pandora, 1984), 275.

9. Davis, *Muang Metaphysics*, 55.

10. The minimal impact of surnames is suggested in Walter F. Vella and Dorothy B. Vella, *Chaiyo! King Vajiravudh and the Development of Thai Nationalism* (Honolulu: University of Hawai'i Press, 1978), 135.

11. Anan Ganjanapan, "Phithi Wai Phi Mueang Lae Amnat Rat Nai Lanna" [Spirit worship and state power in Lanna], in *Sangkhom Lae Watthanatham Nai Prathet Thai* [Society and culture in Thailand], ed. Princess Maha Chakri Sirindhorn Anthropology Centre (Bangkok: Princess Maha Chakri Sirindhorn Anthropology Centre, 1999); Chalatchai Ramitanon, *Phi Chao Nai* [Aristocratic spirits] (Chiang Mai: Ming Mueang Publishing House, 2002).

12. B. J. Terwiel, "The Origin and Meaning of the Thai 'City Pillar'," *Journal of the Siam Society* 66, no. 2 (1978).

13. Anan, "Spirit Worship and State Power"; H. L. Shorto, "The 32 Myos in the Medieval Mon Kingdom," *Bulletin of the School of Oriental and African Studies* 26, no. 3 (1963); Terwiel, "The Origin and Meaning of the Thai 'City Pillar.'"

14. Donald K. Swearer, Sommai Premchit, and Phaithoon Dokbuakaew, *Sacred Mountains of Northern Thailand and Their Legends* (Chiang Mai: Silkworm Books, 2004).

15. Gehan Wijeyewardene, *Place and Emotion in Northern Thai Ritual Behaviour* (Bangkok: Pandora, 1986), 131.

16. Turton, "Matrilineal Descent Groups," 244, 246, 255.

17. Wijeyewardene, *Place and Emotion*, 213.

18. That is not to say that there are not elements of gender rivalry sometimes expressed in the *pu nya* cults. See, for example, Cohen and Wijeyewardene, "Introduction," 256–57.

19. Chalatchai, *Aristocratic Spirits*.

20. Shigeharu Tanabe, "Spirits and Ideological Discourse: The Tai Lu Guardian Cults in Yunnan," *Sojourn* 3, no. 1 (1988): 3.

21. Anan, "Spirit Worship and State Power."

22. Turton, "Matrilineal Descent Groups," 253.

CHAPTER 4. CONTRACTS, PRIVATE CAPITAL, AND THE STATE

1. Northern Meteorological Centre, "Average Rainfall in Chiang Mai (Millimetres)," accessed 6 April 2010, http://www.cmmet.tmd.go.th/.

2. Government of Thailand, "Phon Krathop Krathiam Jaak Kan Poet Talat Seri Thai-Jin" [The impact on garlic of the Thai-China Free Trade Agreement] (report, Bangkok, 2003); Government of Thailand, "Sathanakan Kratiam Nai Changwat Chiangmai Pi 2550" [The garlic situation in Chiang Mai Province in 2007] (report, Bangkok, 2007).

3. Benchaphun et al., "Production System and Productivity of Land Use." Potatoes provide even better returns than garlic. They have been tried in Ban Tiam, but growing them has not been successful.

4. Office of Agricultural Economics, "Basic Data on Agricultural Economics," 63.

5. A quota was placed on garlic imports from China, with a 57 percent tariff on imports above quota, but production costs in China were so low and garlic smuggling so widespread that the quota was expected to offer little effective protection: Chayodom Sabhasri, Somprawin Manprasert, and Thanee Chaiwat, *ASEAN and China Free Trade Area: Implications for Thailand* (Bangkok: Faculty of Economics, Chulalongkorn University, 2005), 16.

6. Based on data on garlic yield from Food and Agriculture Organization of the United Nations (FAOSTAT), production, crops: garlic, accessed 22 August 2010, http://faostat.fao.org.

7. Office of Agricultural Economics, "Basic Data on Agricultural Economics," 20.

8. Benchaphun et al., "Production System and Productivity of Land Use," 60.

9. Peter Warr and Archanun Kohpaiboon, "Distortions to Agricultural Incentives in a Food Exporting Country: Thailand" (manuscript, Crawford School, College of Asia and the Pacific, Australian National University, 2007), 8.

10. Michael J. Watts, "Life under Contract: Contract Farming, Agrarian Restructuring, and Flexible Accumulation," in *Living under Contract: Contract Farming and Agrarian Transformation in Sub-Saharan Africa*, ed. P. D. Little and M. J. Watts (Madison: University of Wisconsin Press, 1994), 64.

11. Roger A. J. Clapp, "Representing Reciprocity, Reproducing Domination: Ideology and the Labour Process in Latin American Contract Farming," *Journal of Peasant Studies* 16, no. 1 (1988): 6.

12. Murray, "From Dependency to Reform," 199–201.

13. Tanya Korovkin, "Peasants, Grapes, and Corporations: The Growth of Contract Farming in a Chilean Community," *Journal of Peasant Studies* 19, no. 2 (1992): 250.

14. David Glover and Kenneth C. Kusterer, *Small Farmers, Big Business: Contract Farming and Rural Development* (Houndmills, Basingstoke: Macmillan, 1990), 132.

15. Nigel Key and David Runsten, "Contract Farming, Smallholders, and Rural Development in Latin America: The Organization of Agroprocessing Firms and the Scale of Outgrower Production," *World Development* 27, no. 2 (1999): 396.

16. Glover and Kusterer, *Small Farmers*, 131.

17. Ben White, "Agroindustry and Contract Farmers in Upland West Java," *Journal of Peasant Studies* 24, no. 3 (1997): 131–32.

18. Sompop Manarungsan and Suebskun Suwanjindar, "Contract Farming and Outgrower Schemes in Thailand," in *Contract Farming in Southeast Asia: Three Country Studies*, ed. David Glover and Teck Ghee Lim (Kuala Lumpur: Institute for Advanced Studies, University of Malaya, 1992), 22–24.

19. My survey may not have captured all garlic cultivation, but it certainly captured the vast majority of it.

20. "Thai Food Hit by Garlic Crisis," *The Nation*, 2 March 2008.

21. In inflation-adjusted terms this was slightly lower than the peak reached in 1996.

22. Manager On Line, "Kasettrakon Pak Lak Na Sala Klang Chiangmai Rong Rat Poet Chamnam Krathiam" [Farmers protest in front of Chiangmai City Hall asking the government to purchase their garlic], *Manager On Line*, accessed 24 June 2009, http://www.ftawatch.org/news/view.php?id=13291.

23. Office of Agricultural Economics, "Kratiam Haeng Yai" [Large dried garlic], accessed 24 April 2008, http://www.oae.go.th/warning%20garlic.htm.

24. Prachatham, "Kasettrakon Chiangmai Chi Ratthaban Rapphitchop Rakha Krathiam Toktam" [Chiangmai farmers urge government to take responsibility for the fall of garlic price], *Prachatham*, 8 April 2008, accessed 23 August 2009, http://www.prachatham.com/detail.htm?code=n4_08042008_01.

25. Scott, *Weapons of the Weak*, 183.

26. Ibid., 248–72.

27. Ibid., 180.

28. Sherry B. Ortner, "Resistance and the Problem of Ethnographic Refusal," *Comparative Studies in Society and History* 37, no. 1 (1995).

29. J. Sumberg and C. Okali, eds., *Farmers' Experiments: Creating Local Knowledge* (Boulder, Colo.: Lynne Rienner Publishers, 1997).

30. Holly High, "Village in Laos: An Ethnographic Account of Poverty and Policy among the Mekong's Flows" (PhD diss., Department of Anthropology, Research School of Pacific and Asian Studies, Australian National University, 2005), 216–22, 228–30.

31. Ibid., 234–35.

CHAPTER 5. THE POLITICAL ECONOMY OF PROJECTS

1. The golden apple snail (*Pomacea canaliculata*) is an invasive pest that infests rice fields in many parts of Asia and damages rice crops by eating through the stems of the growing plants.

2. James Ferguson, *The Anti-politics Machine: "Development," Depoliticization, and Bureaucratic Power in Lesotho* (Minneapolis: University of Minnesota Press, 1994), 273.

3. Tania Li, *The Will to Improve: Governmentality, Development, and the Practice of Politics* (Durham, N.C.: Duke University Press, 2007), 270.

4. Sherry B. Ortner, *Anthropology and Social Theory: Culture, Power, and the Acting Subject* (Durham, N.C.: Duke University Press, 2006), 145.

5. Peter Miller and Nikolas Rose, "Governing Economic Life," *Economy and Society* 19, no. 3 (1990).

6. *Tu* is the word used in northern Thailand to refer to a Buddhist monk.

7. See, for example, Philip Abrams, "Notes on the Difficulty of Studying the State," *Journal of Historical Sociology* 1, no. 1 (1988); James Ferguson and Akhil Gupta, "Spatializing States: Toward an Ethnography of Neoliberal Governmentality," *American Ethnologist* 29, no. 4 (2002); Timothy Mitchell, "Society, Economy, and the State Effect," in *The Anthropology of the State: A Reader*, ed. Aradhana Sharma and Akhil Gupta (Malden, Mass.: Blackwell, 2006); and Michel-Rolph Trouillot, "The Anthropology of the State in the Age of Globalization: Close Encounters of the Deceptive Kind," *Current Anthropology* 42, no. 1 (2001).

CHAPTER 6. COMMUNITY, LEGIBILITY, AND ELIGIBILITY

1. Émile Durkheim, *The Elementary Forms of the Religious Life* (London: George Allen and Unwin, 1915), 200.

2. Ibid., 220.

3. Ibid., 206, 207.

4. Cohen, *The Symbolic Construction of Community*, 28–33.

5. Ibid., 21.

6. Signe Howell, "Community beyond Place: Adoptive Families in Norway," in *Realizing Community: Concepts, Social Relationships, and Sentiments*, ed. Vered Amit (London: Routledge, 2002), 94.

7. Peter Vandergeest, "Gifts and Rights: Cautionary Notes on Community Self-Help in Thailand," *Development and Change* 22, no. 3 (1991): 427–30.

8. Stanley Jeyaraja Tambiah, *Buddhism and the Spirit Cults in Northeast Thailand* (Cambridge: Cambridge University Press, 1970), 342.

9. Durkheim, *The Elementary Forms of the Religious Life*, 214–15.

10. Jeffrey C. Alexander, "Cultural Pragmatics: Social Performance between Ritual and Strategy," *Sociological Theory* 22, no. 2 (2004).

11. Abigaël Pesses, "Women Abilities: Feminism and the Ethics of Sustainable Development among Karen Highlanders," *Tai Culture* 19 (2007): 183–84.

12. Craig J. Reynolds, "The Origins of Community in the Thai Discourse of Global Governance," in *Tai Lands and Thailand: Community and State in Southeast Asia*, ed. Andrew Walker (Singapore: National University of Singapore Press, 2009), 30–35.

13. Ibid., 34.

14. Data from the Organization for Cooperation and Economic Development (OECD), Query Wizard for International Development Statistics (QWIDS), accessed 1 November 2010, http://stats.oecd.org/qwids/.

15. James C. Scott, *Seeing Like a State: How Certain Schemes to Improve the Human Condition Have Failed*, Yale Agrarian Studies (New Haven, Conn.: Yale University Press, 1998).

16. Patricia Cheesman, "Textiles and Clothing of the Lao-Tai Peoples as Community Markers" (presentation to the 306th Meeting of the Informal Northern Thai Group, 14 October 2008), accessed 25 March 2009, http://www.intgcm.thehost server.com/diary2008_306th.html.

17. Rigg et al., "Reconfiguring Rural Spaces."

18. Ibid., 374.

19. Ibid., 376–77.

20. Chatterjee, *The Politics of the Governed*, 75.

CHAPTER 7. THE RURAL CONSTITUTION

1. For a good critical overview of discussions of vote buying, see William A. Callahan, "The Discourse of Vote Buying and Political Reform in Thailand," *Pacific Affairs* 71, no. 1 (2005).

2. Andrew Walker, "The 'Karen Consensus,' Ethnic Politics, and Resource-Use Legitimacy in Northern Thailand," *Asian Ethnicity* 2, no. 2 (2001).

3. Benedict J. Kerkvliet, *Everyday Politics in the Philippines: Class and Status Relations in a Central Luzon Village* (Lanham, Md.: Rowman and Littlefield, 2002).

4. Ibid., 11.

5. Ibid., chapter 8.

6. Benedict J. Kerkvliet, *The Power of Everyday Politics: How Vietnamese Peasants Transformed National Policy* (Ithaca, N.Y.: Cornell University Press, 2005).

7. Kerkvliet, *Everyday Politics in the Philippines*, 242–45.

8. Two were for the village headman, four for local government elections, two for provincial assembly elections, three for House of Representatives elections, and two for Senate elections.

9. In exploring the everyday politics of elections in Thailand, I am not starting completely from scratch. See, for example, Nishizaki, *Political Authority and Provincial Identity*; Katherine A Bowie, "Standing in the Shadows: Of Matrilocality and the Role of Women in a Village Election in Northern Thailand," *American Ethnologist* 35, no. 1 (2008); and Arghiros, *Democracy, Development, and Decentralization*.

10. In response to this constitutional obsession, the historian and public intellectual Nidhi Eoseewong wrote in 1991 about Thailand's "cultural constitution." In contrast to formal written charters, which are easily set aside by coup makers, the cultural constitution reflects the more enduring "ways of life, ways of thinking, and values" that underpin the key institutions in Thailand's political life. Nidhi Eoseewong, "The Thai Cultural Constitution," *Kyoto Review of Southeast Asia* 3 (2003).

11. Pasuk Phongpaichit, "Developing Social Alternatives: Walking Backwards into a Klong" (paper presented at the conference Thailand Update: Thailand beyond the Crisis, Australian National University, Canberra, 21 April 1999), 6.

12. Each mayoral candidate had a team of candidates running for council membership.

13. The word *mahachon* means "the masses."

14. Votes were counted at the constituency level, so village-level counts are not available.

15. For details of this scheme, see chapter 2, note 17.

16. Agricultural budget is from chart 4 in chapter 1. Agricultural GDP is from the World Bank's World Development Indicators Online, accessed 22 June 2010, http://data.worldbank.org/data-catalog/world-development-indicators.

17. Previously, lower house votes (but not Senate votes) had been combined and counted at constituency level, in an effort to reduce the alleged impact of vote buying. But the postcoup government, despite a vigorous campaign against vote buying, changed the rules to allow for vote counts at booth level.

18. Benedict J. Kerkvliet and Resil B. Mojares, "Themes in the Transition from Marcos to Aquino: An Introduction," in *From Marcos to Aquino: Local Perspectives on Political Transition in the Philippines*, ed. Benedict J. Kerkvliet and Resil B. Mojares (Manila: Ateneo de Manila University Press, 1991), 10.

19. Max Gluckman, *Custom and Conflict in Africa* (Oxford: Basil Blackwell, 1955).

CONCLUSION

1. United Nations Development Program, *Human Security*, table A1.4.

2. Kengkij Kitirianglarp and Kevin Hewison, "Social Movements and Political Opposition in Contemporary Thailand," *Pacific Review* 22, no. 4 (2009).

3. Sattha Sarattha, "7 Hetphon Thi Tham Hai Khi Thuk Chai Pen Awut [7 reasons why shit is used as a weapon]," *Prachatai*, 3 October 2010, accessed 28 October 2010, http://www.prachatai3.info/journal/2010/03/28065.

4. Robert Woodrow, "The Down-Trodden Rural Poor of Thailand: It's Not Quite What You Think," *New Mandala*, 10 May 2010, accessed 23 October 2010, http://asia pacific.anu.edu.au/newmandala/2010/05/10/the-rebellion-of-thailands-middle-income-peasants/.

5. Chatterjee, *The Politics of the Governed*, 41.

6. Partha Chatterjee, "Beyond the Nation? Or Within?," *Social Text* 56 (Autumn 1998): 60.

7. Nissim Mannathukkaren, "The 'Poverty' of Political Society: Partha Chatterjee and the People's Plan Campaign in Kerala, India," *Third World Quarterly* 31, no. 2 (2010).

8. Neera Chandhoke, "Review of Chatterjee, Partha, 'Empire and Nation: Selected Essays,'" H-Net Reviews, August 2010, accessed 14 September 2010, http://www.h-net.org/reviews/showrev.php?id=30477.

9. Larry Diamond, "Toward Democratic Consolidation: Rethinking Civil Society," *Journal of Democracy* 5, no. 3 (1994): 5.

10. Ibid., 6.

11. Ibid.; Archon Fung, "Associations and Democracy: Between Theories, Hopes, and Realities," *Annual Review of Sociology* 29 (2003).

12. Adrian C. Mayer, "The Significance of Quasi-Groups in the Study of Complex Societies," in *The Social Anthropology of Complex Societies*, ed. Michael Banton (London: Tavistock Publications, 1966).

13. Muthiah Alagappa, "Civil Society and Political Change: An Analytical Framework," in *Civil Society and Political Change in Asia: Expanding and Contracting Democratic Space*, ed. Muthiah Alagappa (Stanford: Stanford University Press, 2004), 32.

14. Fung, "Associations and Democracy."

15. Diamond, "Toward Democratic Consolidation," 11.

16. Paul Ginsborg, *Democracy: Crisis and Renewal* (London: Profile Books, 2008), 27–28.

17. Ibid., 34.

18. Fung, "Associations and Democracy," 525.

19. Ginsborg, *Democracy*, 44, 48.

20. Ibid., 71.

21. Chatterjee, *The Politics of the Governed*, 74.

22. Ibid.

23. Tim Meisburger, *Constitutional Reform and Democracy in Thailand: A National Survey of the Thai People* (Bangkok: Asia Foundation, 2009).

24. Robert Albritton and Thawilwadee Bureekul, "The State of Democracy in Thailand," *New Mandala*, 18 September 2008, accessed 28 October 2010, http://asiapacific.anu.edu.au/newmandala/wp-content/uploads/2008/09/state-of-democracy.pdf; Robert B. Albritton and Thawilwadee Bureekul, "Developing Democracy under a New Constitution in Thailand," in *Asian Barometer: A Comparative Survey of Democracy, Governance, and Development* (Taipei: Asian Barometer Project Office, National Taiwan University and Academia Sinica, 2004).

Bibliography

Abrams, Philip. "Notes on the Difficulty of Studying the State." *Journal of Historical Sociology* 1, no. 1 (1988): 58–89.

Alagappa, Muthiah. "Civil Society and Political Change: An Analytical Framework." In *Civil Society and Political Change in Asia: Expanding and Contracting Democratic Space*, edited by Muthiah Alagappa, 25–57. Stanford: Stanford University Press, 2004.

Albritton, Robert B., and Thawilwadee Bureekul. "Developing Democracy under a New Constitution in Thailand." In *Asian Barometer: A Comparative Survey of Democracy, Governance, and Development.* Taipei: Asian Barometer Project Office, National Taiwan University and Academia Sinica, 2004.

———. "The State of Democracy in Thailand." *New Mandala*, 18 September 2008. Accessed 28 October 2010. http://asiapacific.anu.edu.au/newmandala/wp-content/uploads/2008/09/state-of-democracy.pdf.

Alexander, Jeffrey C. "Cultural Pragmatics: Social Performance between Ritual and Strategy." *Sociological Theory* 22, no. 2 (2004): 527–73.

Alpha Research. *Thailand in Figures.* Bangkok: Tera International, various years.

Ammar Siamwalla, Suthad Setboonsarng, and Direk Patamasiriwat. *Thai Agriculture: Resources, Institutions, and Policies.* Bangkok: Thailand Development Research Institute Foundation, 1991.

Anan Ganjanapan. "Phithi Wai Phi Mueang Lae Amnat Rat Nai Lanna" [Spirit worship and state power in Lanna]. In *Sangkhom Lae Watthanatham Nai Prathet Thai* [Society and culture in Thailand], edited by Princess Maha Chakri Sirindhorn Anthropology Centre, 150–61. Bangkok: Princess Maha Chakri Sirindhorn Anthropology Centre, 1999.

Anderson, Benedict R. O'G. "The Idea of Power in Javanese Culture." In *Culture and Politics in Indonesia*, edited by Claire Holt, Benedict R. O'G. Anderson, and James Siegel, 1–70. Ithaca, N.Y.: Cornell University Press, 1972.

Anderson, Kym, and Will Martin. "Distortions to Agricultural Incentives in China and Southeast Asia." Agricultural Distortions Working Papers, no. 69, World Bank, 2008.

Anderson, Kym, and Ernesto Valenzuela. "Estimates of Global Distortions to Agricultural Incentives, 1955 to 2007." World Bank, 2008. Accessed 1 October 2010. http://cies.adelaide.edu.au/agdistortions/database/report/.

Anek Laothamatas. "A Tale of Two Democracies: Conflicting Perceptions of Elections and Democracy in Thailand." In The Politics of Elections in Southeast Asia, edited by R. H. Taylor, 201–23. Washington, D.C.: Woodrow Wilson Center Press, 1996.

Arghiros, Daniel. Democracy, Development, and Decentralization in Provincial Thailand. Richmond, UK: Curzon, 2001.

Arghiros, Daniel, and Joanne Moller. "Thai Rural Enterprise Development Strategies in the 1990s: A Critical Appraisal." Sojourn: Journal of Social Issues in Southeast Asia 15, no. 2 (2000): 153–83.

Attachak Sattayanurak. "Thobthuan Kan Mai Nai Praden Rueng Chonchan" [Let's reassess the issue of class]. On Open, 30 April 2010. Accessed 15 November 2010. http://www.onopen.com/attachak/10-04-30/5360.

Baker, Chris. "Thailand's Assembly of the Poor: Background, Drama, Reaction." South East Asia Research 8, no. 1 (2000): 5–29.

Bank for Agriculture and Cooperatives. Annual Reports. Bangkok: BAAC, various years.

Bank of Thailand. "Laeng Thi Ma Lae Chai Pai Khong Ngoen Thun Khong Thanakhan Phue Kankaset Lae Sahakon Kankaset" [Operations of the Bank for Agriculture and Agricultural Co-Operatives]. Accessed 7 July 2011. http://www.bot.or.th/Thai/Statistics/Discontinued/Pages/MoneyBanking.aspx.

———. "Ngoen Ku Hai Yuem Khong Thanakhan Phanit Chamnaek Tam Praphet Thurakit" [Private bank lending by business type]. Accessed 28 November 2010. http://www2.bot.or.th/statistics/ReportPage.aspx?reportID=27&language=th.

Basu, Deepankar. "Some Comments on Partha Chatterjee's Theoretical Framework." Radical Notes Journal, 31 October 2008. Accessed 29 August 2010. http://radical-notes.com/journal/2008/10/31/some-comments-on-partha-chatterjees-theoretical-framework/.

Bell, Peter F. "'Cycles' of Class Struggle in Thailand." In Thailand: Roots of Conflict, edited by Andrew Turton, Jonathan Fast, and Malcolm Caldwell, 51–79. Nottingham: Spokesman, 1978.

Benchaphun Ekasingh, Chapika Sungkapitux, Jirawan Kitchaicharoen, and Pornsiri Suebpongsang. Competitive Commercial Agriculture in the Northeast of Thailand. Chiang Mai: Faculty of Agriculture, Chiang Mai University, 2007.

Benchaphun Ekasingh, Kuson Thong-ngam, Tanya Promburom, and Supakit Sinchaikul. "Rabop Kan Phalit Lae Phalittaphap Nai Kan Chai Thi Din Khong Kasettrakon Changwat Chiangmai Chiangrai Lae Lamphun" [The production system and productivity of land use by farmers in Chiangmai, Chiangrai, and Lampun provinces]. Paper presented at the conference Su Rabob Ahan Thi Plotphai Sang

Mulakha Phoem Lae Chai Sapphayakon Yang Yangyuen [Toward a safe food system, added value, and sustainable use of natural resources], Pang Suan Kaew Hotel, Chiang Mai, 2004.

Borwornsak Uwanno. "Thai Political Situation: Wherefrom and Whereto." Paper presented at the panel discussion "Thai Political Situation: Wherefrom and Whereto?," cohosted by the Royal Thai Embassy and the SOAS Thai Society, School of Oriental and African Studies, London, 29 January 2010.

Bowie, Katherine A. *Rituals of National Loyalty: An Anthropology of the State and the Village Scout Movement in Thailand.* New York: Columbia University Press, 1997.

———. "Standing in the Shadows: Of Matrilocality and the Role of Women in a Village Election in Northern Thailand." *American Ethnologist* 35, no. 1 (2008): 136–53.

Bryceson, Deborah Fahy. "Disappearing Peasantries? Rural Labour Redundancy in the Neo-liberal Era and Beyond." In *Disappearing Peasantries? Rural Labour in Africa, Asia, and Latin America,* edited by Deborah Fahy Bryceson, Cristóbal Kay, and Jos E. Mooij, 1–36. London: Intermediate Technology Publications, 2000.

———. "The Scramble in Africa: Reorienting Rural Livelihoods." *World Development* 30, no. 5 (2002): 725–39.

Burch, David. "Globalized Agriculture and Agri-Food Restructuring in Southeast Asia: The Thai Experience." In *Globalization and Agri-Food Restructuring: Perspectives from the Australasia Region,* edited by David Burch, Geoffrey Lawrence, and Roy E. Rickson, 323–44. Aldershot: Avebury, 1996.

Bureau of the Budget. *Rairap Raichai Priapthiap Ngoppraman Pracham Pi* [A comparison of the government's anuual revenue and expenditures]. Bangkok: Bureau of the Budget, various years.

Callahan, William A. "The Discourse of Vote Buying and Political Reform in Thailand." *Pacific Affairs* 71, no. 1 (2005): 95–113.

Chalatchai Ramitanon. *Phi Chao Nai* [Aristocratic spirits]. Chiang Mai: Ming Mueang Publishing House, 2002.

Chandhoke, Neera. "Review of Chatterjee, Partha, 'Empire and Nation: Selected Essays.'" H-Net Reviews, August 2010. Accessed 14 September 2010. http://www.h-net.org/reviews/showrev.php?id=30477.

Chang Noi. "A New Cold War Underway in Thailand." *The Nation,* 29 November 2007.

———. "Politics and Thailand's Wealth Gap." *The Nation,* 2 November 2009.

Chatterjee, Partha. "Beyond the Nation? Or Within?" *Social Text* 56 (Autumn 1998): 57–69.

———. "Peasant Cultures of the Twenty-First Century." *Inter-Asia Cultural Studies* 9, no. 1 (2008): 116–26.

———. *The Politics of the Governed: Reflections on Popular Politics in Most of the World.* New York: Columbia University Press, 2004.

Chatthip Nartsupha. *The Thai Village Economy in the Past.* Chiang Mai: Silkworm Books, 1999.

Chayodom Sabhasri, Somprawin Manprasert, and Thanee Chaiwat. *ASEAN and China Free Trade Area: Implications for Thailand.* Bangkok: Faculty of Economics, Chulalongkorn University, 2005.

Cheesman, Patricia. "Textiles and Clothing of the Lao-Tai Peoples as Community Markers." Presentation to the 306th Meeting of the Informal Northern Thai Group, 14 October 2008. Accessed 25 March 2009. http://www.intgcm.thehostserver.com/diary2008_306th.html.

Clapp, Roger A. J. "Representing Reciprocity, Reproducing Domination: Ideology and the Labour Process in Latin American Contract Farming." *Journal of Peasant Studies* 16, no. 1 (1988): 5–39.

Cohen, Anthony P. *The Symbolic Construction of Community.* London: Tavistock, 1985.

Cohen, Paul. "The Politics of Economic Development in Northern Thailand, 1967–1978." PhD dissertation, University of London, 1981.

Cohen, Paul, and Gehan Wijeyewardene. "Introduction." "Spirit Cults and the Position of Women in Northern Thailand," special issue, *Mankind* 14, no. 4 (1984): 249–62.

———, eds. "Spirit Cults and the Position of Women in Northern Thailand." Special issue, *Mankind* 14, no. 4 (1984).

Corden, W. M. "The Exchange Rate System and the Taxation of Trade." In *Thailand: Social and Economic Studies in Development,* edited by T. H. Silcock, 151–69. Canberra: Australian National University Press, 1967.

Davis, Richard B. *Muang Metaphysics: A Study of Northern Thai Myth and Ritual.* Bangkok: Pandora, 1984.

Department of Community Development. *Rai-Ngan Khunaphap Chiwit Khong Khon Thai Pi 2551: Chak Khomun Khwam Champen Phuenthan* [Report of Thai People's Quality of Life in 2008: From Basic Needs Data]. Bangkok: Ministry of Interior, 2008.

Diamond, Larry. "Toward Democratic Consolidation: Rethinking Civil Society." *Journal of Democracy* 5, no. 3 (1994): 4–17.

Doner, Richard F. *The Politics of Uneven Development: Thailand's Economic Growth in Comparative Perspective.* Cambridge: Cambridge University Press, 2009.

Durkheim, Émile. *The Elementary Forms of the Religious Life.* London: George Allen and Unwin, 1915.

Eberhardt, Nancy. *Imagining the Course of Life: Self-Transformation in a Shan Buddhist Community.* Honolulu: University of Hawai'i Press, 2006.

Elson, R. E. *The End of the Peasantry in Southeast Asia: A Social and Economic History of Peasant Livelihood, 1800–1990s.* Houndmills, Basingstoke: Macmillan, 1997.

Evans, Peter. "Government Action, Social Capital, and Development: Reviewing the Evidence on Synergy." *World Development* 24, no. 6 (1996): 1119–32.

Fan, Shenggen, Somchai Jitsuchon, and Nuntaporn Methakunnavut. "The Importance of Public Investment for Reducing Poverty in Middle-Income Countries: The Case of Thailand." Development Strategy and Governance Division Discussion Papers, no. 7, International Food Policy Research Institute, 2004.

Farrelly, Nicholas. "Tai Community and Thai Border Subversions." In *Tai Lands and Thailand: Community and State in Southeast Asia*, edited by Andrew Walker, 67–86. Singapore: National University of Singapore Press, 2009.

Ferguson, James. *The Anti-politics Machine: "Development," Depoliticization, and Bureaucratic Power in Lesotho*. Minneapolis: University of Minnesota Press, 1994.

Ferguson, James, and Akhil Gupta. "Spatializing States: Toward an Ethnography of Neoliberal Governmentality." *American Ethnologist* 29, no. 4 (2002): 981–1002.

Food and Agriculture Organization of the United Nations [FAOSTAT]. http://fao stat.fao.org/.

Fry, Gerald W. "Decentralization as a Management and Development Strategy: A Thai Case Study." *Asian Journal of Public Administration* 5, no. 2 (1983): 44–53.

Fung, Archon. "Associations and Democracy: Between Theories, Hopes, and Realities." *Annual Review of Sociology* 29 (2003): 515–39.

Ginsborg, Paul. *Democracy: Crisis and Renewal*. London: Profile Books, 2008.

Glover, David, and Kenneth C. Kusterer. *Small Farmers, Big Business: Contract Farming and Rural Development*. Houndmills, Basingstoke: Macmillan, 1990.

Gluckman, Max. *Custom and Conflict in Africa*. Oxford: Basil Blackwell, 1955.

Government of Thailand. "Phon Krathop Krathiam Jaak Kan Poet Talat Seri Thai-Jin" [The impact on garlic of the Thai-China Free Trade Agreement]. Report, Bangkok, 2003.

———. "Sathanakan Kratiam Nai Changwat Chiangmai Pi 2550" [The garlic situation in Chiang Mai Province in 2007]. Report, Bangkok, 2007.

Grace, Brewster. "Recent Developments in Thai Rice Production." *American Universities Field Staff Report, Southeast Asia Series* 23, no. 3 (1975): 1–9.

Grandstaff, Terry B., Somluckrat Grandstaff, Viriya Limpinuntana, and Nongluck Suphanchaimat. "Rainfed Revolution in Northeast Thailand." *Southeast Asian Studies* 46, no. 3 (2008): 289–376.

Haas, Mary R. *Thai-English Student's Dictionary*. Stanford: Stanford University Press, 1964.

Haberkorn, Tyrell. *Revolution Interrupted: Farmers, Students, Law, and Violence in Northern Thailand*. Madison: University of Wisconsin Press, 2011.

Hanks, Lucien M. "Merit and Power in the Thai Social Order." *American Anthropologist* 64, no. 6 (1962): 1247–61.

———. "The Thai Social Order as Entourage and Circle." In *Change and Persistence in Thai Society: Essays in Honor of Lauriston Sharp*, edited by G. William Skinner and A. Thomas Kirsch, 197–218. Ithaca, N.Y.: Cornell University Press, 1975.

Hayami, Yujiro. "An Emerging Agricultural Problem in High-Performing Asian Economies." Policy Research Working Papers, no. 4312, World Bank Development Research Group, Trade Team, 2007.

Hewison, Kevin. "Neo-liberalism and Domestic Capital: The Political Outcome of the Economic Crisis in Thailand." *Journal of Development Studies* 41, no. 2 (2005): 310–30.

High, Holly. "Village in Laos: An Ethnographic Account of Poverty and Policy among the Mekong's Flows." PhD dissertation, Department of Anthropology, Research School of Pacific and Asian Studies, Australian National University, 2005.

Hirsch, Philip. *Development Dilemmas in Rural Thailand.* Singapore: Oxford University Press, 1990.

Hobsbawm, E. J. *Age of Extremes: The Short Twentieth Century, 1914–1991.* London: Michael Joseph, 1994.

Holt, John. *Spirits of the Place: Buddhism and Lao Religious Culture.* Honolulu: University of Hawai'i Press, 2009.

Howell, Signe. "Community beyond Place: Adoptive Families in Norway." In *Realizing Community: Concepts, Social Relationships, and Sentiments,* edited by Vered Amit, 84–104. London: Routledge, 2002.

Hyden, Goran, Jusius Court, and Ken Mease. *Political Society and Governance in Sixteen Developing Countries.* World Governance Survey Discussion Papers, no. 5. London: Overseas Development Institute, 2003.

Ikemoto, Yukio, and Mine Uehara. "Income Inequality and Kuznets' Hypothesis in Thailand." *Asian Economic Journal* 14, no. 4 (2000): 421–43.

International Rice Research Institute. *Background Paper: The Rice Crisis—What Needs to Be Done?* Los Banos: IRRI, 2008.

———. "Table 3: Paddy Rice Yield (t/ha), by Country and Geographical Region, 1961–2007." *World Rice Statistics* (2008).

Kajisa, Kei, and Takamasa Akiyama. *The Evolution of Rice Price Policies over Four Decades: Thailand, Indonesia, and the Philippines.* Tokyo: Foundation for Advanced Studies on International Development, 2003.

Kasian Tejapira. "Toppling Thaksin." *New Left Review* 39 (May–June 2006): 5–37.

Kearney, Michael. *Reconceptualizing the Peasantry: Anthropology in Global Perspective.* Boulder, Colo.: Westview Press, 1996.

Kengkij Kitirianglarp. "Kan Tosu Khrang Ni Khue Songkhram Thang Chonchan Thi Pranipranom Mai Dai" [The fight this time is class war without compromise]. *Prachatai,* 31 March 2010. Accessed 12 November 2010. http://www.prachatai3 .info/journal/2010/03/28605.

Kengkij Kitirianglarp and Kevin Hewison. "Social Movements and Political Opposition in Contemporary Thailand." *Pacific Review* 22, no. 4 (2009): 451–77.

Kerkvliet, Benedict J. *Everyday Politics in the Philippines: Class and Status Relations in a Central Luzon Village.* Lanham, Md.: Rowman and Littlefield, 2002.

———. *The Power of Everyday Politics: How Vietnamese Peasants Transformed National Policy.* Ithaca, N.Y.: Cornell University Press, 2005.

Kerkvliet, Benedict J., and Resil B. Mojares. "Themes in the Transition from Marcos to Aquino: An Introduction." In *From Marcos to Aquino: Local Perspectives on Political*

Transition in the Philippines, edited by Benedict J. Kerkvliet and Resil B. Mojares, 1–12. Manila: Ateneo de Manila University Press, 1991.

Key, Nigel, and David Runsten. "Contract Farming, Smallholders, and Rural Development in Latin America: The Organization of Agroprocessing Firms and the Scale of Outgrower Production." *World Development* 27, no. 2 (1999): 381–401.

Kirsch, A. Thomas. "Complexity in the Thai Religious Sytem: An Interpretation." *Journal of Asian Studies* 36, no. 2 (1977): 241–66.

Korovkin, Tanya. "Peasants, Grapes, and Corporations: The Growth of Contract Farming in a Chilean Community." *Journal of Peasant Studies* 19, no. 2 (1992): 228–54.

Krueger, Anne O. "Political Economy of Agricultural Policy." *Public Choice* 87, no 1/2 (1996): 163–75.

Kuhonta, Erik Martinez. "The Political Economy of Equitable Development in Thailand." *American Asian Review* 21, no. 4 (2003): 69–108.

Larsson, Tomas. "Security and the Politics of Property Rights in Thailand." Manuscript, Department of Politics and International Studies, University of Cambridge, 2010.

Lenin, V. I. *The Development of Capitalism in Russia.* Moscow: Progress Publishers, [1899] 1960.

Li, Tania. *The Will to Improve: Governmentality, Development, and the Practice of Politics.* Durham, N.C.: Duke University Press, 2007.

Lipton, Michael. *Why Poor People Stay Poor: A Study of Urban Bias in World Development.* London: Temple Smith, 1977.

Manager On Line. "Kasettrakon Pak Lak Na Sala Klang Chiangmai Rong Rat Poet Chamnam Krathiam" [Farmers protest in front of Chiangmai City Hall asking the government to purchase their garlic]. *Manager On Line,* n.d. Accessed 24 June 2009. http://www.ftawatch.org/news/view.php?id=13291.

Mannathukkaren, Nissim. "The 'Poverty' of Political Society: Partha Chatterjee and the People's Plan Campaign in Kerala, India." *Third World Quarterly* 31, no. 2 (2010): 295–314.

Mayer, Adrian C. "The Significance of Quasi-Groups in the Study of Complex Societies." In *The Social Anthropology of Complex Societies*, edited by Michael Banton, 97–121. London: Tavistock Publications, 1966.

McMorran, M. V. "Northern Thai Ancestral Cults: Authority and Aggression." "Spirit Cults and the Position of Women in Northern Thailand," special issue, *Mankind* 14, no. 4 (1984): 308–14.

McVey, Ruth Thomas. *Money and Power in Provincial Thailand.* Copenhagen: Nordic Institute of Asian Studies, 2000.

Medhi Krongkaew, Suchittra Chamnivickorn, and Isriya Nitithanprapas. "Economic Growth, Employment, and Poverty Reduction Linkages: The Case of Thailand." Issues in Employment and Poverty Discussion Papers, no. 20, International Labour Organization, 2006.

Meisburger, Tim. *Constitutional Reform and Democracy in Thailand: A National Survey of the Thai People*. Bangkok: Asia Foundation, 2009.

Miller, Peter, and Nikolas Rose. "Governing Economic Life." *Economy and Society* 19, no. 3 (1990): 1–31.

Missingham, Bruce D. *The Assembly of the Poor in Thailand: From Local Struggles to National Protest Movement*. Chiang Mai: Silkworm Books, 2003.

Mitchell, Timothy. "Society, Economy, and the State Effect." In *The Anthropology of the State: A Reader*, edited by Aradhana Sharma and Akhil Gupta, 169–86. Malden, Mass.: Blackwell, 2006.

Moerman, Michael. "A Thai Village Headman as Synaptic Leader." In *Modern Thai Politics*, edited by Clark D. Neher, 229–50. Cambridge, Mass.: Schenkman Publishing, 1979.

Montesano, Michael J. "Market Society and the Origins of the New Thai Politics." In *Money and Power in Provincial Thailand*, edited by Ruth McVey, 74–96. Singapore: Institute for Southeast Asian Studies, 2000.

Mulder, Niels. *Everyday Life in Thailand: An Interpretation*. Bangkok: Duang Kamol, 1979.

Murray, Warwick E. "From Dependency to Reform and Back Again: The Chilean Peasantry during the Twentieth Century." In *Latin American Peasants*, edited by Henry Veltmeyer and Tom Brass, 185–221. London: Frank Cass, 2003.

Nagai, Fumio, Kazuyo Ozaki, and Yoichiro Kimata. *JICA Program on Capacity Building of Thai Local Authorities*. Tokyo: Japan International Cooperation Agency, 2007.

National Statistics Office. "The Labor Force Survey, Whole Kingdom, Quarter 4, Oct.–Dec. 2006, Table 14." National Statistics Office, Bangkok, 2006.

———. *Northern Region Industrial Survey*. Bangkok: National Statistics Office, 2007.

———. *Report of the 2007 Household Socio-economic Survey*. Bangkok: National Statistics Office, 2007.

———. *Sathiti Khomun Khwam Yakchon lae Kan Krachai Raidai, 2531–2552* [Data on poverty and income distribution, 1998–2009]. Bangkok: National Economic and Social Development Board, 2010.

———. *Statistical Yearbook, Thailand*. Bangkok: National Statistics Office, various years.

———. *The 2003 Agricultural Census*. Bangkok: National Statistics Office of Thailand, 2003.

Neher, Clark D. "The Politics of Change in Rural Thailand." *Comparative Politics* 4, no. 2 (1972): 201–16.

Nidhi Eoseewong. "The Thai Cultural Constitution." *Kyoto Review of Southeast Asia* 3 (2003). http://kyotoreview.cseas.kyoto-u.ac.jp/issue/issue2/index.html.

Nishizaki, Yoshinori. *Political Authority and Provincial Identity in Thailand: The Making of Banharn-Buri*. Studies on Southeast Asia. Ithaca, N.Y.: Southeast Asia Program, Cornell University, 2011.

Northern Meteorological Centre. "Average Rainfall in Chiang Mai (Millimetres)." Accessed 6 April 2010. http://www.cmmet.tmd.go.th/.

Office of Agricultural Economics. *Khomun Phuenthan Setthakit Kan Kaset Pi 2552* [Basic data on agricultural economics, 2009]. Bangkok: Ministry of Agriculture, 2009.

———. "Kratiam Haeng Yai" [Large dried garlic]. Accessed 24 April 2008. http://www.oae.go.th/warning%20garlic.htm.

———. "Rakha Sinkha Kaset" [Agricultural commodity prices]. Accessed 10 June 2009. http://www.oae.go.th/oae_report/price/price_month.php.

Office of the National Economic and Social Development Board. *Gross Regional and Provincial Products, 2008 Edition.* Bangkok: NESDB, 2008.

———. *Phaen Phattana Setthakit Lae Sangkhom Chabap Thi 1, Raya Thi 2 Pho.So. 2507–2509* [The First Economic and Social Development Plan, Second Stage, 1964–1966]. Bangkok: NESDB, 1964.

———. "Phak Phanuak Kho: Kan Khamnuan Sen Khwam Yakchon" [Appendix C: The calculation of the poverty line]. In *Rai-Ngan Kan Pramoen Khwam Yakchon Pi 2551* [Report of poverty assessment in 2008]. Bangkok: NESDB, 2008.

Organization for Cooperation and Economic Development. Query Wizard for International Development Statistics (QWIDS). Accessed 1 November 2010. http://stats.oecd.org/qwids/.

Ortner, Sherry B. *Anthropology and Social Theory: Culture, Power, and the Acting Subject.* Durham, N.C.: Duke University Press, 2006.

———. "Resistance and the Problem of Ethnographic Refusal." *Comparative Studies in Society and History* 37, no. 1 (1995): 173–93.

Otsuka, Keijiro, and Takashi Yamano. "Introduction to the Special Issue on the Role of Nonfarm Income in Poverty Reduction: Evidence from Asia and East Africa." *Agricultural Economics* 35, no. 3 (2006): 393–97.

Pasuk Phongpaichit. "Developing Social Alternatives: Walking Backwards into a Klong." Paper presented at the conference Thailand Update: Thailand beyond the Crisis, Australian National University, Canberra, 21 April 1999.

Paulson, Anna L. "Insurance Motives for Migration: Evidence from Thailand." Working paper, Kellogg Graduate School of Management, Northwestern University, 2000.

Pesses, Abigaël. "Women Abilities: Feminism and the Ethics of Sustainable Development among Karen Highlanders." *Tai Culture* 19 (2007): 183–96.

Phillips, Herbert P. *Thai Peasant Personality: The Patterning of Interpersonal Behavior in the Village of Bang Chan.* Berkeley: University of California Press, 1965.

Piya Hanvoravongchai and William C. Hsiao. "Thailand: Achieving Univeral Coverage with Social Health Insurance." In *Social Health Insurance for Developing Nations,* edited by William C. Hsiao and R. Paul Shaw, 133–54. Washington, D.C.: World Bank, 2007.

Potter, Jack M. *Thai Peasant Social Structure.* Chicago: University of Chicago Press, 1976.

Prachatham. "Kasettrakon Chiangmai Chi Ratthaban Rapphitchop Rakha Krathiam Toktam" [Chiangmai farmers urge government to take responsibility for the fall of

garlic prices]. *Prachatham*, 8 April 2008. Accessed 23 August 2009. http://www
.prachatham.com/detail.htm?code=n4_08042008_01.

"Red Rage Rising." *Bangkok Post*, 13 March 2010.

Reynolds, Craig J. "The Origins of Community in the Thai Discourse of Global Governance." In *Tai Lands and Thailand: Community and State in Southeast Asia*, edited by Andrew Walker, 27–43. Singapore: National University of Singapore Press, 2009.

Rigg, Jonathan. *Living with Transition in Laos: Market Integration in Southeast Asia.* Routledge Contemporary Southeast Asia. London: Routledge, 2005.

Rigg, Jonathan, Suriya Veeravongs, Lalida Veeravongs, and Piyawadee Rohitarachoon. "Reconfiguring Rural Spaces and Remaking Rural Lives in Central Thailand." *Journal of Southeast Asian Studies* 39, no. 3 (2008): 355–81.

Robinson, Andrew. "Review of the Politics of the Governed: Reflections on Popular Politics in Most of the World by Partha Chatterjee (2004)." *Contemporary Political Theory* 7, no. 1 (2008): 114–19.

Rosen, George. *Peasant Society in a Changing Economy: Comparative Development in Southeast Asia and India.* Urbana: University of Illinois Press, 1975.

Sattha Sarattha. "7 Hetphon Thi Tham Hai Khi Thuk Chai Pen Awut" [7 reasons why shit is used as a weapon]. *Prachatai*, 3 October 2010. Accessed 28 October 2010. http://www.prachatai3.info/journal/2010/03/28065.

Sauwalak Kittiprapas. "Social Impacts of Financial and Economic Crisis in Thailand." Report, East Asian Development Network Regional Project on the Social Impact of the Asian Financial Crisis, 2002.

Scott, James C. *The Art of Not Being Governed: An Anarchist History of Upland Southeast Asia.* Yale Agrarian Studies. New Haven, Conn.: Yale University Press, 2009.

———. *The Moral Economy of the Peasant: Rebellion and Subsistence in Southeast Asia.* New Haven, Conn.: Yale University Press, 1976.

———. *Seeing Like a State: How Certain Schemes to Improve the Human Condition Have Failed.* Yale Agrarian Studies. New Haven, Conn.: Yale University Press, 1998.

———. *Weapons of the Weak: Everyday Forms of Peasant Resistance.* New Haven, Conn.: Yale University Press, 1985.

Shanin, Teodor. "Introduction." In *Peasants and Peasant Societies*, edited by Teodor Shanin, 11–19. Harmondsworth: Penguin Books, 1971.

Sharp, Lauriston, and Lucien M. Hanks. *Bang Chan: Social History of a Rural Community in Thailand.* Ithaca, N.Y.: Cornell University Press, 1978.

Shigetomi, Shinichi. "Thailand: Toward a Developed, Rice-Exporting Country." In *The World Food Crisis and the Strategies of Asian Rice Exporters*, edited by Shinichi Shigetomi, Kensuke Kubo, and Kazunari Tsukada, 73–93. Chiba: Institute of Developing Economies, 2011.

Shorto, H. L. "The 32 Myos in the Medieval Mon Kingdom." *Bulletin of the School of Oriental and African Studies* 26, no. 3 (1963): 572–91.

Somchai Phatharathananunth. *Civil Society and Democratization: Social Movements in Northeast Thailand.* Copenhagen: Nordic Institute of Asian Studies, 2006.

Sompop Manarungsan and Suebskun Suwanjindar. "Contract Farming and Out-grower Schemes in Thailand." In *Contract Farming in Southeast Asia: Three Country Studies*, edited by David Glover and Teck Ghee Lim, 10–70. Kuala Lumpur: Institute for Advanced Studies, University of Malaya, 1992.

Somporn Isvilanonda and Nipon Poapongsakorn. *Rice Supply and Demand in Thailand: The Future Outlook*. Bangkok: Thailand Development Research Institute, 1995.

Sonthi Boonyaratglin. "Sarup Kan Banyai Phiset, 26 Kanyayon 2550" [Summary of the special lecture, 26 September 2007]. Secret Thai government document circulated by e-mail, 2007.

Sumberg, J., and C. Okali, eds. *Farmers' Experiments: Creating Local Knowledge*. Boulder, Colo.: Lynne Rienner Publishers, 1997.

Swearer, Donald K., Sommai Premchit, and Phaithoon Dokbuakaew. *Sacred Mountians of Northern Thailand and Their Legends*. Chiang Mai: Silkworm Books, 2004.

Tambiah, Stanley Jeyaraja. *Buddhism and the Spirit Cults in Northeast Thailand*. Cambridge: Cambridge University Press, 1970.

Tanabe, Shigeharu. "Spirits and Ideological Discourse: The Tai Lu Guardian Cults in Yunnan." *Sojourn* 3, no. 1 (1988): 1–25.

Tannenbaum, Nicola Beth. *Who Can Compete against the World? Power-Protection and Buddhism in Shan Worldview*. Ann Arbor, Mich.: Association for Asian Studies, 1995.

Teerana Bhongmakapat. "Income Distribution in a Rapidly Growing Economy of Thailand." *Chulalongkorn Journal of Economics* 5, no. 2 (1993): 109–35.

Terwiel, B. J. "The Origin and Meaning of the Thai 'City Pillar.'" *Journal of the Siam Society* 66, no. 2 (1978): 159–71.

"Thai Food Hit by Garlic Crisis." *The Nation*, 2 March 2008.

Trouillot, Michel-Rolph. "The Anthropology of the State in the Age of Globalization: Close Encounters of the Deceptive Kind." *Current Anthropology* 42, no. 1 (2001): 125–38.

Turton, Andrew. "The Current Situation in the Thai Countryside." In *Thailand: Roots of Conflict*, edited by Andrew Turton, Jonathan Fast, and Malcolm Caldwell, 104–42. Nottingham: Spokesman, 1978.

———. "Limits of Ideological Domination and the Formation of Social Consciousness." In *History and Peasant Consciouness in South East Asia*, edited by Andrew Turton and Shigeharu Tanabe, 19–73. Osaka: National Museum of Ethnology, 1984.

———. "Local Powers and Rural Differentiation." In *Agrarian Transformation: Local Processes and the State in Southeast Asia*, edited by Gillian Hart, Andrew Turton, and Benjamin White, 70–79. Berkeley: University of California Press, 1989.

———. "Matrilineal Descent Groups and Spirit Cults of the Thai-Yuan in Northern Thailand." *Journal of the Siam Society* 60, no. 2 (1972): 217–56.

———. "Thailand: Agrarian Bases of State Power." In *Agrarian Transformation: Local Processes and the State in Southeast Asia*, edited by Gillian Hart, Andrew Turton and Benjamin White, 53–69. Berkeley: University of California Press, 1989.

Ueda, Yoko. *Local Economy and Entrepreneurship in Thailand: A Case Study of Nakhon Ratchasima.* Japan: Kyoto University Press, 1995.

United Nations Development Program. *Human Security, Today and Tomorrow: Thailand Human Development Report, 2009.* Bangkok: UNDP, 2010.

———. *Sufficiency Economy and Human Development: Thailand Human Development Report, 2007.* Bangkok: UNDP, 2007.

Vandergeest, Peter. "Gifts and Rights: Cautionary Notes on Community Self-Help in Thailand." *Development and Change* 22, no. 3 (1991): 421–43.

Vella, Walter F., and Dorothy B. Vella. *Chaiyo! King Vajiravudh and the Development of Thai Nationalism.* Honolulu: University of Hawai'i Press, 1978.

Waleerat Suphannachart and Peter Warr. "Research and Productivity in Thai Agriculture." Working Papers in Trade and Development, no. 2009/11, Arndt-Corden Division of Economics, College of Asia and the Pacific, Australian National University, 2009.

Walker, Andrew. "The 'Karen Consensus,' Ethnic Politics, and Resource-Use Legitimacy in Northern Thailand." *Asian Ethnicity* 2, no. 2 (2001): 145–62.

Walker, Andrew, and Nicholas Farrelly. "Northern Thailand's Specter of Eviction." *Critical Asian Studies* 40, no. 3 (2008): 373–97.

Warr, Peter. "Boom, Bust, and Beyond." In *Thailand beyond the Crisis,* edited by Peter Warr, 3–65. London: Routledge, 2004.

———. "Productivity Growth in Thailand and Indonesia: How Agriculture Contributes to Economic Growth." Working Papers in Economics and Development Studies, no. 200606, Department of Economics, Padjadjaran University, 2006.

———. "Thailand's Crisis Overload." *Southeast Asian Affairs* 2009 (2009): 334–54.

Warr, Peter, and Archanun Kohpaiboon. "Distortions to Agricultural Incentives in a Food Exporting Country: Thailand." Manuscript, Crawford School, College of Asia and the Pacific, Australian National University, 2007.

Watts, Michael J. "Life under Contract: Contract Farming, Agrarian Restructuring, and Flexible Accumulation." In *Living under Contract: Contract Farming and Agrarian Transformation in Sub-Saharan Africa,* edited by P. D. Little and M. J. Watts, 21–77. Madison: University of Wisconsin Press, 1994.

White, Ben. "Agroindustry and Contract Farmers in Upland West Java." *Journal of Peasant Studies* 24, no. 3 (1997): 100–136.

Wijeyewardene, Gehan. "Matriclans or Female Cults: A Problem in Northern Thai Ethnography." *Mankind* 11, no. 1 (1977): 19–25.

———. *Place and Emotion in Northern Thai Ritual Behaviour.* Bangkok: Pandora, 1986.

Wolf, Eric. R. *Peasants.* Englewood Cliffs, N.J.: Prentice-Hall, 1966.

Woodrow, Robert. "The Down-Trodden Rural Poor of Thailand: It's Not Quite What You Think." *New Mandala,* 10 May 2010. Accessed 23 October 2010. http://asia pacific.anu.edu.au/newmandala/2010/05/10/the-rebellion-of-thailands-middle-income-peasants/.

World Bank. *Thailand Economic Monitor, April 2005*. Bangkok: World Bank, 2005.
————. *Thailand Social Monitor: Improving Secondary Education*. Washington, D.C.: World Bank, 2006.
————. World Development Indicators Online. Various access dates. http://data .worldbank.org/data-catalog/world-development-indicators.
Yamada, Unichi. "Capital Outflow from the Agriculture Sector in Thailand." Policy Research Working Papers, no. 1910, World Bank, 1998.
Yang, Mayfair Mei-Hui. "The Gift Economy and State Power in China." *Comparative Studies in Society and History* 31, no. 1 (1989): 25–54.
Yang, Shu-Yuan. "Imagining the State: An Ethnographic Study." *Ethnography* 6, no. 4 (2005): 487–516.
Young, Stephen B. "The Northeastern Thai Village: A Non-participatory Democracy." In *Modern Thai Politics*, edited by Clark D. Neher, 251–67. Cambridge, Mass.: Schenkman Publishing, 1979.

Index

Page numbers in bold italics indicate illustrations and captions.

NEW PERSPECTIVES IN SOUTHEAST ASIAN STUDIES

The Burma Delta: Economic Development and
Social Change on an Asian Rice Frontier, 1852–1941
MICHAEL ADAS

From Rebellion to Riots: Collective Violence on Indonesian Borneo
JAMIE S. DAVIDSON

The Floracrats: State-Sponsored Science and
the Failure of the Enlightenment in Indonesia
ANDREW GOSS

Revolution Interrupted: Farmers, Students, Law,
and Violence in Northern Thailand
TYRELL HABERKORN

Amazons of the Huk Rebellion: Gender, Sex, and
Revolution in the Philippines
VINA A. LANZONA

Policing America's Empire: The United States, the Philippines,
and the Rise of the Surveillance State
ALFRED W. MCCOY

An Anarchy of Families: State and Family in the Philippines
Edited by ALFRED W. MCCOY

The Hispanization of the Philippines: Spanish Aims and
Filipino Responses, 1565–1700
JOHN LEDDY PHELAN

Pretext for Mass Murder: The September 30th Movement and
Suharto's Coup d'État in Indonesia
JOHN ROOSA

The Social World of Batavia: Europeans and
Eurasians in Colonial Indonesia, second edition
JEAN GELMAN TAYLOR

29678161R00176

Made in the USA
Lexington, KY
03 February 2014